Lotus® Freelance Graphics

Release 2 for Windows™
Illustrated

Lotus® Freelance Graphics

Release 2 for Windows™ Illustrated

Katherine Murray

Course Technology

Course Technology, Inc. One Main Street, Cambridge, MA 02142

An International Thomson Publishing Company

I(T)P

Lotus Freelance Graphics Release 2 for Windows Illustrated © 1995 Course Technology, Inc.

Managing Editor	Marjorie Schlaikjer
Product Manager	Kim Crowley
Developmental Editor	Mary-Terese Cozzola
Director of Production	Myrna D'Addario
Production Editor	Donna Whiting
Desktop Publishing Supervisor	Debbie Masi
Desktop Publishing Specialist	Andrea Star Greitzer
Copyeditor	Jennifer Hooper
Proofreader	Mark Vodnik
Indexer	Alexandra Nickerson
Product Testing and Support Supervisor	Jeff Goding
Technical Reviewers	James Valente
	Mark Vodnik
	Chris Greacen
Prepress Production	Gex, Inc.
Manufacturing Manager	Elizabeth Martinez
Instructional Designer	Debbie Krivoy
Text Designer	Leslie Hartwell
Cover Designer	John Gamache

Trademarks

Course Technology and the open book logo are registered trademarks of Course Technology, Inc.
I(T)P The ITP logo is a trademark under license.

Lotus Freelance Graphics Release 2 is a registered trademark of Lotus Development Corporation and Windows is a registered trademark of Microsoft Corporation.

Some of the product names used in this book have been used for identification purposes only and may be trademarks or registered trademarks of their respective manufacturers and sellers.

Disclaimer

Course Technology, Inc. reserves the right to revise this publication and make changes from time to time in its content without notice.

ISBN 1-56527-262-5

Printed in the United States of America

10 9 8 7 6 5 4 3 2

From the Publisher

At Course Technology, Inc., we believe that technology will transform the way that people teach and learn. We are very excited about bringing you, college professors and students, the most practical and affordable technology-related products available.

The Course Technology Development Process

Our development process is unparalleled in the higher education publishing industry. Every product we create goes through an exacting process of design, development, review, and testing.

Reviewers give us direction and insight that shape our manuscripts and bring them up to the latest standards. Every manuscript is quality tested. Students whose background matches the intended audience work through every keystroke, carefully checking for clarity, and pointing out errors in logic and sequence. Together with our technical reviewers, these testers help us ensure that everything that carries our name is error-free and easy to use.

Course Technology Products

We show both *how* and *why* technology is critical to solving problems in college and in whatever field you choose to teach or pursue. Our time-tested, step-by-step instructions provide unparalleled clarity. Examples and applications are chosen and crafted to motivate students.

The Course Technology Team

This book will suit your needs because it was delivered quickly, efficiently, and affordably. In every aspect of business, we rely on a commitment to quality and the use of technology. Every employee contributes to this process. The names of all our employees are listed below: Tim Ashe, David Backer, Stephen M. Bayle, Josh Bernoff, Michelle Brown, Ann Marie Buconjic, Jody Buttafoco, Kerry Cannell, Jim Chrysikos, Barbara Clemens, Susan Collins, John M. Connolly, Kim Crowley, Myrna D'Addario, Lisa D'Alessandro, Howard S. Diamond, Kathryn Dinovo, Joseph B. Dougherty, MaryJane Dwyer, Chris Elkhill, Don Fabricant, Kate Gallagher, Laura Ganson, Jeff Goding, Laurie Gomes, Eileen Gorham, Andrea Greitzer, Catherine Griffin, Tim Hale, Roslyn Hooley, Nicole Jones, Matt Kenslea, Susannah Lean, Suzanne Licht, Laurie Lindgren, Kim Mai, Margaret Makowski, Elizabeth Martinez, Debbie Masi, Don Maynard, Dan Mayo, Kathleen McCann, Jay McNamara, Mac Mendelsohn, Laurie Michelangelo, Kim Munsell, Amy Oliver, Micheal Ormsby, Kristine Otto, Debbie Parlee, Kristin Patrick, Charlie Patsios, Jodi Paulus, Darren Perl, Kevin Phaneuf, George J. Pilla, Cathy Prindle, Nancy Ray, Marjorie Schlaikjer, Christine Spillett, Michelle Tucker, David Upton, Mark Valentine, Karen Wadsworth, Anne Marie Walker, Renee Walkup, Tracy Wells, Donna Whiting, Janet Wilson, Lisa Yameen.

Preface

Course Technology, Inc. is proud to present this new book in its Illustrated Series. *Lotus Freelance Graphics Release 2 for Windows Illustrated* provides a highly visual, hands-on introduction to Freelance Graphics. The book is designed as a learning tool for Freelance Graphics novices but will also be useful as a source for future reference.

Organization and Coverage

Lotus Freelance Graphics Release 2 for Windows Illustrated contains a Windows overview and seven units that cover basic Freelance skills. In these units students learn how to plan, design, create, and modify a presentation. They work with text, graphics, charts, and tables, and learn to organize and present an effective presentation.

Approach

Lotus Freelance Graphics Release 2 for Windows Illustrated distinguishes itself from other textbooks with its highly visual approach to computer instruction.

Lessons: Information Displays

The basic lesson format of this text is the "information display," a two-page lesson that is sharply focused on a specific task. This sharp focus and the precise beginning and end of a lesson make it easy for students to study specific material. Modular lessons are less overwhelming for students, and they provide instructors with more flexibility in planning classes and assigning specific work. The units are also modular and can be presented in any order.

Each lesson, or "information display," contains the following elements:

Introduction — Concise text that introduces the basic principles discussed in the lesson and integrates the brief case study scenario. Procedures are easier to learn when concepts fit into a framework.

Numbered steps — Clear step-by-step directions explain how to complete the specific task. When students follow the numbered steps, they quickly learn how each procedure is performed and what the results will be.

Reference tables — These are quickly accessible summaries of key terms, SmartIcon shortcuts, or keyboard alternatives connected with the lesson material. Students can refer easily to this information when working on their own projects at a later time.

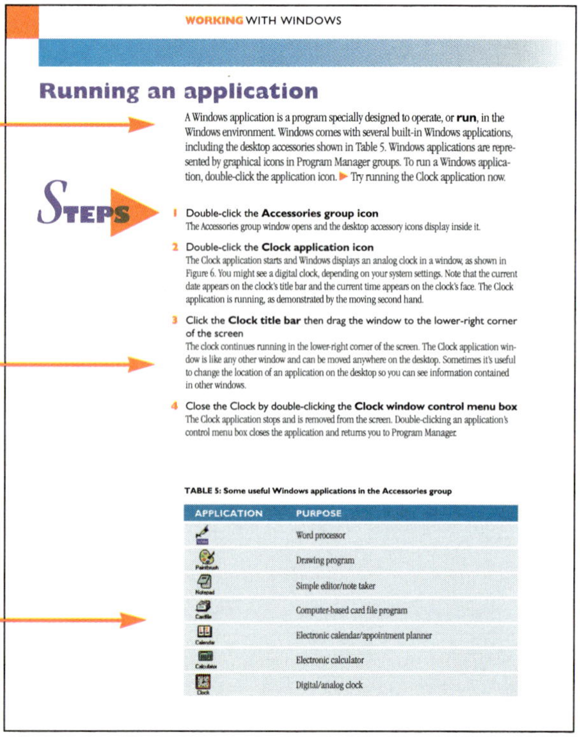

WORKING WITH WINDOWS

Running an application

A Windows application is a program specially designed to operate, or **run**, in the Windows environment. Windows comes with several built-in Windows applications, including the desktop accessories shown in Table 5. Windows applications are represented by graphical icons in Program Manager groups. To run a Windows application, double-click the application icon. ▶ Try running the Clock application now.

STEPS

1 Double-click the **Accessories group icon**
The Accessories group window opens and the desktop accessory icons display inside it.

2 Double-click the **Clock application icon**
The Clock application starts and Windows displays an analog clock in a window, as shown in Figure 6. You might see a digital clock, depending on your system settings. Note that the current date appears on the clock's title bar and the current time appears on the clock's face. The Clock application is running, as demonstrated by the moving second hand.

3 Click the **Clock title bar** then drag the window to the lower-right corner of the screen
The clock continues running in the lower-right corner of the screen. The Clock application window is like any other window and can be moved anywhere on the desktop. Sometimes it's useful to change the location of an application on the desktop so you can see information contained in other windows.

4 Close the Clock by double-clicking the **Clock window control menu box**
The Clock application stops and is removed from the screen. Double-clicking an application's control menu box closes the application and returns you to Program Manager.

TABLE 5: Some useful Windows applications in the Accessories group

APPLICATION	PURPOSE
[illegible]	Word processor
Paintbrush	Drawing program
Notepad	Simple editor/note taker
Cardfile	Computer-based card file program
Calendar	Electronic calendar/appointment planner
Calculator	Electronic calculator
Clock	Digital/analog clock

Features

Lotus Freelance Graphics Release 2 for Windows Illustrated is an exceptional textbook because it contains the following features:

- "Read This Before You Begin" Pages — These pages, one for the Windows section and one before Unit 1, provide essential information that both students and instructors need to know before they begin working through the units.
- Windows Overview — The Working with Windows introduction provides an overview so students can begin working in the Windows environment right away. This introductory section introduces students to the graphical user interface and helps them learn basic skills they can use in all Windows applications.
- Real-World Case — The case study used throughout the textbook is designed to be "real-world" in nature and representative of the kinds of activities that students will encounter when creating presentations. With a real-world case, the process of producing effective presentations will be more meaningful to students.
- End of Unit Material — Each unit concludes with a meaningful Concepts Review that tests students' understanding of what they learned in the unit. The Concepts Review is followed by Applications Review, which provides students with additional hands-on practice of the skills they learned in the unit. The Applications Review is followed by Independent Challenges, which pose case problems for students to solve. The Independent Challenges allow students to learn by exploring, and develop critical thinking skills.

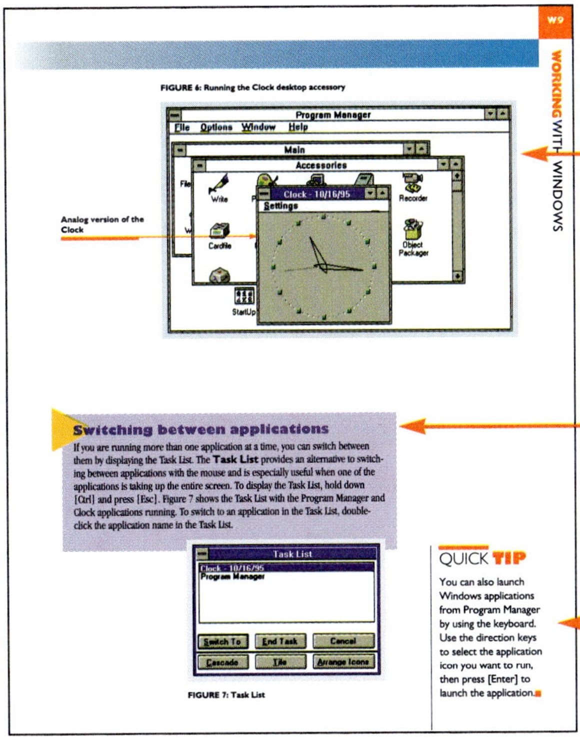

Screen shots — Large-size, full-color representations of what the student's screen should look like after completing the numbered steps.

Related topics — Concise information that either expands on one component of the major lesson skill, or describes an independent task that is in some way related to the major lesson skill. These often include both text and screen shots.

Quick Tips and Trouble? — Shortcuts and hints for using Lotus Freelance Graphics more effectively, as well as troubleshooting advice to fix common problems that might occur.

The Student Disks

The Student Disks bundled with the instructor's copy of this book contain all the data files students need to complete the step-by-step lessons.

Adopters of this text are granted the right to post the Student Disks on any standalone computer or network used by students who have purchased this product.

For more information on the Student Disks, see the section in this book called "Read This Before You Begin Lotus Freelance Graphics 2."

The Supplements

Instructor's Manual — The Instructor's Manual is quality-assurance tested. It includes:

- Answers and solutions to all lessons, Concept Reviews, Application Reviews, and Independent Challenges
- A disk containing solutions to all of the lessons, Concept Reviews, Application Reviews, and Independent Challenges
- Unit notes, which contain tips from the author about the instructional progression of each lesson
- Transparency masters of key concepts

Test Bank — The Test Bank contains 50 questions per unit in true/false, multiple choice, and fill-in-the-blank formats, plus two essay questions. Each question has been quality assurance tested by students to achieve clarity and accuracy.

Electronic Test Bank — The Electronic Test Bank allows instructors to edit individual test questions, select questions individually or at random, and print out scrambled versions of the same test to any supported printer.

Acknowledgments

This book is the culmination of the creativity, insight, and careful evaluation of a number of talented people. Many thanks to Kim Crowley for her keen ability to amass, distribute, coordinate, and control this project as it threatened to take on a life of its own; to Mary-Terese Cozzola for her invaluable developmental suggestions and redirections; to Marjorie Schlaikjer for her developmental guidance and understanding of the Illustrated series; and to Donna Whiting, the production editor on the project, and to John Purcell and Rick Ender, the academic advisors; James Valente for quality assurance testing, and to Mark Vodnik for quality assurance testing and proofreading. Their many helpful insights and catches have made this a better and more accurate book. Thanks also to Jennifer Hooper, copyeditor; Sandy Nickerson, indexer; and Kathy Finnegan and Jane Pedicini for word processing.

Brief Contents

Contents

TABLES

Read This Before You Begin Working with Windows

To the Student

The Working with Windows section gives you practice using the main features of Windows, the control program that lets you work easily with your computer and many programs you run. You need copies of the Student Disks to complete this section.

Your instructor might provide you with your own copies of the Student Disks, or might make the Student Disk files available to you over a network in your school's computer lab. See your instructor or your technical support person for further information.

To the Instructor

Student Disks

The instructor's copy of this book is bundled with three Student Disks, which contain all the files your students need to complete the step-by-step lessons in this book. Your students will not need the Student Disk files to complete this Working with Windows section, but they will need Student Disk #1 to create a practice directory called MY_FILES. As your students work through the text and begin using the two other Student Disks, they will need to create the MY_FILES directory on these disks as well.

If you choose to make the Student Disk files available to students over a network, then be sure to tell students where you want them to create the MY_FILES directory. For more information on the Student Disks, refer to the "Read This Before You Begin Lotus Freelance Graphics 2" page.

Screens

This Working with Windows section assumes students will use the default Windows setup. If you want your students' screen to look like those in the figures, set up the Program Manager window to look like Figure 1, and make sure the Clock accessory is in analog mode with the title bar displayed at the top.

OBJECTIVES

- Start Windows
- Use the mouse
- Use Program Manager groups
- Run an application
- Resize a window
- Use menus and dialog boxes
- Save a file
- Use File Manager
- Arrange windows and icons
- Exit Windows

Working WITH WINDOWS

Microsoft Windows 3.1 is the **graphical user interface** (GUI) that works hand in hand with MS-DOS to control the basic operation of your computer and the programs you run on it. Windows is a comprehensive control program that helps you run useful, task-oriented programs known as **applications**. This introduction will help you to learn basic skills that you can use in all Windows applications. First you'll learn how to start Windows and how to use the mouse in the Windows environment. Next you'll get some hands-on experience with Program Manager, and you'll learn how to work with groups, run an application, resize a window, use menus and dialog boxes, save files, use File Manager, and arrange windows and icons. Then you'll learn how to exit a Windows application and exit Windows itself.

Starting Windows

Windows is started, or **launched**, from MS-DOS with the Win command. Once started, Windows takes over most of the duties of MS-DOS and provides a graphical environment in which you run your applications. Windows has several advantages over MS-DOS. As a graphical interface, it uses meaningful pictures and symbols known as **icons** to replace hard-to-remember commands. Windows lets you run more than one application at a time, so you can run, for example, a word processor and a spreadsheet at the same time and easily share data between them. ▶ Each application is represented in a rectangular space called a **window**. The Windows environment also includes several useful desktop accessories, including Clock and Notepad, which you can use for day-to-day tasks. ▶ Try starting Windows now.

STEPS

1 **Turn on your computer**
The computer displays some technical information as it starts up and tests its circuitry. MS-DOS starts automatically, then displays the **command prompt** (usually C:\>). The command prompt gives you access to MS-DOS commands and applications. If your computer is set up so that it automatically runs Windows when it starts, the command prompt will not display. You can then skip Step 2.

2 **Type win then press [Enter]**
This command starts Windows. The screen momentarily goes blank while the computer starts Windows. An hourglass displays, indicating Windows is busy processing a command. Then the Windows Program Manager displays on your screen, as shown in Figure 1. Your screen might look slightly different depending on which applications are installed on your computer.

TABLE 1:
Elements of the Windows desktop

DESKTOP ELEMENT	DESCRIPTION
Program Manager	The main control program of Windows. All Windows applications are started from the Program Manager.
Window	A rectangular space framed by a double border on the screen. The Program Manager is framed in a window.
Application icon	The graphic representation of a Windows application.
Title bar	The area directly below the window's top border that displays the name of a window or application.
Sizing buttons	Buttons in the upper-right corner of a window that you can use to minimize or maximize a window.
Menu bar	The area under the title bar on a window. The menu bar provides access to most of an application's commands.
Control menu box	A box in the upper-left corner of each window; provides a menu used to resize, move, maximize, minimize, or close a window. Double-clicking this box closes a window or an application.
Mouse pointer	An arrow indicating the current location of the mouse on the desktop.

FIGURE 1: Program Manager window

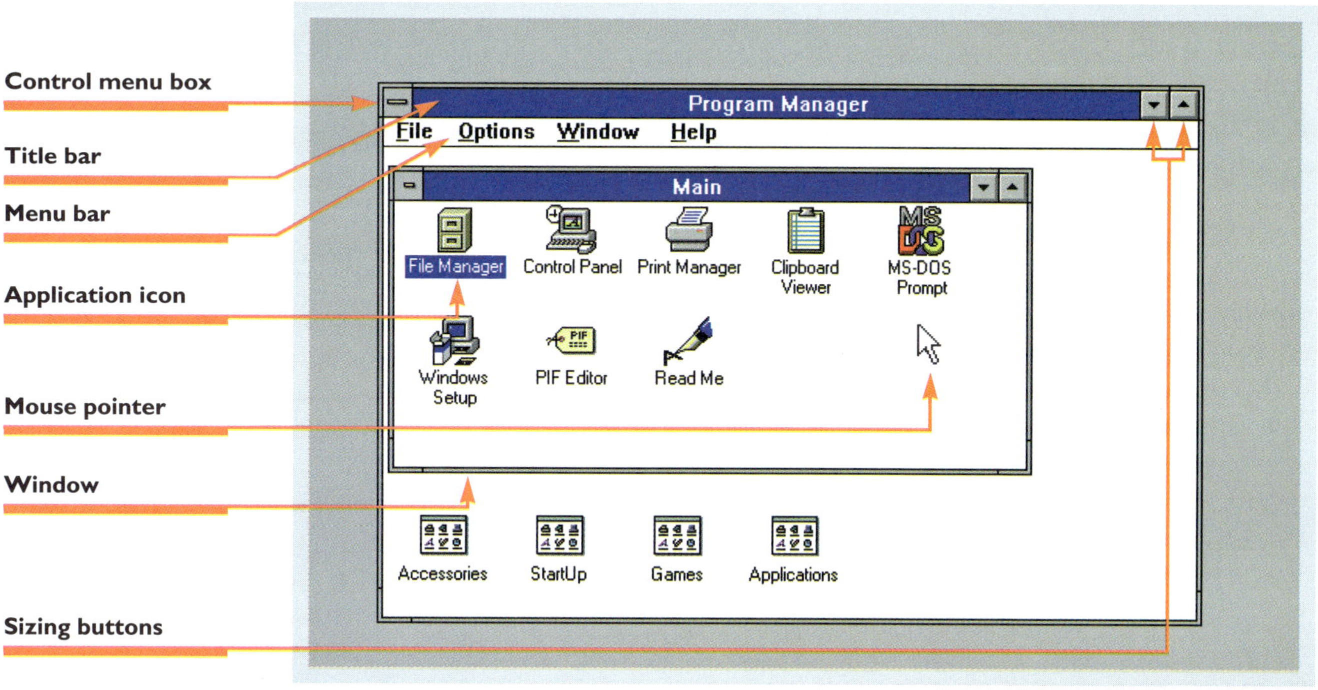

The Windows desktop

The entire screen area on the monitor represents the Windows desktop. The **desktop** is an electronic version of a desk that provides workspace for different computing tasks. Windows allows you to customize the desktop to support the way you like to work and to organize the applications you need to run. Use Table 1 to identify the key elements of the desktop, referring to Figure 1 for their locations. Because the Windows desktop can be customized, your desktop might look slightly different.

Using the mouse

The **mouse** is a handheld input device that you roll on your desk to position the mouse pointer on the Windows desktop. When you move the mouse on your desk, the **mouse pointer** on the screen moves in the same direction. The buttons on the mouse are used to select icons and choose commands, and to indicate the work to be done in applications. Table 2 lists the four basic mouse techniques. Table 3 shows some common mouse pointer shapes. ▶ Try using the mouse now.

STEPS

1. **Locate the mouse pointer on the Windows desktop and move the mouse across your desk**
   Watch how the mouse pointer moves on the Windows desktop in response to your movements. Try moving the mouse pointer in circles, then back and forth in straight lines.

2. **Position the mouse pointer over the Control Panel icon in the Main group window**
   Positioning the mouse pointer over an icon is called **pointing.** The Control Panel icon is a graphical representation of the Control Panel application, a special program that controls the operation of the Windows environment. If the Control Panel icon is not visible in the Main group window, point to any other icon. The Program Manager is customizable so the Control Panel could be hidden from view.

3. **Press and release the left mouse button**
   Pressing and releasing the mouse button is called **clicking**. When you position the mouse pointer on an icon in Program Manager then click, you **select** the icon. When the Control Panel icon is selected, its title is highlighted, as shown in Figure 2. If you clicked an icon that caused a menu to open, click the icon again to close the menu. You'll learn about menus later. Now practice a mouse skill called **dragging**.

4. **With the icon selected, press and hold the left mouse button and move the mouse down and to the right**
   The icon moves with the mouse pointer, as shown in Figure 3. When you release the mouse button, the icon relocates in the group window.

5. **Drag the Control Panel icon back to its original position**

TABLE 2:
Basic mouse techniques

TECHNIQUE	HOW TO DO IT
Pointing	Move the mouse pointer to position it over an item on the desktop.
Clicking	Press and release the mouse button.
Double-clicking	Press and release the mouse button twice quickly.
Dragging	Point at an item, press and hold the mouse button, move the mouse to a new location, then release the mouse button.

FIGURE 2: Selecting an icon

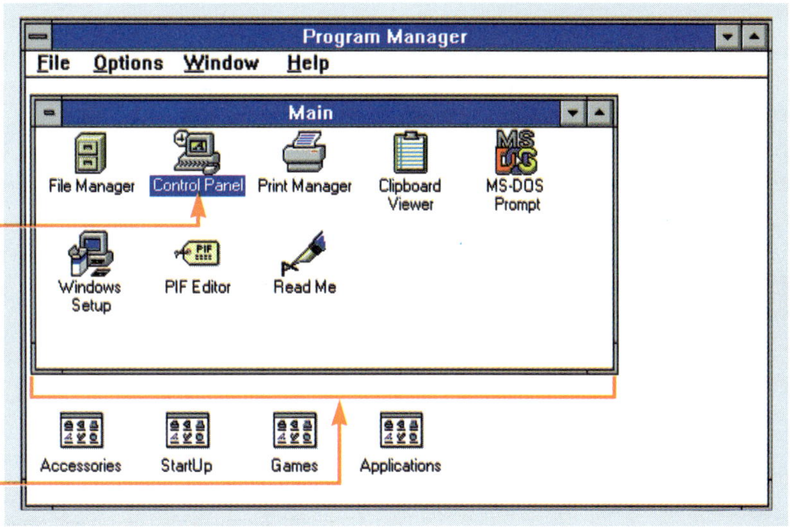

FIGURE 3: Dragging an icon

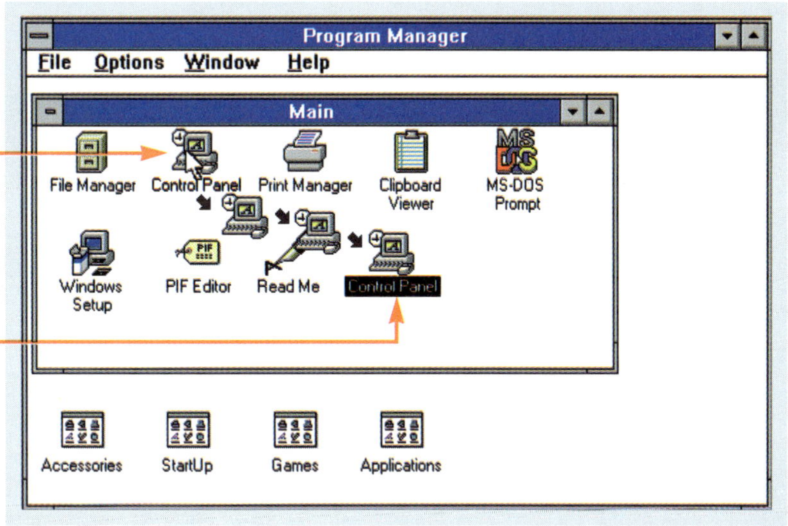

TABLE 3: Common mouse pointer shapes

SHAPE	USED TO
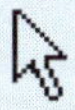	Select items, choose commands, start applications, and work in applications.
	Position mouse pointer for editing or inserting text. This icon is called an insertion point.
	Indicate Windows is busy processing a command.
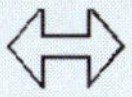	Change the size of a window. This icon appears when mouse pointer is on the border of a window.

Using Program Manager groups

In Program Manager, you launch applications and organize your applications into windows called groups. A **group** can appear as an open window or as an icon in the Program Manager window. Each group has a name related to its contents, and you can reorganize the groups to suit your needs. The standard Windows groups are described in Table 4. ▶ Try working with groups now.

STEPS

1. **If necessary, double-click the Main group icon to open the Main group window**
   The Main group icon is usually located at the bottom of the Program Manager window.

2. **Double-click the Accessories group icon**
   When you double-click the Accessories group icon, it expands into the Accessories group window, as shown in Figure 4. Now move the Accessories group window to the right.

3. **Click the Accessories group window title bar and drag the group window to the right**
   An outline of the window moves to the right with the mouse. When you release the mouse button, the Accessories group window moves to the location you've indicated. Moving a window lets you see what is beneath it. Any window in the Windows environment can be moved with this technique.

4. **Click the title bar of the Main group window**
   The Main group window becomes the **active window**, the one you are currently working in. Other windows, including the Accessories group window, are considered background windows. Note that the active window has a highlighted title bar. Program Manager has a highlighted title bar because it is the **active application**.

5. **Activate the Accessories group window by clicking anywhere in that window**
   The Accessories group window moves to the foreground again. Now try closing the Accessories group window to an icon.

6. **Double-click the control menu box in the Accessories group window**
   When you double-click this box, the Accessories group window shrinks to an icon and the Main group window becomes the active window. Double-clicking the control menu box is the easiest way to close a window or an application.

TABLE 4: Standard Windows groups

GROUP NAME	CONTENTS
Main	Applications that control how Windows works; the primary Windows group.
Accessories	Useful desktop accessories for day-to-day tasks.
StartUp	Programs that run automatically when Windows is started.
Games	Game programs for Windows.
Applications	Group of applications found on your hard disk.

FIGURE 4: Accessories group expanded into a window

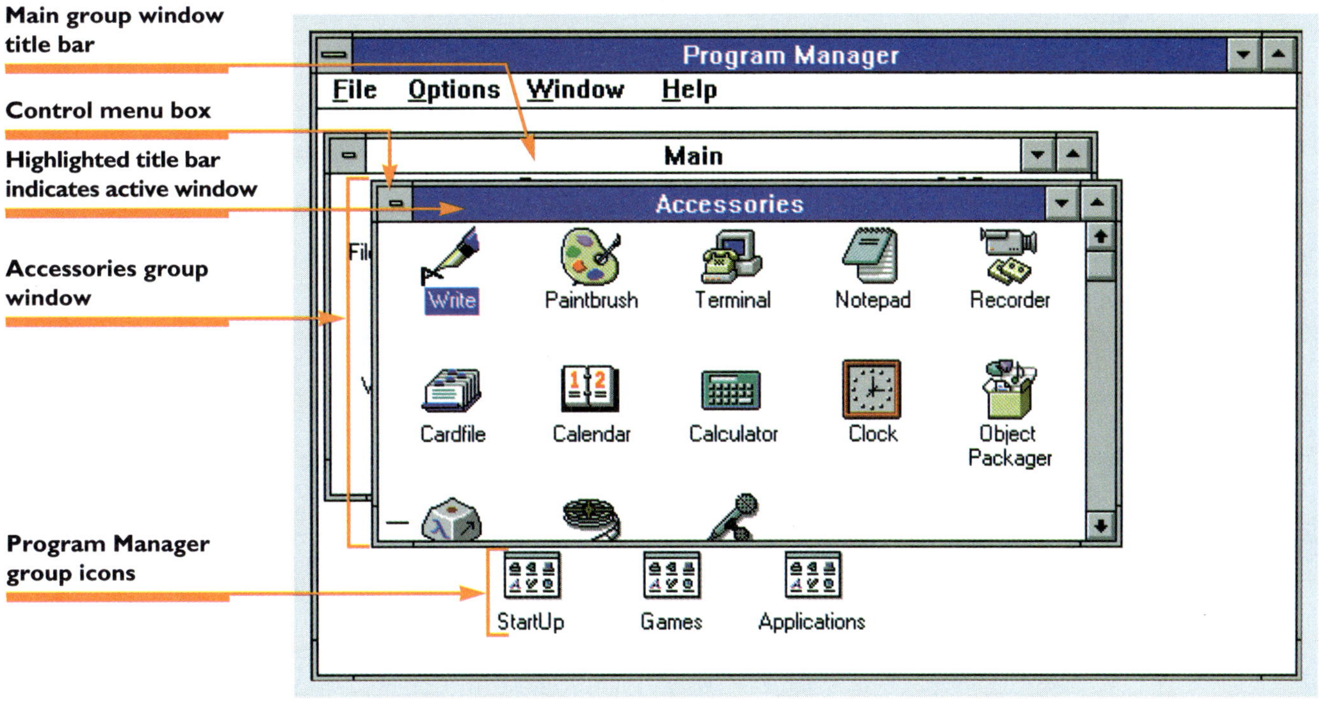

Scroll bars

If a group contains more icons than can be displayed at one time, **scroll bars** appear on the right and/or bottom edges of the window to give you access to the remaining icons, as shown in Figure 5. Vertical or horizontal arrows appear at the ends of the bars. To use scroll bars, click the vertical or horizontal arrows that point in the direction you want the window to scroll or drag the scroll box along the scroll bar. Scroll bars appear whenever there is more information than can fit in a window. You'll see them in many Windows applications.

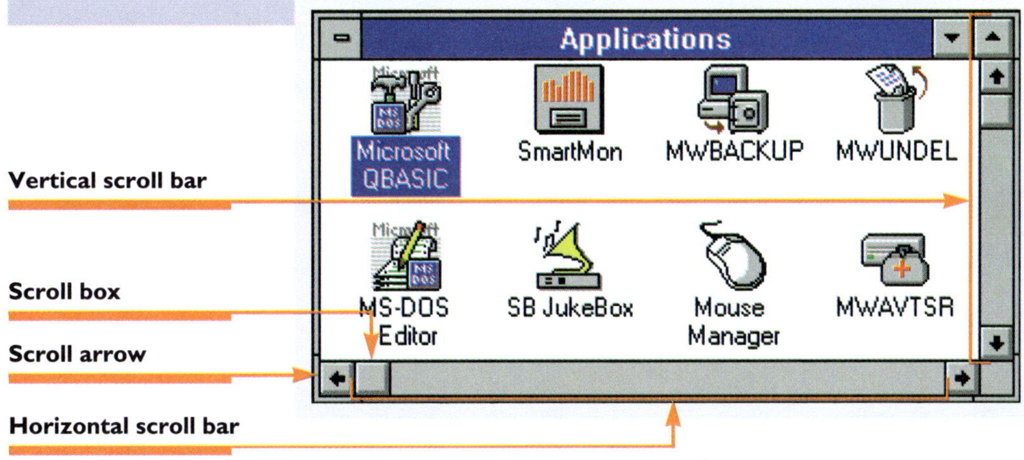

FIGURE 5: Vertical and horizontal scroll bars on a window

QUICK **TIP**

You can use the direction keys on the keyboard to scroll the contents of the active window. To scroll vertically, press [↑] or [↓]. To scroll horizontally, press [←] or [→].

Running an application

A Windows application is a program specially designed to operate, or **run**, in the Windows environment. Windows comes with several built-in Windows applications, including the desktop accessories shown in Table 5. Windows applications are represented by graphical icons in Program Manager groups. To run a Windows application, double-click the application icon. ▶ Try running the Clock application now.

STEPS

1 Double-click the **Accessories group icon**
The Accessories group window opens and the desktop accessory icons display inside it. You may need to move the Main window to see the Accessories group icon.

2 Double-click the **Clock application icon**
The Clock application starts and Windows displays an analog clock in a window, as shown in Figure 6. You might see a digital clock, depending on your system settings. Note that the current date appears on the clock's title bar and the current time appears on the clock's face. The Clock application is running, as demonstrated by the moving second hand.

3 Click the **Clock title bar** then drag the window to the lower-right corner of the screen
If the clock does not have a title bar, double-click the clock to display the title bar. The clock continues running in the lower-right corner of the screen. The Clock application window is like any other window and can be moved anywhere on the desktop. Sometimes it's useful to change the location of an application on the desktop so you can see information contained in other windows.

4 Close the Clock by double-clicking the **Clock window control menu box**
The Clock application closes and is no longer visible on the screen. Double-clicking an application's control menu box closes the application and returns you to the application's group window.

TABLE 5: Some common Windows applications in the Accessories group

APPLICATION	PURPOSE
Write	Word processor
Paintbrush	Drawing program
Notepad	Simple editor/note taker
Cardfile	Card file program
Calendar	Electronic calendar/appointment planner
Calculator	Calculator
Clock	Digital/analog clock

FIGURE 6: Running the Clock desktop accessory

Analog version of the Clock

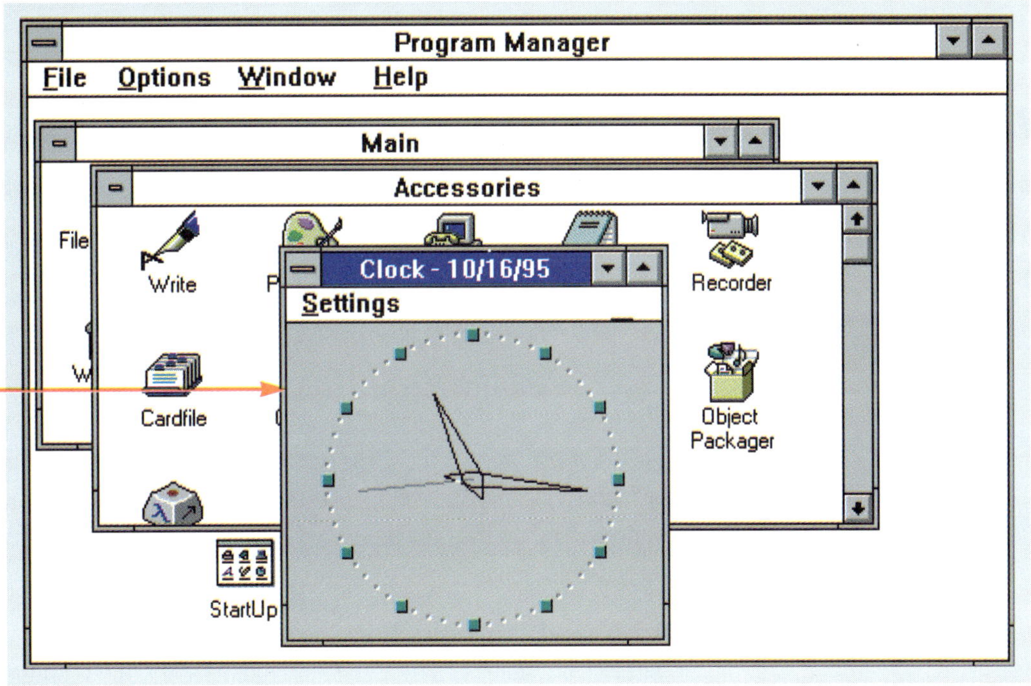

Switching between applications

If you are running more than one application at a time, you can switch between them by displaying the Task List. The **Task List** provides an alternative to switching between applications with the mouse and is especially useful when one of the applications is taking up the entire screen. To display the Task List, hold down [Ctrl] and press [Esc]. Figure 7 shows the Task List with the Program Manager and Clock applications running. To switch to an application in the Task List, double-click the application name in the Task List.

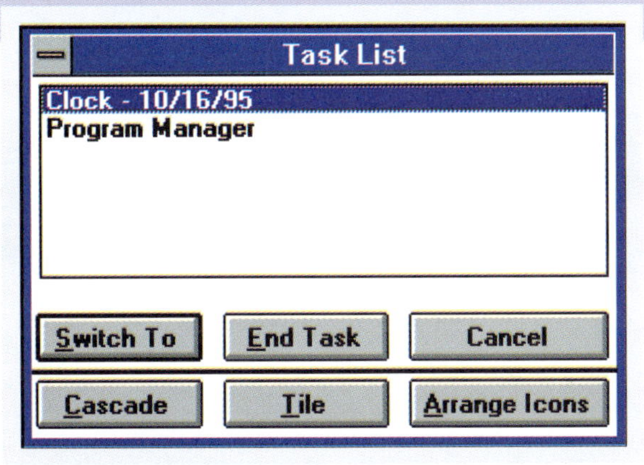

FIGURE 7: Task List

Resizing a window

The Windows desktop can get cluttered with icons and windows if you use lots of applications. Each window is surrounded by a standard border and sizing buttons that allow you to minimize, maximize, and restore windows as needed. The sizing buttons are shown in Table 6. They help you keep the desktop organized. ▶ Try sizing the Clock window now.

STEPS

1. Double-click the **Clock application icon**
   The Clock application restarts.
2. Click the **Minimize button** in the upper-right corner of the Clock window
   The Minimize button is the sizing button on the left. When you **minimize** the clock, it shrinks to an icon at the bottom of the screen, as shown in Figure 8. Notice that the Clock icon continues to show the right time, even as an icon. Windows applications continue to run after you minimize them.
3. Double-click the **Clock icon** to restore the Clock window to its original size
   The clock is restored to its original size, and the application continues to run.
4. Click the **Maximize button** in the upper-right corner of the Clock window
   The Maximize button is the sizing button to the right of the Minimize button. When you **maximize** the clock, it takes up the entire screen, as shown in Figure 9. Although it's unlikely you'll want to maximize this application very often, you'll find the ability to maximize other Windows applications very useful.
5. Click the **Restore button** in the upper-right corner of the Clock window
   The Restore button, as shown in Figure 9, is located to the right of the Minimize button *after* an application has been maximized. The Restore button returns an application to its original size.
6. Double-click the **Clock window control menu box** to close the application

TABLE 6:
Buttons for managing windows

BUTTON	PURPOSE
	Minimizes an application to an icon on the bottom of the screen.
	Maximizes an application to its largest possible size.
	Restores an application, returning it to its original size.

FIGURE 8: Minimized Clock application as an icon

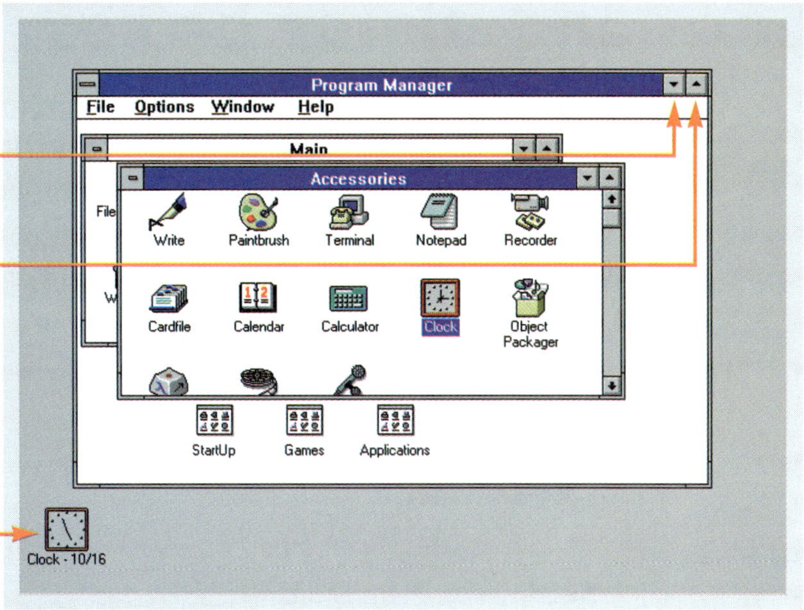

Minimize button

Maximize button

Minimized clock with current time and date

FIGURE 9: Maximized clock filling entire screen

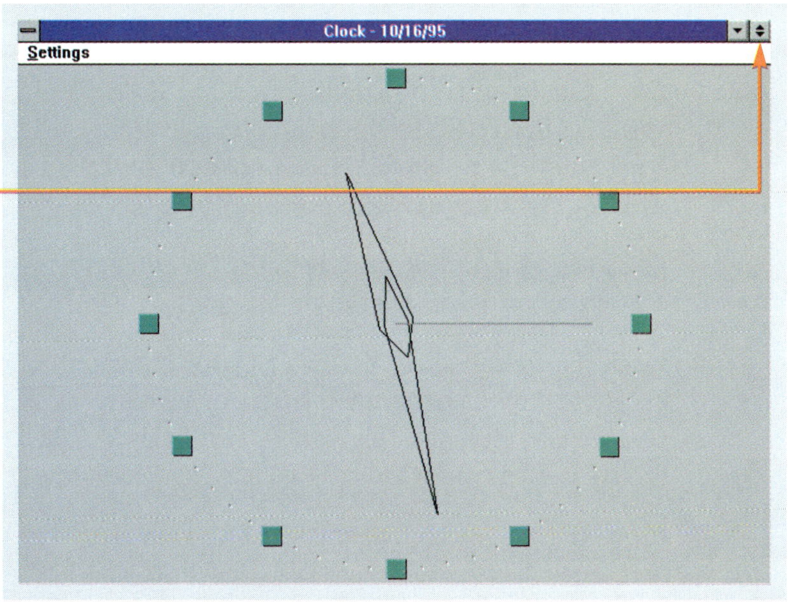

Restore button appears after a window has been maximized

Changing the dimension of a window

The dimension of a window can also be changed, but the window will always be a rectangle. To change the dimension of a window, position the mouse pointer on the window border you want to modify. The mouse pointer changes to ⇔. Drag the border in the direction you want to change. Figure 10 shows the width of the Clock window being increased, which will make the clock face larger.

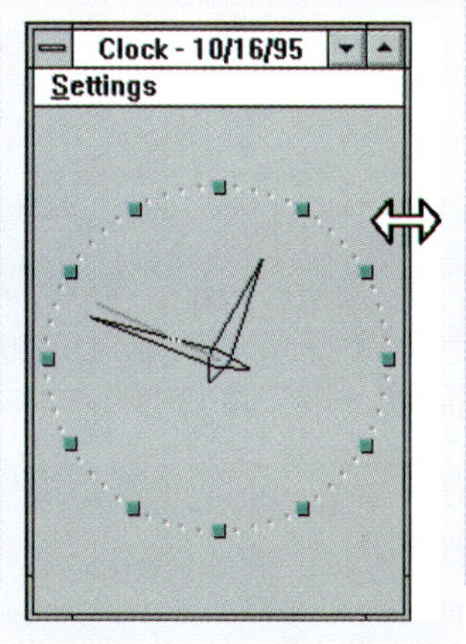

FIGURE 10: Increasing the width of the Clock window

Using menus and dialog boxes

A **menu** is a list of commands that you can use to accomplish certain tasks. Each Windows application has its own set of menus, which are listed on the **menu bar** along the top of the application window. Sometimes when you select a command from a menu, the application needs more information before it can complete the task, in which case a **dialog box** opens, giving you more options. See Table 7 for some of the typical conventions used on menus and dialog boxes. ▶ Try using the Control Panel which lets you customize your Windows desktop.

STEPS

1 Click the **Main group window** to make it active, then double-click the **Control Panel icon**
Drag other windows out of the way, if necessary. The Control Panel window opens.

2 Click **Settings** on the menu bar
A menu displays listing all the commands that let you adjust different aspects of your desktop. See Table 7.

3 Click **Desktop** to display the Desktop dialog box
This dialog box provides options to customize your desktop. See Figure 11. Next, locate the Screen Saver section of the dialog box. A **screen saver** is a moving pattern that fills your screen after your computer has not been used for a specified amount of time.

4 Click the **Name list arrow** in the Screen Saver section
A list of available screen saver patterns displays.

5 Click the screen saver pattern of your choice, then click **Test**
The Test button is a **command button**. The two most common command buttons are OK and Cancel which you'll see in almost every dialog box. The screen saver pattern you chose displays. It will remain on the screen until you move the mouse or press a key.

6 Move the mouse to exit the screen saver
Next, you'll adjust the cursor blink rate in the Cursor Blink Rate section. The **cursor** is the vertical line that shows you where you are on the screen. See Figure 11.

7 Drag the scroll box all the way to the right of the scroll bar, then click the **left arrow** in the scroll bar a few times
By moving the scroll box between Slow and Fast on the scroll bar, you can adjust the cursor blink rate to suit your needs.

8 Click **OK** to save your changes and close the dialog box
Clicking OK accepts your changes; clicking Cancel rejects your changes. Now you can exit the Control Panel.

9 Double-click the **Control Panel control menu box** to close this window

FIGURE 11:
Desktop dialog box

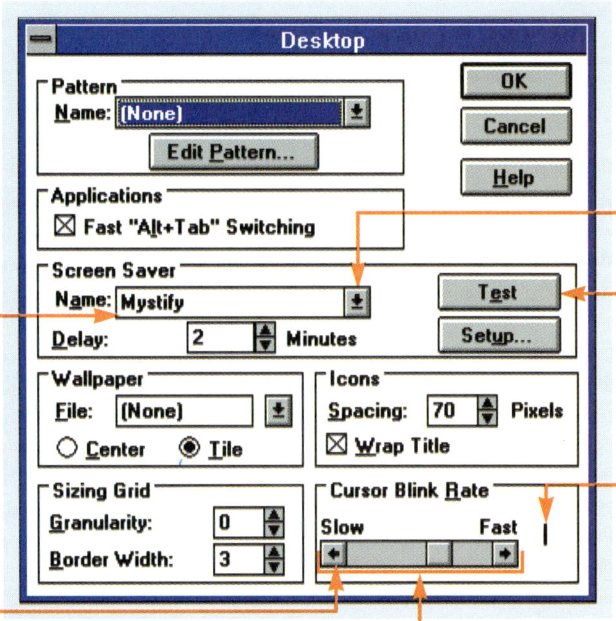

QUICK TIP

If you are in a computer lab, you might want to return the desktop settings you changed to their original state.

TABLE 7: Typical items on menus and dialog boxes

ITEM	MEANING	EXAMPLE
Dimmed command	A menu command that is not currently available.	Undo
Ellipsis	Choosing this menu command opens a dialog box that asks for further information.	Paste Special...
Triangle	Clicking this button opens a cascading menu containing an additional list of menu commands.	Axis ▶
Keyboard shortcut	A keyboard alternative for executing a menu command.	Cut Ctrl+X
Underlined letter	Pressing the underlined letter executes this menu command.	Copy Right
Check box	Clicking this square box turns a dialog box option on or off.	☒ Wrap Title
Text box	A box in which you type text.	tours.wk4
Radio button	Clicking this small circle selects a single dialog box option.	◉ Tile
Command button	Clicking this button executes this dialog box command.	OK
List box	A box containing a list of items. To choose an item, click the list arrow, then click the desired item.	c: ms-dos_5

Saving a file

The documents you create using a computer are stored in the computer's random access memory (RAM). **RAM** is temporary storage space that is erased when the computer is turned off. To store a document permanently, you need to save it to a disk. You can either save your work to a 3.5-inch or a 5.25-inch disk that you insert into the disk drive of your computer (i.e., drive A or B), or a hard disk, which is a disk built into the computer (usually drive C). Your instructor has provided you with a Student Disk to use as you proceed through the lessons in this book. This book assumes that you will save all of your files to your Student Disk. Refer to the Read This Before You Begin page immediately preceding this section for more information on your Student Disk. ▶ In this lesson, you'll create a simple document using Notepad, then you will save the document to your Student Disk. **Notepad** is a simple text editor that lets you create memos, record notes, or edit text files. A **text file** is a document containing words, letters, or numbers, but no special computer instructions, such as formatting.

STEPS

1. Insert your Student Disk into drive A or drive B
   Check with your instructor if you aren't sure which drive you should use.
2. Click the **Accessories group window** to activate it
3. Double-click the **Notepad application icon** to start Notepad
   The Notepad application starts, and the Notepad window displays. Now, enter some text.
4. Type **Today I started working with Notepad.** then press **[Enter]**
   Your screen should look like Figure 12.
5. Click **File** on the Notepad menu bar, then click **Save**
   The Save As dialog box displays, as shown in Figure 13. In this dialog box you enter a name for your file and specify where you want to save it.
6. Type **MYNOTES** in the File Name text box
   Your entry replaces the highlighted (selected) *.txt. Notepad will automatically add the extension when you click OK. Now you need to specify the drive where your Student Disk is located.
7. Click the **Drives list arrow** to display the drives on your computer, then click **a:** or **b:**, depending on which drive contains your Student Disk
   Notice that the list of files that are on your Student Disk displays below the File Name text box.
8. Click **OK**
   The Save As dialog box closes and MYNOTES is now saved on your Student Disk.
9. Click **File** on the Notepad menu bar, then click **Exit** to close Notepad

FIGURE 12: Notepad window with text entered

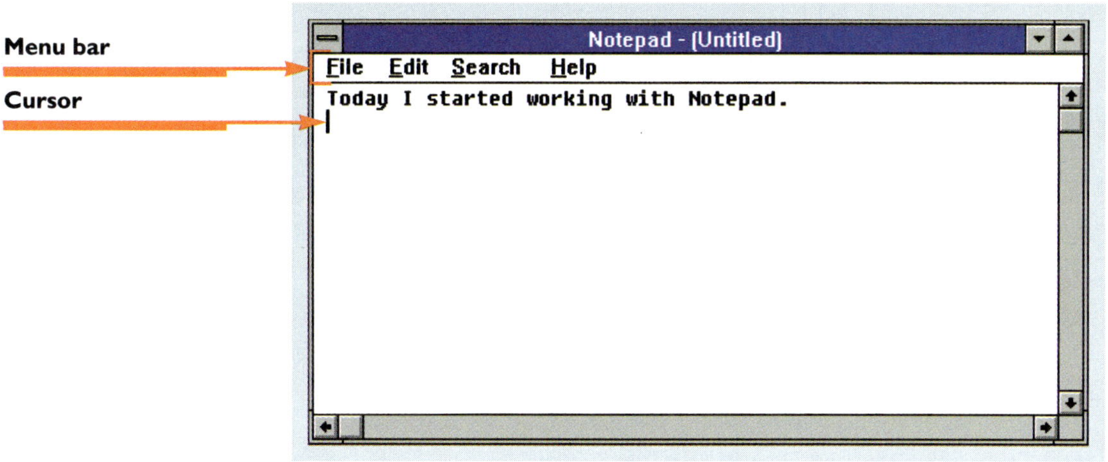

FIGURE 13: Save As dialog box

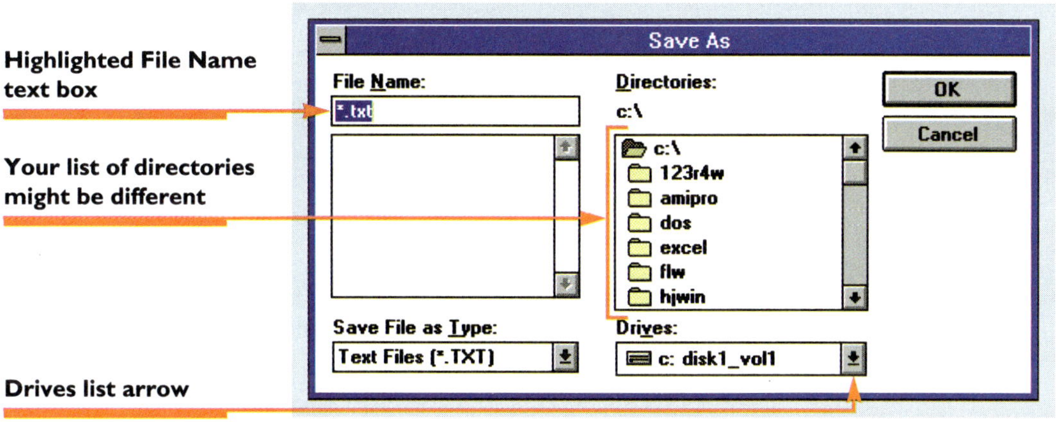

QUICK TIP

Save your work often, at least every 15 minutes and before printing.

Using File Manager

File Manager is an application included with Windows that can help you organize files and directories. A **directory** is like a file folder—it is a part of a disk where you can store a group of related files. For example, you might want to create a directory called PROJECT1 and store all of the files relating to a particular project in that directory. You can use File Manager to create the directory, then move the related files into it. ▶ Use File Manager to create a directory called MY_FILES on your Student Disk and then move the Notepad file you created and saved in the previous lesson into that directory. Make sure your Student Disk is in drive A or drive B before beginning the steps.

STEPS

1. Double-click the **Main program group icon**, or if it is already open, click the **Main group window** to activate it
2. Double-click the **File Manager application icon** in the Main group window
   File Manager opens to display the directory window, as shown in Figure 14. Your File Manager will contain different files and directories. The directory window is divided by the split bar. The left side of the window displays the structure of the current drive, or the directory tree. The right side of the window displays a list of files in the selected directory. See Table 8 for a description of the various icons used in the directory window. The status bar displays the information about the current drive and directory and other information to help you with file management tasks.
3. Click the **drive icon** that corresponds to the drive containing your Student Disk
   The contents of your Student Disk displays. Now create a directory on this disk.
4. Click **File** on the menu bar, then click **Create Directory**
   The Create Directory dialog box displays listing the current directory, which in this case is the top level directory indicated by the backslash (\). You will type a new directory name in the text box provided. Directory names can have up to 11 characters but cannot include spaces, commas, or backslashes.
5. Type **MY_FILES** in the Name text box, then click **OK**
   You can type in the directory name in either uppercase or lowercase letters. The new directory appears in both sides of the directory window.
6. Press and hold the mouse button to select MYNOTES.TXT, then drag the file into the MY_FILES directory on the left side of the window
   The mouse pointer changes as you drag the file, as shown in Figure 15. Don't worry if you move a file to the wrong place; simply drag it again to the correct location. (You can drag it to the MY_FILES directory in either the left or right side of the window.)
7. Click **Yes** in the Confirm Mouse Operation dialog box
   Notice that the file no longer appears in the list of files. Now check that the file is in the newly created directory.
8. Double-click the **MY_FILES icon**
   The file appears in the list of files. If you want, you can use this directory throughout this book to store the files that you save. Now that you have created a directory and moved a file into it, you can exit File Manager.
9. Double-click the **control menu box** to exit File Manager

FIGURE 14: File Manager

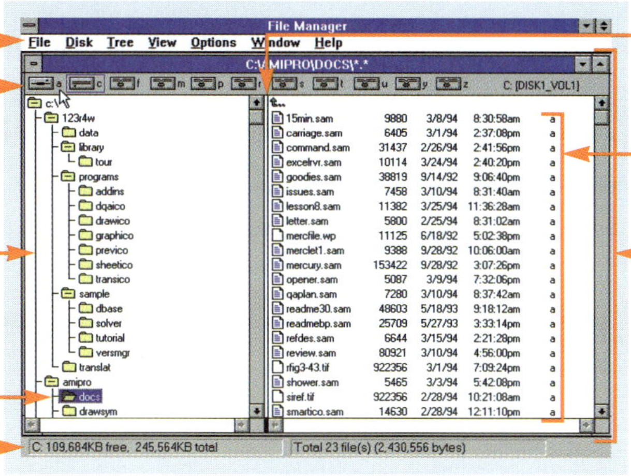

FIGURE 15: Dragging a file to a new location

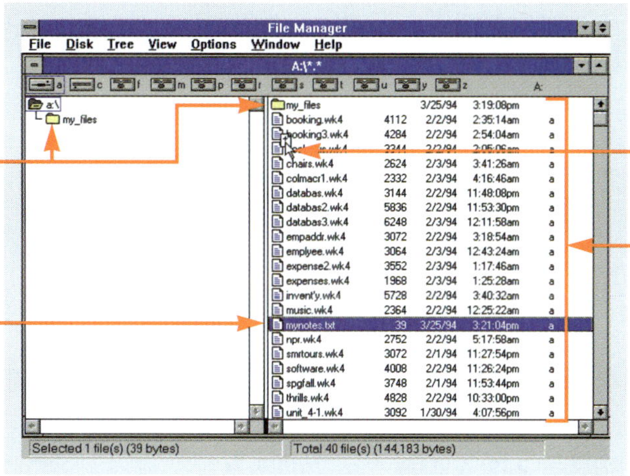

TABLE 8: Directory window icons

ICON	DESCRIPTION
	Displays the contents of a directory one level up in the directory tree.
	Represents a directory.
	Represents a directory that contains additional directories not displayed in the directory tree.
	Represents a directory that contains additional directories that are displayed in the directory tree.
	Represents an open directory. The files in this directory are listed in the right side of the directory window.
	Represents an application file. These files start applications or start programs.
	Represents a document file associated with an application. When you open this file, the application that you used to create it starts.
	Represents other document files.

QUICK TIP

To select a group of files, click the first file, then press [Shift] and click the last file. To select noncontiguous files (files not next to each other in the file list), click the first file, then press [Ctrl] and click each additional file.

Arranging windows and icons

If your desktop contains many groups that you open regularly, you might find that the open windows clutter your desktop. The Tile and Cascade commands on the Window menu let you view all your open group windows at once in an organized arrangement. You can also use the Window menu to open all the program groups installed on your computer. ▶ Once you are comfortable working with Windows, you might decide to reorganize your group windows. You can easily move an icon from one group window to another by dragging it with the mouse. In the following steps, you'll drag the Clock icon from the Accessories group window to the StartUp group window. The StartUp group window contains programs that automatically start running when you launch Windows.

STEPS

1 Click the **Program Manager Maximize button** to maximize this window, then click **Window** on the menu bar

The Window menu opens, as shown in Figure 16, displaying the commands Cascade, Tile, and Arrange Icons, followed by a numbered list of the program groups installed on your computer. You might see a check mark next to one of the items, indicating that this program group is the active one. Locate StartUp on the numbered list. If you don't see StartUp, click More Windows at the bottom of the list, then double-click StartUp in the dialog box that displays. If you still can't find StartUp, see your instructor or technical support person for assistance.

2 Click **StartUp**

The StartUp group window opens. Depending on how your computer is set up, you might see some program icons already in this window. At this point, your screen is getting cluttered with three program group windows open (Main, Accessories, and StartUp). Use the Cascade command to arrange them in an orderly way.

3 Click **Window** on the menu bar, then click **Cascade**

The windows display in a layered arrangement, with the title bars of each showing. This formation is neatly organized and shows all your open group windows, but it doesn't allow you to easily drag the Clock icon from the Accessories group window to the StartUp group window. The Tile command arranges the windows so that the contents of all the open windows are visible.

4 Click **Window** on the menu bar, then click **Tile**

The windows are now positioned in an ideal way to copy an icon from one window to another. Before continuing to step 5, locate the Clock icon in the Accessories group window. If you don't see the icon, use the scroll bar to bring it into view.

5 Drag the Clock application icon from the Accessories group window to the StartUp group window

Your screen now looks like Figure 17. The Clock application will automatically start the next time Windows is launched. If you are working on your own computer and want to leave the Clock in the StartUp group, skip Step 6 and continue to the next lesson, "Exiting Windows." If you are working in a computer lab, move the Clock icon back to its original location in the Accessories group window.

6 Drag the Clock application icon from the StartUp group window to the Accessories group window

The Clock icon is now back in the Accessories group.

FIGURE 16:
Window menu

Check mark indicates the active program group

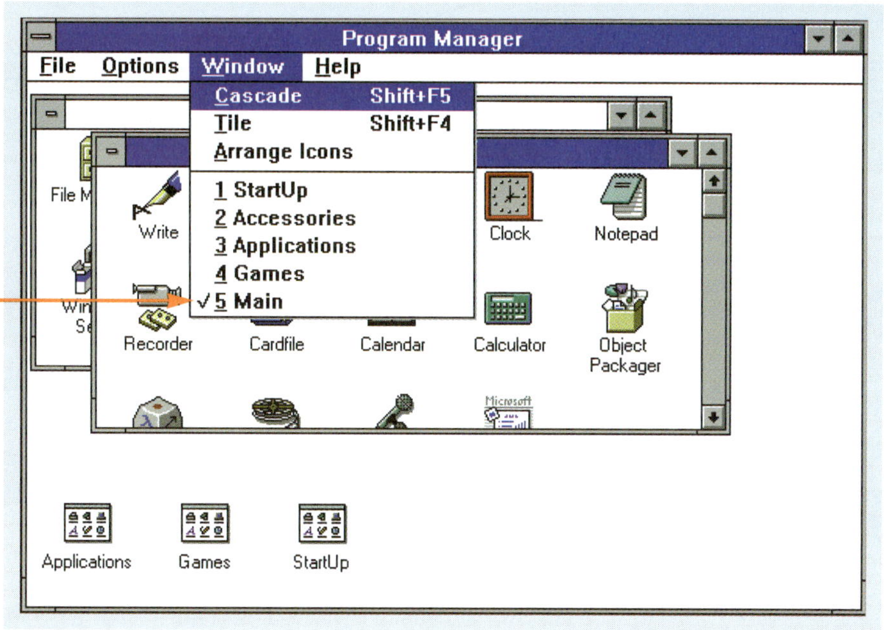

FIGURE 17:
Tiled group windows

StartUp group window with Clock icon

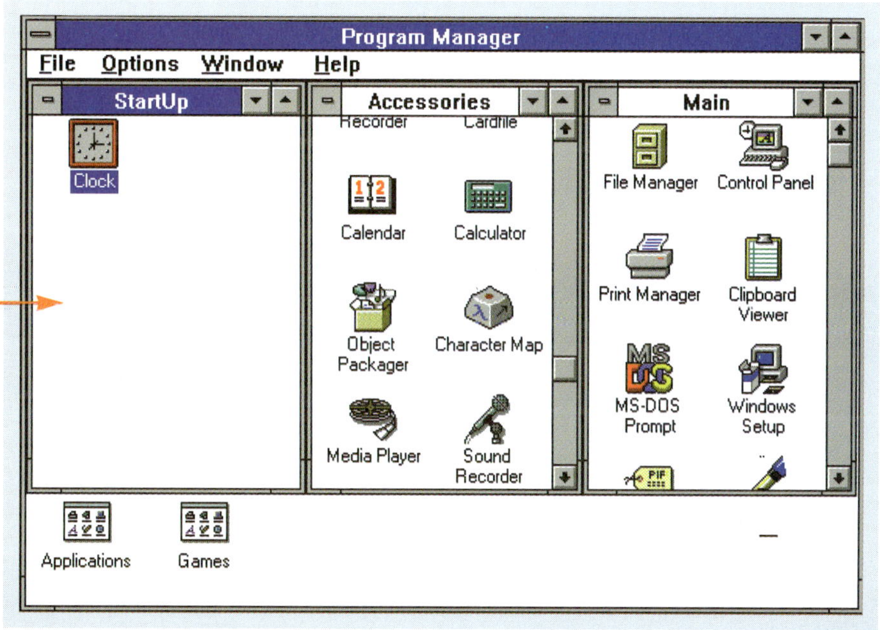

QUICK TIP

To move a copy of an icon from one group window to another, hold down [Ctrl] as you drag the icon.

Exiting Windows

When you are finished working with Windows, close all the applications you are running and exit Windows. Do not turn off the computer while Windows is running; you could lose important data if you turn off your computer too soon. ▶ Now try closing all your active applications and exiting Windows.

STEPS

1. **Close any active applications or group windows by double-clicking the control menu boxes of the open windows, one at a time**
   The windows close. If you have any unsaved changes in your application, a dialog box displays, asking if you want to save them.

2. Click **File** on the Program Manager menu bar
   The File menu displays, as shown in Figure 18.

3. Click **Exit Windows**
   Program Manager displays the Exit Windows dialog box, as shown in Figure 19. You have two options at this point: Click OK to exit Windows, or click Cancel to abort the Exit Windows command and return to the Program Manager.

4. Click **OK** to exit Windows
   Windows finishes its work and the MS-DOS command prompt appears. You can now safely turn off the computer.

FIGURE 18: Exiting Windows using the File menu

Menu bar

Exit Windows command

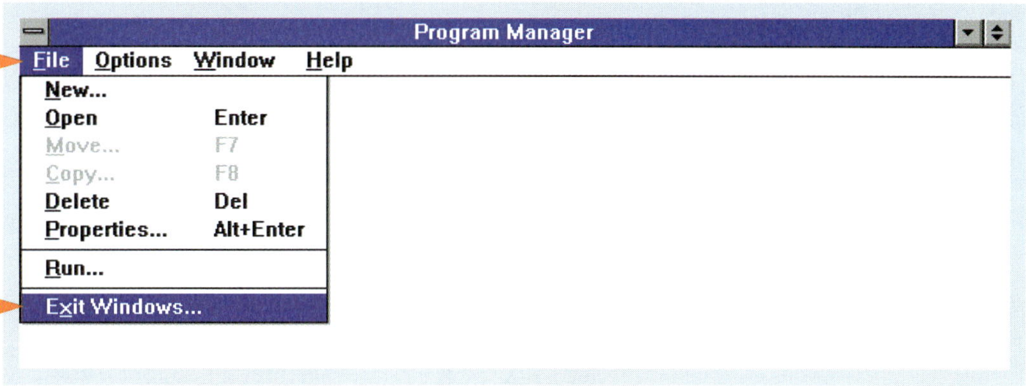

FIGURE 19: Exit Windows dialog box

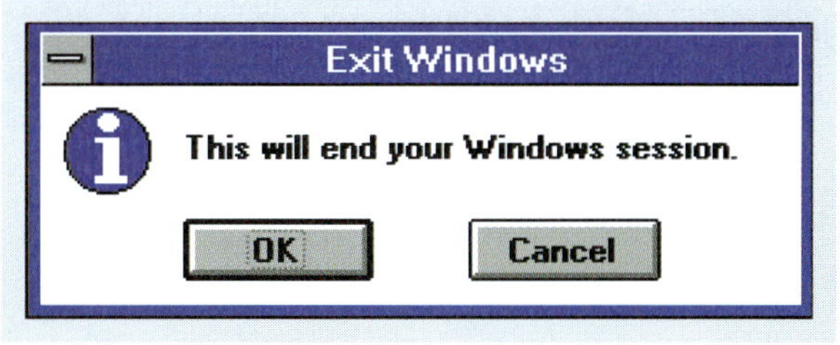

Exiting Windows with the Program Manager control menu box

You can also exit Windows by double-clicking the control menu box in the upper-left corner of the Program Manager window, as shown in Figure 20. After you double-click the control menu box, you see the Exit Windows dialog box. Click OK to exit Windows.

Double-click the control menu box

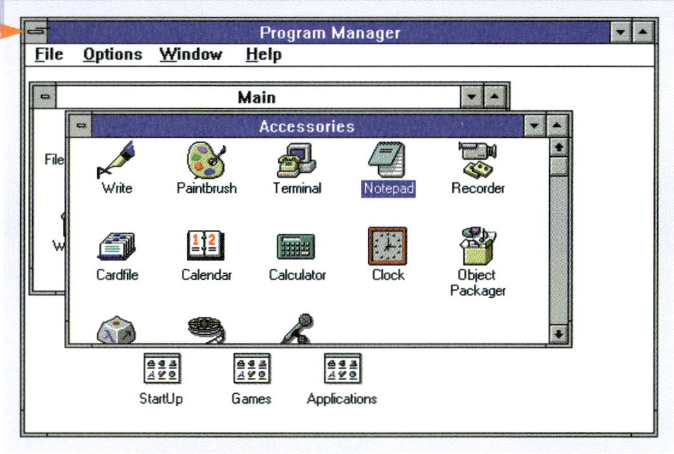

FIGURE 20: Exiting Windows with the Program Manager control menu box

TROUBLE?

If you do not exit from Windows before turning off the computer, you might lose data from the applications you used while you were running Windows. Always close your applications and exit from Windows before turning off your computer. Do not turn off the computer if you are in a computer lab.

CONCEPTS REVIEW

Label each of the elements of the Windows screen shown in Figure 21.

1 ____

2 ____

3 ____

4 ____

5 ____

6 ____

7 ____

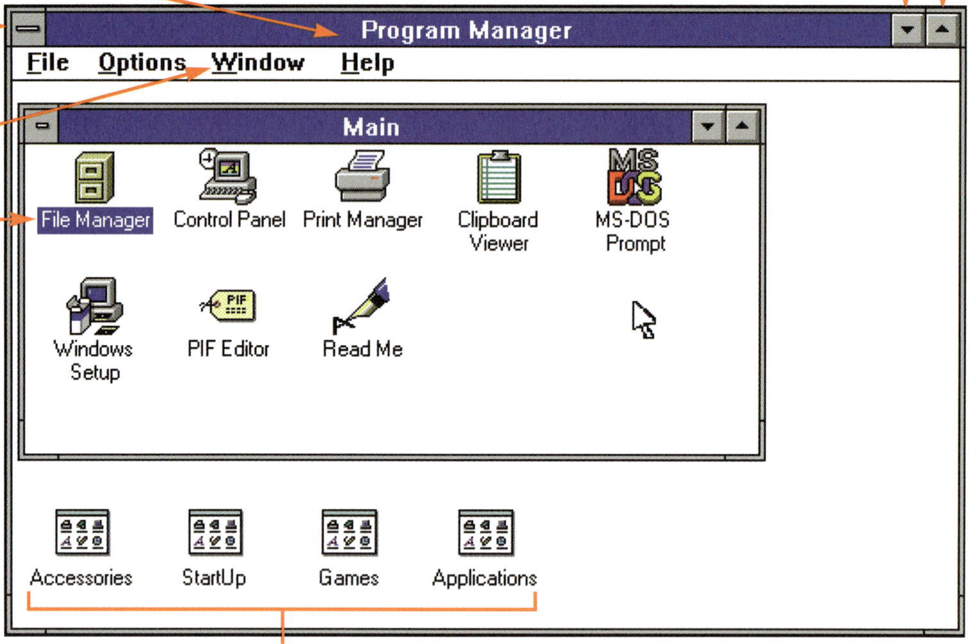

FIGURE 21

Match each of the statements with the term it describes.

8 Shrinks an application window to an icon

9 Displays the name of the window or application

10 Servs as a launching pad for all applications

11 Requests more information that you supply before executing command

12 Lets the user point at screen menus and icons

a. Program Manager
b. Dialog box
c. Mouse
d. Title bar
e. Minimize button

Select the best answer from the list of choices.

13 The acronym GUI means:
- a. Grayed user information
- b. Group user icons
- c. Graphical user interface
- d. Group user interconnect

14 The term for starting Windows is:
- a. Prompting
- b. Launching
- c. Applying
- d. Processing

15 The small pictures that represent items such as applications are:

a. Icons

b. Windows

c. Buttons

d. Pointers

16 All of the following are examples of using a mouse, EXCEPT:

a. Clicking the Maximize button

b. Pressing [Enter]

c. Pointing at the control menu box

d. Dragging the Games icon

17 When Windows is busy performing a task, the mouse pointer changes to a(n):

a. Hand

b. Arrow

c Clock

d. Hourglass

18 The term for moving an item to a new location on the desktop is:

a. Pointing

b. Clicking

c. Dragging

d. Restoring

19 The Clock, Notepad, and Calendar applications in Windows are known as:

a. Menu commands

b. Control panels

c. Sizing buttons

d. Desktop accessories

20 The Maximize button is used to:

a. Return a window to its original size

b. Expand a window to fill the computer screen

c. Scroll slowly through a window

d. Run programs from the main menu

21 What appears if a window contains more information than can be displayed in the window?

a. Program icon

b. Cascading menu

c. Scroll bars

d. Check box

22 A window is active when its title bar is:

a. Highlighted

b. Dimmed

c. Checked

d. Underlined

23 What is the term for changing the dimensions of a window?

a. Selecting

b. Resizing

c. Navigating

d. Scrolling

24 The menu bar provides access to an application's functions through:

a. Icons

b. Scroll bars

c. Commands

d. Control menu box

25 File Manager is a Windows application that lets you:

a. Select a different desktop wallpaper

b. Move a file from one location to another

c. Type entries into a text file

d. Determine what programs begin automatically when you start Windows

26 When your desktop is too cluttered, you can organize it by all the following methods, EXCEPT:

a. Double-clicking the control menu box to close unneeded windows

b. Using the Tile command to view all open group windows

c. Using the Cascade command to open group window title bars

d. Clicking File, clicking Exit Windows, then clicking OK

27 You can exit Windows by double-clicking the:

a. Accessories group icon

b. Program Manager control menu box

c. Main window menu bar

d. Control Panel application

APPLICATIONS REVIEW

1 Start Windows and identify items on the screen.

a. Turn on the computer, if necessary.

b. At the command prompt, type "WIN," then press [Enter]. After Windows loads, the Program Manager displays.

c. Try to identify as many items on the desktop as you can, without referring to the lesson material. Then compare your results with Figure 1.

2 Minimize and restore the Program Manager window.

a. Click the Minimize button. Notice that the Program Manager window reduces to an icon at the bottom of the screen. Now try restoring the window.

b. Double-click the minimized Program Manager icon. The Program Manager window opens.

c. Practice minimizing and restoring other windows on the desktop.

3 Resize and move the Program Manager window.

a. Click anywhere inside the Program Manager window to activate the window.

b. Move the mouse pointer over the lower-right corner of the Program Manager window. Notice that the mouse pointer changes to a double-ended arrow.

c. Press and hold the mouse button and drag the corner of the window up and to the right until the Program Manager takes up the top third of your screen.

d. Drag the Program Manager title bar to reposition the window at the bottom of the screen.

4 Practice working with menus and dialog boxes.

a. Click Window on the Program Manager menu bar, then click Accessories (if you can't find it in the menu, click More Windows, then double-click it from the list that appears, scrolling if necessary).

b. Double-click the Calculator icon to open the Calculator application.

c. Click numbers and operators as you would on a handheld calculator to perform some simple arithmetic operations, like 22 multiplied by 3.99, to see how much it would cost to take a bus of 22 employees on the way back from a conference to a fast-food place for a quick lunch. (Multiplication is indicated by an asterisk *.)

d. Double-click the Calculator control menu box when you are finished.

5 Practice working with files:

a. Open File Manager from the Main group window.

b. Be sure your Student Disk is in drive A or drive B, then double-click the drive icon containing your Student Disk.

c. Double-click the drive C icon, then choose Tile from the Window menu. The open drive windows display, one above the other. If you have more windows open, double-click their control menu boxes to close them, then choose Tile again.

d. Double-click the c:\ folder icon on the left side of the drive C window, then scroll down the left side of the drive C window using the vertical scroll bar to see the available directories. When you see the Windows folder icon, double-click it to see the directories and files available in the Windows folder.

e. Scroll down the right side of the drive C window using the vertical scroll bar to see the files contained in the Windows folder. If you needed to copy a file from the Windows folder to your Student Disk, you could drag it from the list of files in the drive C window to the drive A window, but don't do so now.

6 Exit Windows.

a. Close any open application by double-clicking the application's control menu box.

b. Double-click the control menu box in the upper-left corner of the Program Manager window. The Exit Windows dialog box displays.

c. Click OK. Windows closes and the DOS command prompt displays.

INDEPENDENT CHALLENGE

Windows 3.1 provides an on-line tutorial which can help you master essential Windows controls and concepts. The tutorial features interactive lessons that teach you how to use Windows elements such as the mouse, Program Manager, menus, and icons. The tutorial also covers how to use Help.

The tutorial material you should use depends on your level of experience with Windows. Some users might want to review the basics of the Windows work area. Others might want to explore additional Windows topics, such as managing files and customizing windows.

Ask your instructor or technical support person about how to use the Windows tutorial.

Lotus® Freelance Graphics

Release 2 for Windows™

Read This Before You Begin Lotus Freelance Graphics 2

To the Student

The exercises and examples in this book feature several ready-made Lotus Freelance Graphics files which are contained on the two Student Disks provided to your instructor. To complete the step-by-step lessons in this book, you must have these two Student Disks. Your instructor will do one of the following: 1) provide you with your own copies of the disks; 2) have you copy them from a network onto your own floppy disks; 3) have you copy the files from a network into your own subdirectory on the network. Always use your own copies of the lesson and excerise files. See your instructor or technical support person for further information.

Using your own computer

If you are going to work through this book using your own computer, you need a computer system running Microsoft Windows 3.1, Lotus Freelance Graphics Release 2 for Windows, and Student Disks 1 and 2. *You will not be able to complete the step-by-step lessons and exercises in this book using your own computer until you have your own Student Disks.* This book assumes the default settings under a standard installation of Lotus Freelance Graphics Release 2 for Windows.

To the Instructor

Bundled with the instructor's copy of this book are three Student Disks. Student Disk #1 contains all the files your students need to complete the step-by-step lessons in Units 1–4. Student Disk #2 contains files they will need to complete the step-by-step lessons in Units 5–6. Student Disk #3 contains the files they will need to complete Unit 7. As an adopter of this text, you are granted the right to distribute the files on the Student Disks to any student who has purchased a copy of this text. You are free to post all these files to a network or standalone workstations, or simply provide copies of the disks to your students. If you give them disks, be sure to place the Student Disk files for Units 1–4 on one disk, the files for Units 5–6 on a second disk, and the files for Unit 7 on a third disk. If you put them all on one disk, students will run out of disk space. The instructions in this book assume that the students know which drive and directory contain the Student Disk files, so it's important that you provide disk location information before the students start working through the units. You also need to provide instructions about where students should save their modified files.

Using the Student Disk files

To keep the original files on the Student Disks intact, the instructions in this book for opening files require two important steps: (1) Open the existing file and (2) Save it as a new file with a new name in the MY_FILES directory students will create in the Working with Windows section. This procedure ensures that the original file will remain unmodified in case the student wants to redo the exercise. For more information about opening a file and saving it with a new name, please refer to the lesson, "Opening an existing presentation" in Unit 3. For more information on creating the MY_FILES directory, please refer to the lesson, "Using File Manager" in the Working with Windows section.

UNIT 1

OBJECTIVES

- Define presentation graphics
- Start Freelance Graphics for Windows
- Begin a presentation
- Explore the Freelance Graphics screen
- Work with SmartIcons
- Get help
- Exit Freelance Graphics

Getting STARTED WITH FREELANCE GRAPHICS

Now that you are familiar with common Microsoft Windows tasks, you are ready to start working with Freelance Graphics Release 2 for Windows, one of the most popular presentation graphics programs used today. This unit shows you how to start a Freelance Graphics work session and use the mouse and keyboard to select items and get help. ▶ This unit also introduces Conscious Clothing, a small clothing manufacturer wanting to represent its products in the best possible light. The needs of this business will help you see how Freelance Graphics can be used to create effective and professional presentations. ▶

Defining presentation graphics

With a **presentation graphics** program, you use your personal computer to create slides, transparencies, and handouts for all kinds of presentations. Having a professional-looking presentation containing eye-catching charts and graphics will make a big impact on the success of the presentation. ▶ You have recently begun working at Conscious Clothing as assistant to the marketing manager, Tom Leary. Your job involves helping present information on sales, products, and future projections to sales representatives and prospective buyers. Figure 1-1 shows the opening slide of a presentation created using a word processor and a laser printer. Figure 1-2 shows the same information presented using Freelance Graphics for Windows. By using Freelance Graphics you enjoy the many benefits of its features.

- **Present information effectively.**
  Freelance Graphics enables you to take advantage of professional page layouts, color, type styles, and special graphics to help the audience quickly understand your message.

- **Create presentations quickly.**
  With Freelance Graphics, you can sit down with the basic idea for your presentation and create an entire screen show, complete with handouts and speaker notes, in a matter of minutes or hours. Automated features such as SmartMasters help you choose the basic color scheme, background effects, and text styles for your entire presentation.

- **Format pages with confidence.**
  Freelance Graphics lets you choose from a list of preset page formats so you can vary the page style in a presentation with confidence yet still maintain a consistent color scheme and style.

- **Enter information easily.**
  Adding most information in Freelance Graphics is as simple as point, click, and type. You can also import information from other Lotus programs—such as 1-2-3 and Ami Pro—so you never have to type the same data twice.

- **Create effective charts and graphics easily.**
  With Freelance Graphics you can simply choose from a variety of chart styles and special effects to show off your data in the most effective way. Freelance Graphics also gives you the option of including terrific graphics—art imported from other programs or created right there in Freelance Graphics.

- **See a presentation in a new light.**
  A presentation created on paper can only be viewed one way; page after page. With Freelance Graphics, you can look at the presentation from different perspectives—from a full-screen page to a screen showing several pages in reduced size to an outline view of the all the text in the presentation—to make sure you've designed a lively, informative, and effective show.

- **Print in a variety of formats.**
  Coming up with handouts for a hand-made presentation can be more of a headache than the presentation itself. With Freelance Graphics, you can print speaker notes, audience notes, and handouts, with just a few clicks of the mouse button.

FIGURE 1-1: Slide created using a word processor

FIGURE 1-2: Slide created using Freelance Graphics

Starting Freelance Graphics

When you begin to use Freelance Graphics, you must, of course, have access to a computer on which the program has been installed. In most cases, you will simply flip the on/off switch to on (or push the power button), start Windows from the DOS prompt, open the Lotus Applications window, and double-click the Freelance Graphics icon. If you are working on a network or someone has modified the way Windows works on your system, the procedure may be slightly different for you. ▶ You must learn how to use Freelance in order to help successfully market the Conscious Clothing product line. Try starting Freelance Graphics now so you can begin familiarizing yourself with the program. Begin at the Program Manager.

STEPS

1 Locate the **Lotus Applications group icon**
Depending on how the icons in your Program Manager are arranged, the Lotus Applications group icon may be down at the bottom of the screen or mixed in with the other icons. Compare your screen with the one shown in Figure 1-3.

2 Double-click the **Lotus Applications group icon**
The Lotus Applications group icon opens into a window and the Freelance Graphics icon appears. You may have several different icons in your Lotus Applications window. The Freelance Graphics icon is shown in Figure 1-4. This is the icon you will double-click to start the program.

3 Double-click the **Freelance Graphics icon**
Freelance Graphics loads into memory and the opening screen appears. After a moment, the Welcome to Freelance Graphics dialog box appears.

FIGURE 1-3: The Windows Program Manager window

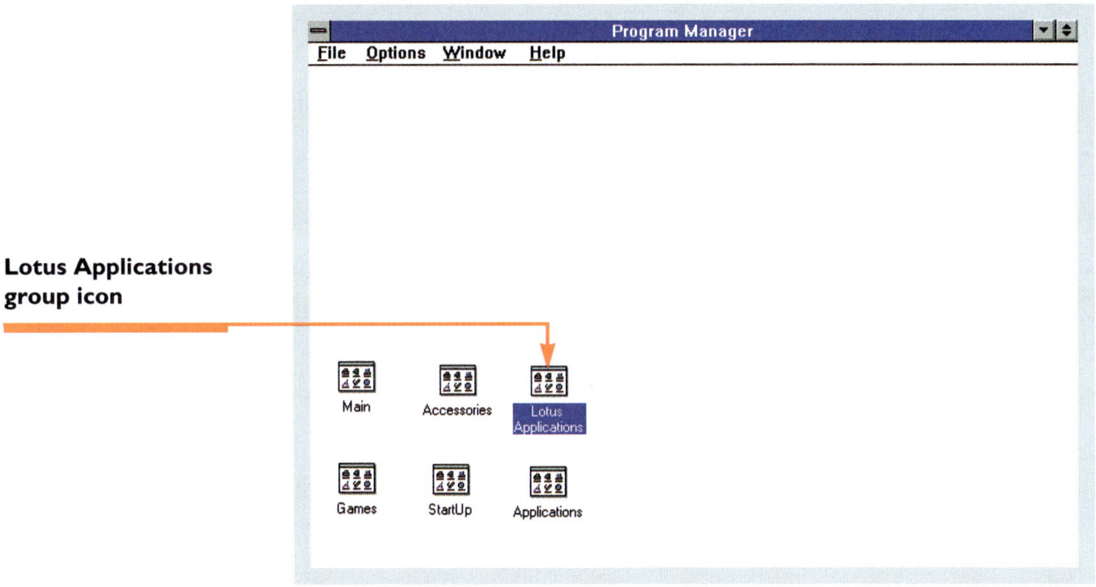

FIGURE 1-4: The Lotus Applications window

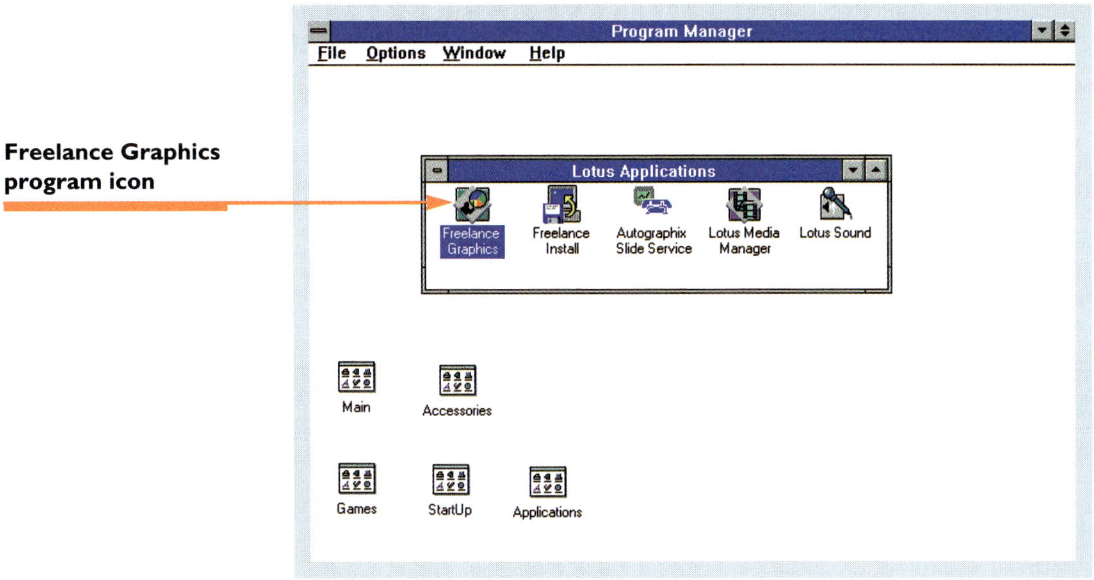

Taking the grand tour

The first time you start Freelance Graphics for Windows, you are greeted by an animated utility, called the Quick Tour, that leads you on a three-minute whirlwind tour through various Freelance Graphics features. This tour is part of an introductory QuickStart that you can take at any time during your Freelance work session. To take the tour, follow the instructions on the screen. To stop the tour at any time, click Quit in the menu bar.

TROUBLE?

If you don't see a Lotus Applications group icon, double-click the Applications window to open it and locate the Freelance Graphics icon.

Beginning a presentation

When you first start Freelance Graphics, the Welcome to Freelance Graphics dialog box appears, as shown in Figure 1-5. Here you choose whether you want to create a new presentation, work with an existing file, or take the QuickStart Tutorial. The Create a New Presentation option is automatically selected for you. ▶ Part of the Freelance Graphics startup process involves choosing a SmartMaster for your presentation. A **SmartMaster** is a predesigned presentation template containing page layouts, color selections, and font choices. Some SmartMasters even contain sample graphics. When you choose one of Freelance Graphics' 60 SmartMasters, the design is already done—all you need to do is enter the text. ▶ In this session, you start a new presentation so that you can explore the various features of Freelance Graphics in preparation for your first Conscious Clothing project. Because the example you create here will not be used in subsequent units, you choose a blank SmartMaster and a simple page layout.

STEPS

1 **In the Welcome to Freelance Graphics dialog box, make sure that Create a New Presentation is selected, and then click OK**

The Choose a Look for Your Presentation dialog box appears. See Figure 1-6. This dialog box presents you with the variety of SmartMasters you can use for your own presentation. When you click a SmartMaster file name, a sample picture of the SmartMaster appears in the preview window in the bottom of the dialog box. The SmartMaster with blank background checkbox enables you to select a background with no color or graphic elements.

2 **Click the SmartMaster with blank background checkbox**

An X appears inside the box, telling Freelance that for this presentation you want to select a SmartMaster with no special color background or graphic elements.

3 **Click OK**

The dialog box closes, but you're not done yet—the Choose Page Layout dialog box appears. See Figure 1-7. This dialog box allows you to select the layout of the page you're adding. Since you're just starting this presentation, the first layout, Title, is automatically selected.

4 **Click OK to leave the layout selected**

The first page of your new presentation displays.

FIGURE 1-5: Welcome to Freelance Graphics dialog box

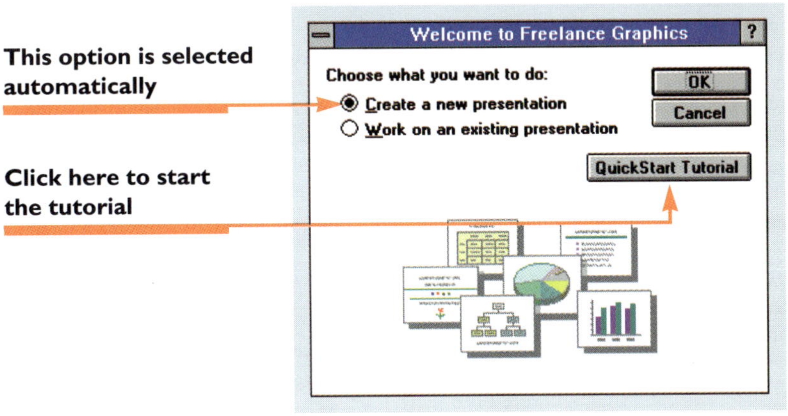

FIGURE 1-6: Choose a Look for Your Presentation dialog box

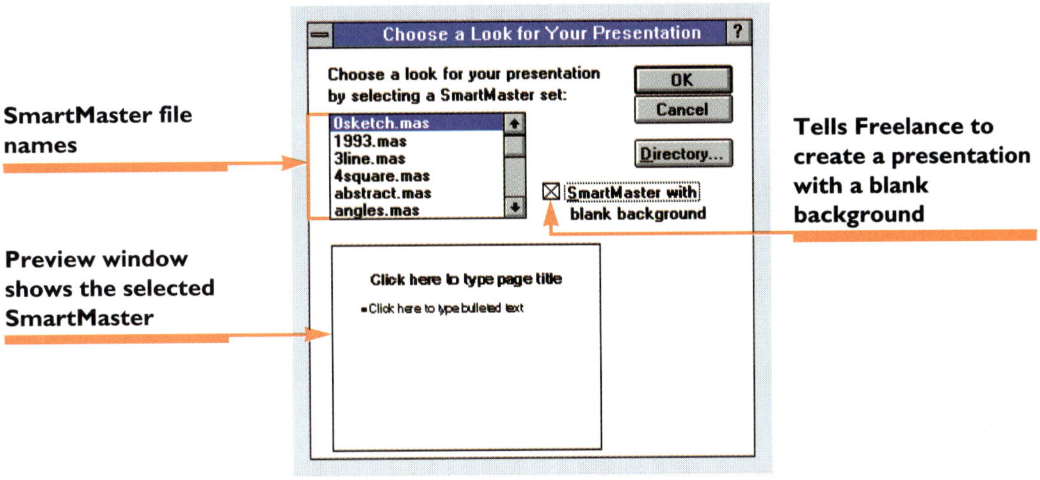

FIGURE 1-7: Choose Page Layout dialog box

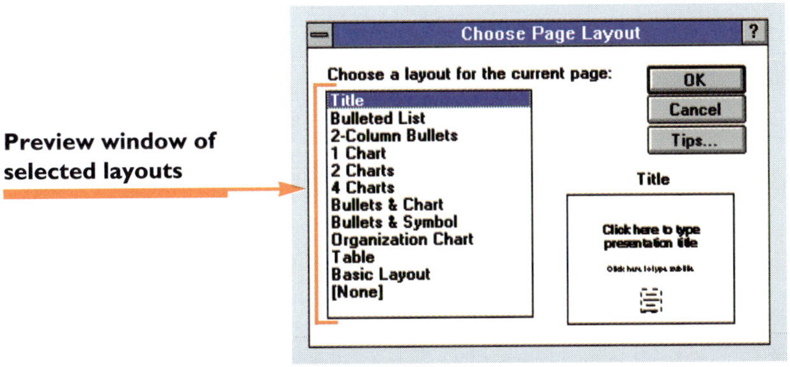

Keyboard shortcuts

You don't have to rely solely on the mouse when you're working your way through dialog boxes; you can also use keyboard shortcuts. In every dialog box, Freelance Graphics underlines one character in each option you select. To choose that option by using the keyboard, press the underlined letter.

Exploring the Freelance Graphics screen

After you finish making your initial selections for SmartMaster set and page layout, Freelance Graphics displays the work area. Although Freelance Graphics provides you with other ways to display the pages in your presentation, this default view, called the **Current Page view**, is the view you'll work with when you add text, graphics, and charts to individual pages. The various elements of the Freelance Graphics screen help you find what you need easily while you are working on your presentation. Take a few minutes to read through the screen components and find them on your screen with the help of Figure 1-8.

- The **presentation window** takes up the major portion of the screen. Inside the white area, you see **Click here to type presentation title**. This is known as **prompt text**, meaning that it's there to prompt you to insert your own text, after which point the prompt text will be replaced with the text you typed. At Conscious Clothing, Tom adds text, graphics, charts, and other objects (like sound or video clips) on the page in the presentation window.
- The **title bar**, at the top of the window, shows the program name (in this case, Freelance Graphics) and the name of the current file. If the file has not yet been saved, **[Untitled1]** appears in place of the file name. Notice that the title bar includes the control menu box and minimize and maximize buttons (which you learned about in the Working with Windows section).
- The **menu bar** contains the menus you'll use while you work with Freelance Graphics. There are 11 menus at your disposal, each of which contain commands relating to a different aspect of your presentation. For example, when you want to edit a chart you've created, look in the Chart menu for applicable commands.
- The **edit line** gives you information about the current page. If you click on prompt text, the edit line tells you that you've selected a "Click here..." text block. The edit line also displays the number of the current page.
- **SmartIcons** are special buttons that help you quickly carry out often-used procedures. By clicking the appropriate SmartIcon, you can open the Print dialog box, copy a text block, boldface selected text, or perform many other common operations.
- The **toolbox** contains a palette of important tools you'll use often in Freelance Graphics. The selection tool, text tool, chart tool, table tool, organizational chart tool, and variety of drawing and symbol tools give you a full complement of essentials for crafting your own presentations.
- The **view buttons** enable you to display your presentation in different ways. The top button displays Current Page view (the view you are looking at now). Other views include Page Sorter view and Outliner view.
- The **page buttons** help you move among pages, choose a different layout, and add a new page easily, without ever opening a menu. Other important buttons in this row include the Color/B&W button, the SmartIcon display button, the typeface button, and the font size button.

FIGURE 1-8: Freelance Graphics screen elements

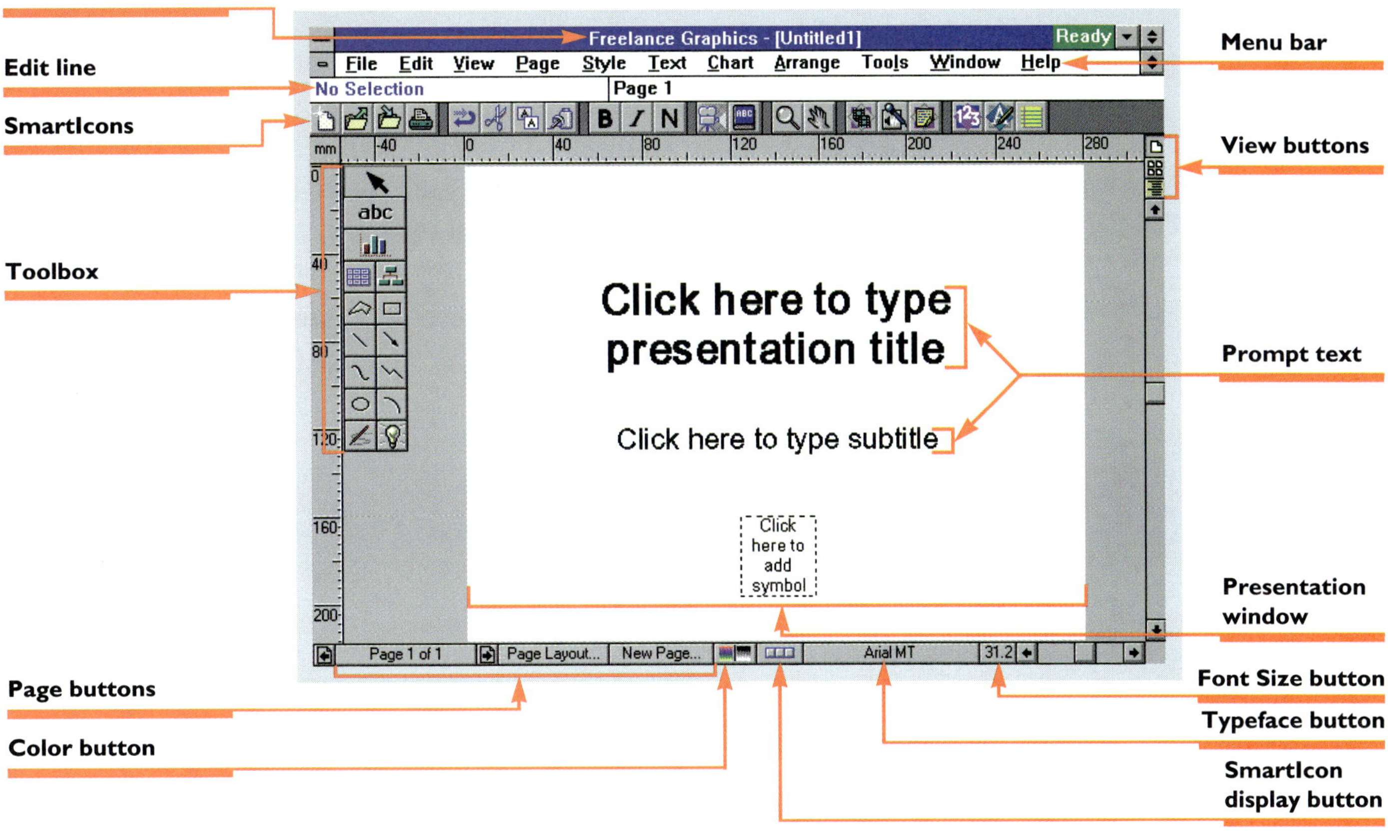

FIGURE 1-9: User Setup dialog box

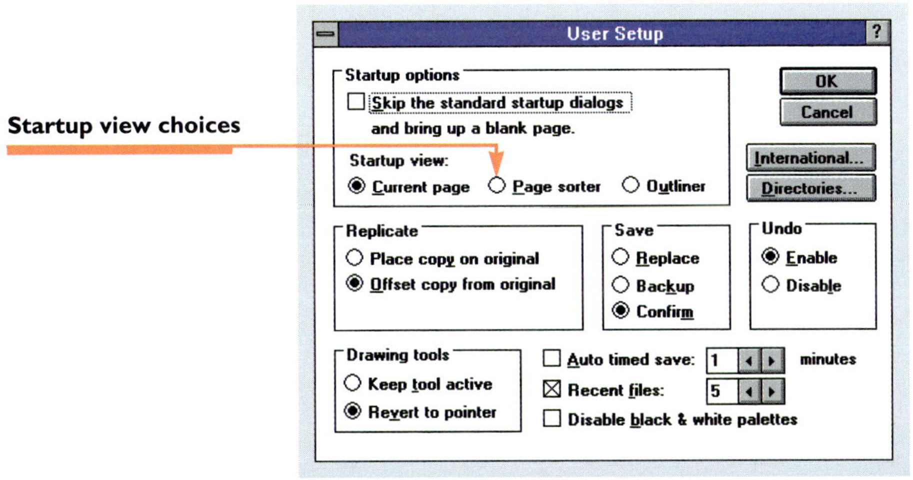

Starting with a different view

Once you get comfortable working with Freelance Graphics, you might find that you prefer working in one of the other available views. You can change the view that is displayed automatically when you start a new presentation by clicking Tools, then User Setup, and clicking the Startup view option you want, as shown in Figure 1-9.

TROUBLE?

If your presentation window doesn't automatically fill the entire screen area, click the maximize button in the far right end of the presentation's title bar.

Working with SmartIcons

Freelance Graphics comes with a set, or palette, of **SmartIcons**, on-screen buttons that let you carry out routine tasks easily. The default SmartIcon palette displayed across the top of the window includes SmartIcons for basic Freelance tasks. But there are many more SmartIcons available. Once you get comfortable with SmartIcons, you may want to create your own sets of SmartIcons that include SmartIcons you use for related tasks like creating and editing charts or working with graphics. ▶ Take a few minutes now and familiarize yourself with the available SmartIcons, so you'll know where to find them when you need them. And use the Italic SmartIcon to change the look of a line of text you enter.

STEPS

1. **Click anywhere on the words Click here to type presentation title**
   The title text box opens over the prompt text, and a blinking cursor marks the point where you will type characters.

2. **Type StreetSmarts**
   The text displays in the box.

3. **Click OK**
   The text box closes, but the text remains selected with small black squares called **handles** on the corners and sides of the box.

4. **Click the Italic SmartIcon**
   Because any formatting changes act on all the text in the box, the text in the box is italicized. Compare your screen to the one shown in Figure 1-10.

5. **Click again**
   This removes the italic style and returns the text to normal. The Bold, Italic, and Normal SmartIcons work as **toggles**, that is, click the SmartIcon once to turn on the feature, and click the SmartIcon a second time to turn it off. Now you're ready to explore all of the SmartIcons available in Freelance Graphics.

6. **Click Tools on the menu bar, then click SmartIcons**
   The SmartIcons dialog box appears, as shown in Figure 1-11. You use the SmartIcons dialog box to create new SmartIcon sets, choose a different set you've created, delete unnecessary SmartIcons from the current palette, change the size of the displayed SmartIcons, or alter the screen position of the SmartIcons.

7. **In the Available Icons list (the list box on the left), scroll down the list by clicking the bottom vertical scroll arrow**
   You see the SmartIcons available for Freelance Graphics tasks.

8. **After you've looked through the available SmartIcons, click OK**
   You are returned to the presentation page. If you added any SmartIcons to the default palette, they will appear in the SmartIcon row.

FIGURE 1-10: Using the Italic SmartIcon

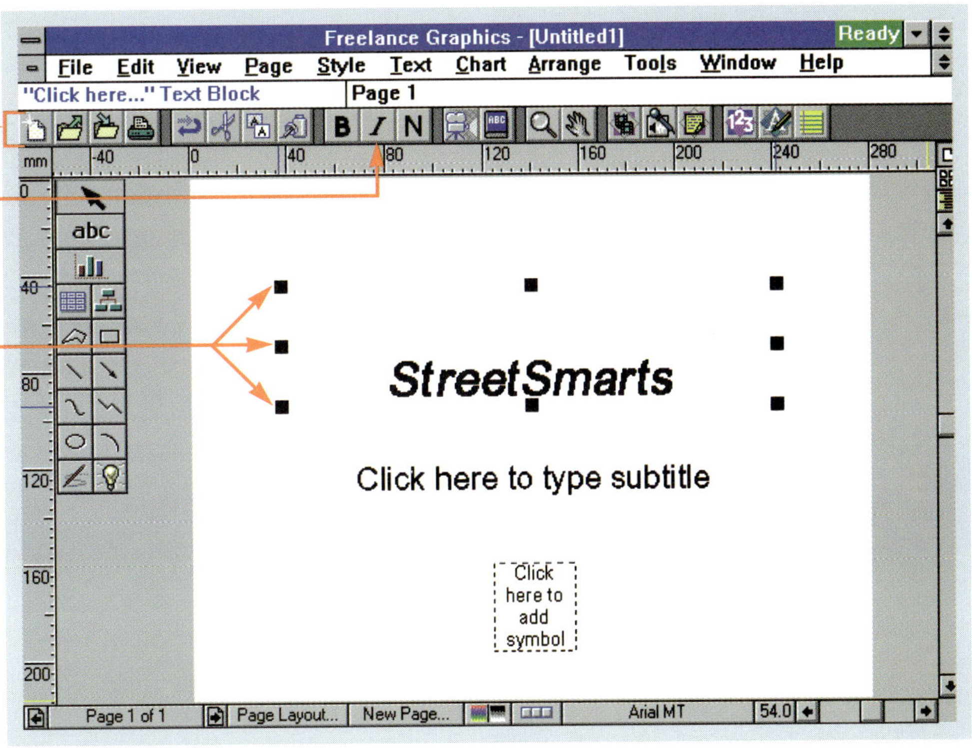

FIGURE 1-11: SmartIcons dialog box

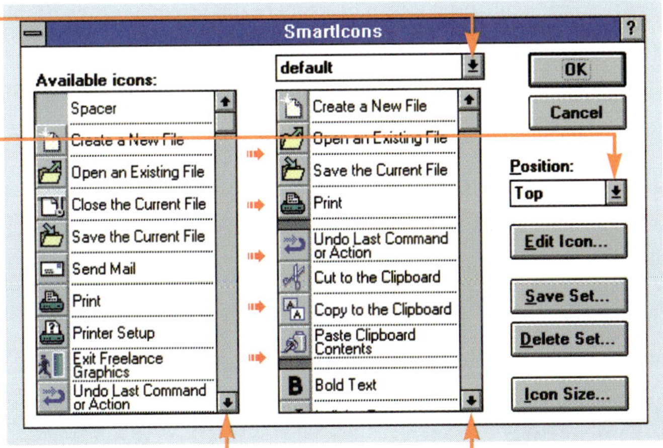

Moving the SmartIcon palette

You can easily change the position of the SmartIcon palette. Click Tools, then SmartIcons. In the SmartIcons dialog box, click the down-arrow button beside the Position box. Click Left, Right, Bottom, or Floating to change the location of the SmartIcon palette.

Getting Help

Freelance Graphics makes sure you always have the help you need. Several different kinds of help are available to you while you are creating and working with your presentations. Table 1-1 introduces you to the different kinds of help always available. ▶ A major part of the presentations you create will involve adding and modifying charts to show financial projects, sales percentages, and cost ratios. You can see how having a set of SmartIcons related to just charts could help save you time when you begin creating charts for your presentations. Take a few minutes now and use the Freelance Graphics Help system to learn more about SmartIcons, specifically, about how to create your own SmartIcon palette to be used for creating charts.

STEPS

1 Click **Help** on the menu bar
The Help menu opens, as shown in Figure 1-12. You see the wide range of Help topics, including Contents, which gives you a help overview, and Search, which enables you to search for specific topics.

2 Click **Contents**
The Freelance Graphics for Windows Help Contents window opens. A list of Help topics is displayed. Find SmartIcons at the bottom of the list.

3 Click **SmartIcons**
The SmartIcons Help overview displays, as shown in Figure 1-13. In addition to a basic definition of SmartIcons and a visual glossary of the SmartIcons available, you see two underlined text passages. When you move the pointer over one of these passages, the pointer changes to a hand, indicating that you can click the passage to see more information. Clicking a term underlined with a dashed line displays its definition.

4 Click the underlined text **Customize the Display of SmartIcons**
The Customize Display of SmartIcons help screen displays. Read through the text to find out more about creating a SmartIcon palette that includes only the SmartIcons you want.

5 Click **File** in the Help menu bar, then click **Exit**
The Help window closes and the presentation page displays again.

TABLE 1-1
Help methods

METHOD	OCCASION	DESCRIPTION
Press F1	Anytime in Freelance Graphics	Displays Help related to the command you are using
Click the ? button in the upper-right corner of a dialog box	When a dialog box is displayed	Shows a Help window listing information relevant to the dialog box procedure
Choose a Help command	When you want to choose the way in which you get Help (How Do I?, Search, Contents)	Displays a Help menu or opening screen
Use the QuickStart	When you want to practice or review a Freelance Graphics procedure	Takes you through a series of lessons

FIGURE 1-12: Help choices

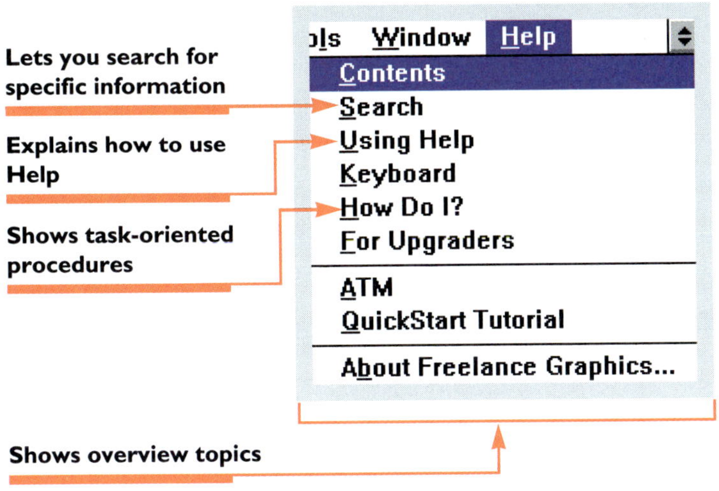

FIGURE 1-13: SmartIcons Help overview

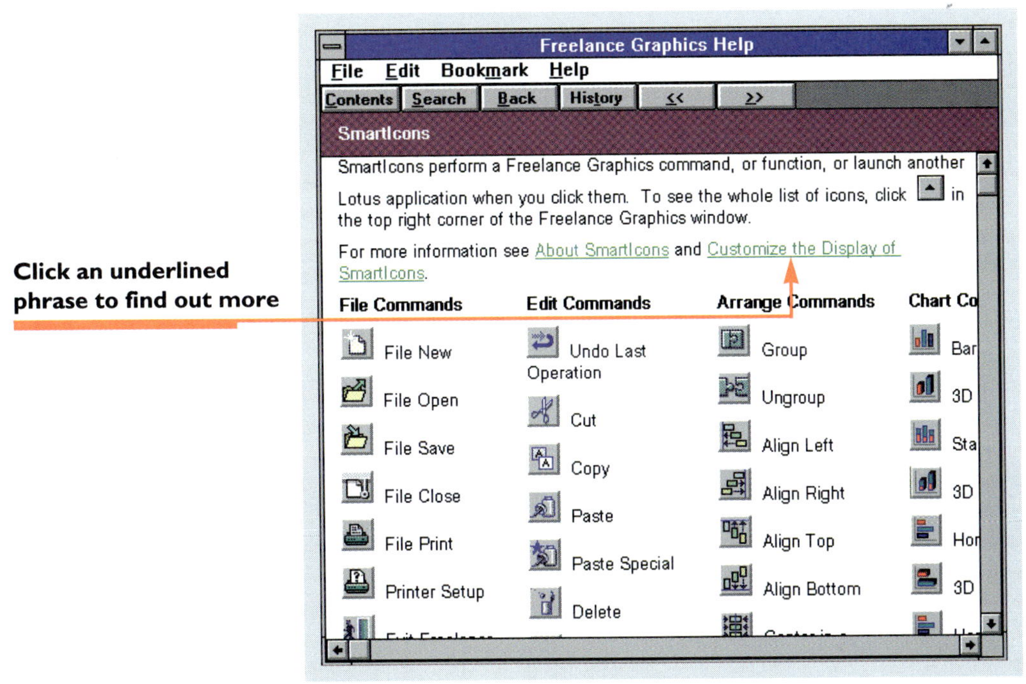

Taking a QuickStart tour

The QuickStart Tutorial, available from the Help menu, includes lessons you can use to learn the basics of creating title and bullet pages, adding charts, creating tables, using the Outliner, and managing presentations. You can go through as many lessons as you want in a single sitting—each lesson takes less than 10 minutes. Start the QuickStart Tutorial by clicking Help in the menu bar and then clicking QuickStart Tutorial. Then choose the topic you want help with.

QUICK TIP

You can print the Help information you display by clicking File in the Help menu bar and clicking Print Topic.

Exiting Freelance Graphics

When you are finished working on your presentation and are ready to shut down for the day, you need to save and close your file and exit Freelance Graphics. In this unit, you explored the various elements of the Freelance Graphics screen and entered a line of text, but since you did not create a sample presentation, there's no need to save a file. ▶ In this case, shutting everything down involves only closing the file and exiting Freelance Graphics. Table 1-2 lists the different close and exit procedures you can use.

STEPS

1. **Click File in the menu bar**
   The File menu opens. See Figure 1-14.
2. **Click Close**
   The Close Window dialog box displays, asking whether you want to save the changes you have made in the file. See Figure 1-15.
3. **Click No**
   The file closes and the main Freelance Graphics window displays.
4. **Click File in the menu bar, then click Exit**
   Freelance Graphics closes and the Lotus Applications group window displays.

TABLE 1-2:
Close and exit procedures

TO DO THIS:	WITH THE KEYBOARD:	WITH THE MOUSE:
Close a file and continue working in Freelance Graphics	Ctrl-F4	Click File, Close or double-click the control menu box in the upper-left corner of the presentation window
Exit Freelance Graphics	Alt-F4	Click File, Exit or double-click the control menu box in the upper-left corner of the Freelance Graphics title bar

FIGURE 1-14: Using the File menu to close a file

Click this to close the current file

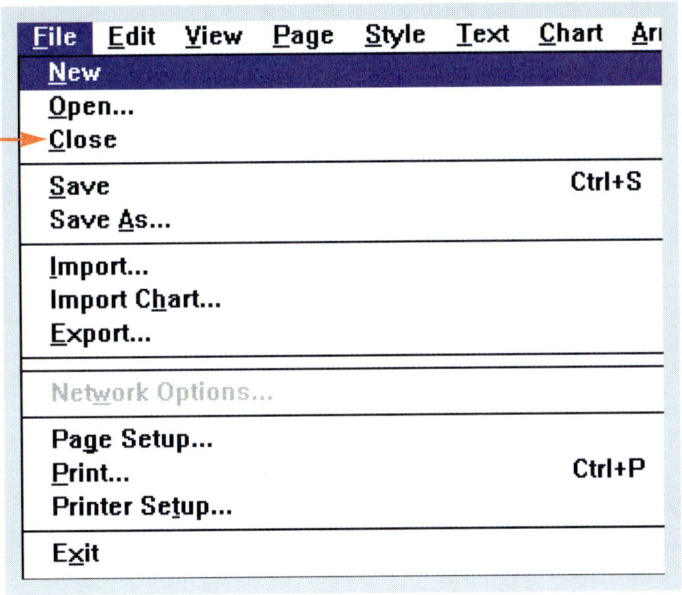

FIGURE 1-15: Close Window dialog box

Click No to close a document without saving

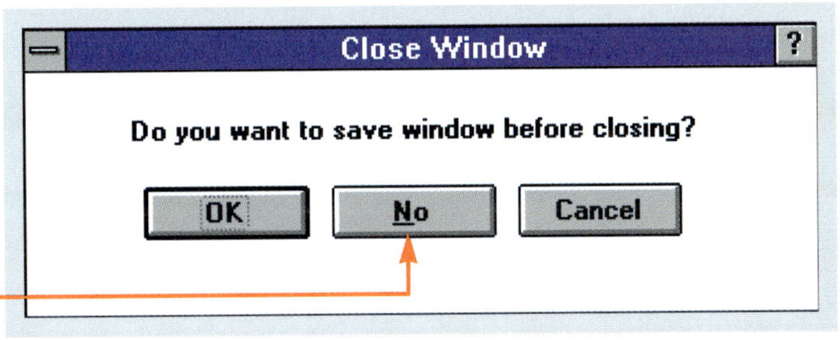

Closing multiple files

Freelance Graphics allows you to have multiple files open at one time. When you close the program, Freelance Graphics asks you if you want to save open files. If you click OK, the program saves the files for you and then closes.

QUICK TIP

If you want to exit Freelance Graphics quickly, click File and Exit. When a dialog box displays, asking whether you want to save modified files, click Yes to save the files or No to abandon your changes.

CONCEPTSREVIEW

Label the Freelance Graphics screen items shown in Figure 1-16.

5 ______

FIGURE 1-16

1 ______

3 ______

4 ______

6 ______

7 ______

2 ______

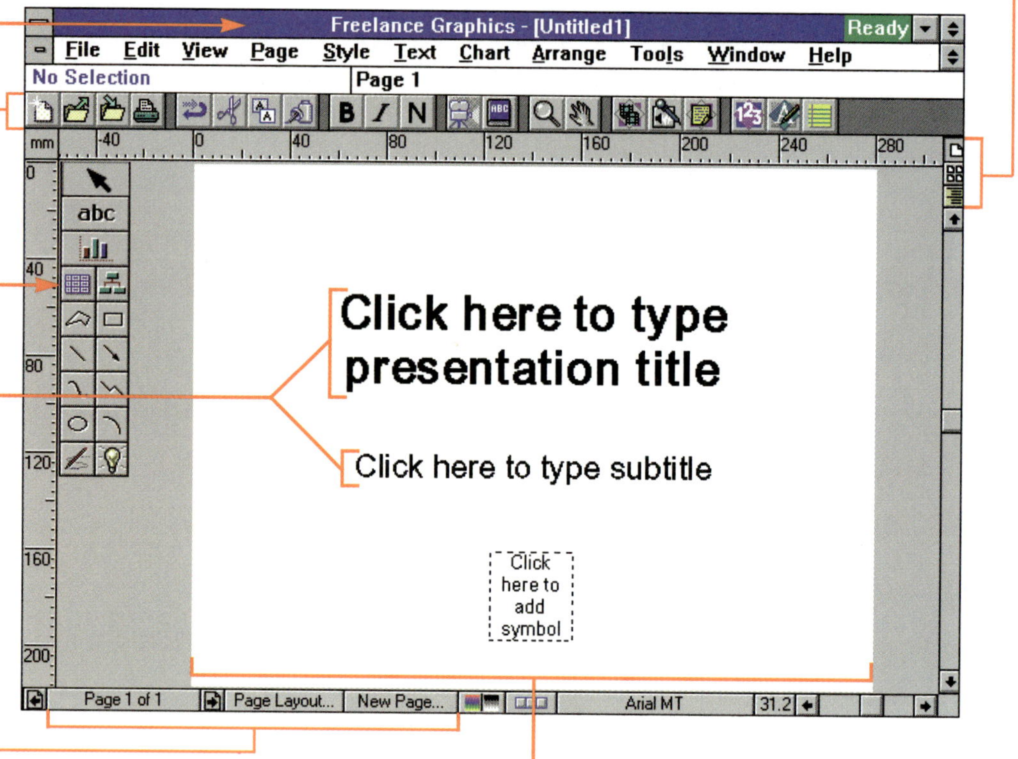

Match each definition with its element.

8 An on-screen button that allows you to perform a routine quickly

9 Text on a page that is replaced when you click on it and type

10 A set of tutorial lessons showing Freelance Graphics tasks

11 The area of the screen showing the current file name

12 An automatic design template with font choices, colors, and page layouts already selected

a. Title bar
b. SmartMaster
c. Prompt text
d. SmartIcon
e. QuickStart

Select the best answer from the list of choices.

13 Presentation graphics software can help you do all the following tasks EXCEPT which one?

a. Create good presentations quickly
b. Use charts effectively
c. Automatically create the content of your presentation
d. Print handouts and audience notes

14 Which of the following statements is FALSE?

a. Freelance Graphics lets you import data from Lotus 1-2-3 and other popular spreadsheets.
b. You can import a chart you created in another program into Freelance Graphics.
c. Freelance Graphics accepts only chart and graphics files from other programs.
d. Freelance Graphics includes buttons that link directly to other Lotus programs.

15 The following tools are included in the toolbox EXCEPT which one?

a. text tool

b. organization chart tool

c. spelling tool

d. symbol tool

16 Which of the following items is NOT a Help command?

a. Search

b. Index

c. Contents

d. How Do I?

17 Which of the following statements is FALSE?

a. You can have more than one presentation file open at one time.

b. Freelance Graphics closes all open files when you click Close.

c. When you exit without first closing and saving the file, Freelance Graphics prompts you to save the file.

d. Exiting Freelance Graphics returns you to the Lotus Applications window.

APPLICATIONS REVIEW

1 Start Freelance Graphics.

a. Turn on your computer and monitor.

b. Type WIN and press [Enter].

c. Open the Program Manager if necessary.

d. Double-click the Lotus Applications group icon.

e. Double-click the Freelance Graphics program icon.

2 Choose a blank presentation.

a. When the Welcome to Freelance Graphics dialog box appears, click OK.

b. Click the SmartMaster with blank background check box, then click OK. The Choose Page Layout dialog box appears.

c. Choose any page layout you'd like to work with. A preview of the layout appears in the window in the lower right corner of the dialog box.

d. Click OK to open the page layout of your choice.

3 Practice working with the Freelance Graphics screen.

a. Move the pointer around on the screen.

b. Locate the Zoom SmartIcon (the magnifying glass).

c. Click the Zoom SmartIcon.

d. Move the pointer to the presentation page area. Notice that the pointer changes to a magnifying glass.

e. Click anywhere on the presentation page (preferably over some text). What happens? See Figure 1-17 for a clue.

f. Click View in the menu bar.

g. Click Full Page. The presentation window returns to normal display.

FIGURE 1-17: Using the Zoom SmartIcon

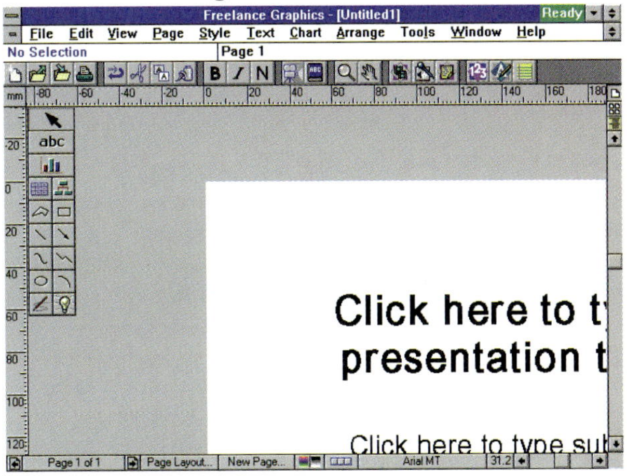

4 Display the SmartIcon choices.

a. Click the SmartIcon button in the bottom of the screen just to the right of the Color/B&W button. Are any SmartIcon sets listed there beside Default?

b. Click Tools in the menu bar.

c. Click SmartIcons. The SmartIcons dialog box appears.

d. Scroll through the list of available SmartIcons; locate the New Page SmartIcon.

e. Drag the New Page SmartIcon to a position in the Default SmartIcon column just above the Bold SmartIcon.

f. Click OK to return to the presentation window. The New Page SmartIcon appears in the SmartIcon palette.

5 Explore Freelance Graphics Help.

a. Click one of the prompt text boxes.

b. Press [F1]. What happened? See Figure 1-18.

c. Close the Help window.

d. Click Help in the menu bar.

e. Choose How Do I?

f. Select Get Started. Another Help window opens.

g. Click Back. The previous How Do I? screen opens.

h. Click File in the menu bar, then click Exit. Help closes.

FIGURE 1-18: Displaying a Help window

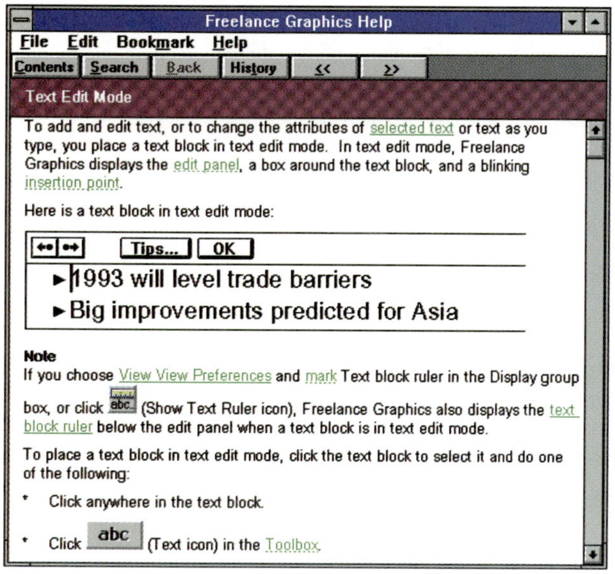

6 Close the current file and exit Freelance Graphics.

a. Click File in the menu bar.

b. Click Close. The Close Window dialog box may ask whether you want to save the current file.

c. Click No.

d. Press [Alt][F4]. Freelance Graphics closes.

INDEPENDENT CHALLENGE 1

Freelance Graphics includes a terrific QuickStart tutorial you can use to familiarize yourself with the various tasks involved in creating a presentation. Each lesson takes just a few minutes to complete and gives you hands-on practice for important procedures like creating a title page, working with presentation pages, and creating tables and charts.

Ask your instructor about taking the Freelance Graphics QuickStart tutorial.

INDEPENDENT CHALLENGE 2

You have volunteered to work for an afternoon in the campaign headquarters of your local congressman. A staff member appears with a stack of papers in hand. "Do you know anything about creating bar charts?" she asks breathlessly. You shake your head. She points to the computer monitor on her desk. "Well, do you know anything about that program?"

Lucky for you, the program gleaming on her screen is Freelance Graphics. And although you don't know how to create a bar chart—yet—you can do something to help. You sit down and begin to create a custom SmartIcon palette that will help the person who creates those bar charts.

To complete this independent challenge,

1. Display the SmartIcons dialog box.
2. Remove all SmartIcons in the Default column, from the Bold SmartIcon to the end of the list.
3. Locate and drag 10 bar chart SmartIcons from the Available Icons list to the Default list.
4. Click the Save Set button; then, in the Name of set box, type bar_charts. Click OK.
5. Return to the presentation window.

Show the new SmartIcon palette to your instructor for approval.

UNIT 2

OBJECTIVES

- Plan a presentation
- Choose a SmartMaster
- Select a page layout
- Choose a color scheme
- Replace prompt text
- View the presentation
- Set display preferences
- Save a presentation
- Print a presentation

Designing A PRESENTATION

Now that you know the basic startup procedure for Freelance Graphics, recognize the screen elements, and understand how to use SmartIcons and the Help system, you are ready to plan and begin your own presentation. Part of planning a presentation involves selecting the look and page layout you want. Once you choose the page layout, you enter text, save, and print the presentation. You can also set display preferences and change the colors in the presentation, if you choose. ▶ You've been asked to design a presentation for a new line of clothing that Tom Leary will present at the next manager's meeting. In this unit, you begin work on the presentation by choosing a SmartMaster and a page layout and creating the first two pages. ▶

Planning a presentation

Before you begin entering text in your presentation, you need to think about what you need to say and how you want to say it. ▶ Because this is your first presentation for Conscious Clothing, you want it to be an impressive one. Make sure you've thought through your presentation by considering the following points before you begin.

- **Identify the overall goal of your presentation.**
  Presentations can entertain, inform, inspire, and educate. Your presentation is informational, explaining a new line of clothing to the managers at Conscious Clothing.

- **Think about the tone of your presentation.**
  The SmartMaster set you choose, the page layouts you select, and the graphics and charts you add all contribute to the tone of your presentation. The tone you create should match your presentation's goal and reflect the presentation topic. Creating an informal presentation with funny sound effects and cartoon-style art would be great for a presentation meant to entertain, but this presentation needs a formal yet highly modern tone that reflects the upbeat style of the clothing line.

- **Remember your audience.**
  You can't please all the people all the time, but you can think about the kind of presentation that will appeal most to the overall age group and experience level of your audience. For this presentation, the audience will be upper-level managers at Conscious Clothing—mostly middle-aged, extremely busy professionals. This means that you need to get the message across quickly and clearly.

- **Write down the important points you need to cover.**
  Make a list of the most important topics to be explained in the presentation. Leave plenty of room between lines. Then go back and add subtopics. You can use this list, called an outline, to create the basic structure of your presentation. Follow the example shown in Figure 2-1 to create your outline.

- **Think about the information you want to display on each page.**
  Once you've finished the outline, you can consider the information you want to include on each page. Which topics require a text explanation? Which can be displayed in a chart? How can you use graphics to enhance the information displayed on a page?

- **Consider where you will give the presentation.**
  Will you be presenting information in front of a large group in a boardroom? In an open lunchroom? In a small office? The size of the room, the amount of light, and the way you present the information will affect the colors and font you choose and the amount of information you display on each page.

- **Sketch a rough plan of the pages in your presentation.**
  When you have a general idea of the topics you'll discuss on each page, draw a series of boxes on a piece of paper. Each box represents one page. Using your outline, sketch out a rough plan of different page layouts, as you see in Figure 2-2. Remember that varying the layout—not putting too many bulleted lists in a row, for example—will make your presentation stronger. The type of page layout you select also affects how much information you can include on a single page.

FIGURE 2-1: Rough outline

1 – Title Page

2 – Overview
- A. Introduction
- B. Presentation Objectives

3 – Introducing Street Smarts
- A. The Look
- B. The Voice
- C. The Meaning

4 – Market Research
- A. Regional
- B. International

5 – Design Strategies
- A. Our Designers
- B. The Process of Design

6 – Manufacturing Information
- A. Material Acquisition
- B. Production Costs
- C. Profit Projections

7 – Availability
- A. Shows
- B. Advertising
- C. Direct Line

8 – Conclusion

FIGURE 2-2: Sketching presentation pages

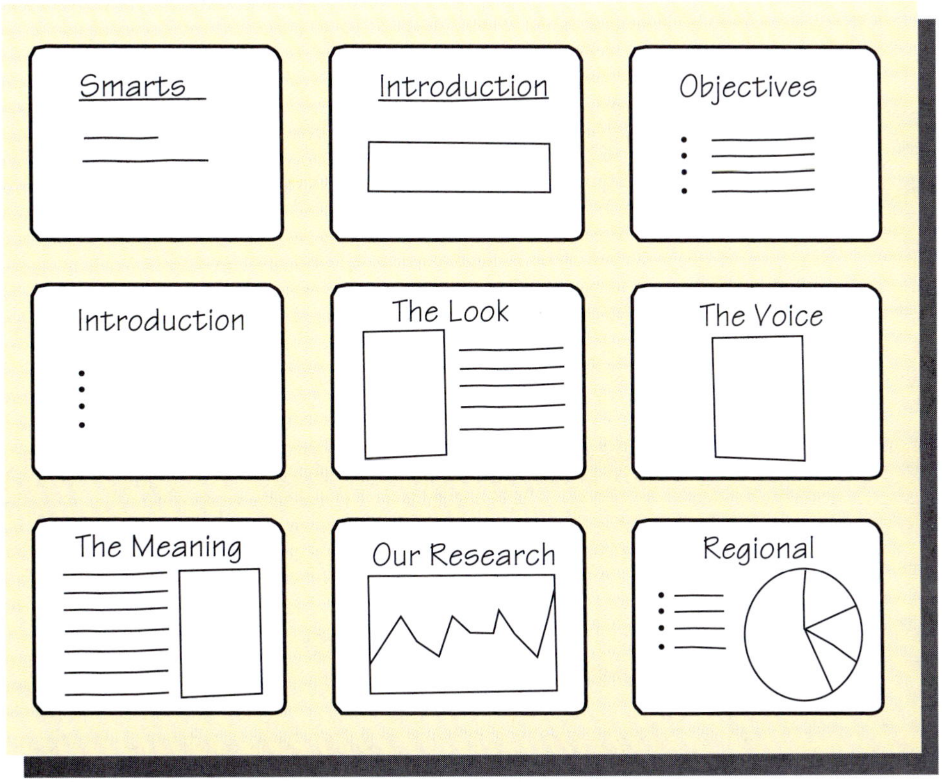

QUICK TIP

When you see an effective presentation, keep a copy of any handouts passed out. You can use a similar design in your own work later.

Choosing a SmartMaster

As you learned in Unit 1, SmartMasters are preset designs you can use for the basis of your own presentation. When you choose one of Freelance Graphics' SmartMasters, the background colors, graphics, and text settings—font, size, style, and color—are already chosen for you. Table 2-1 introduces several SmartMasters and gives an example and comment about the tones they convey. ▶ You need to find a SmartMaster that will suit the tone of the presentation you want to create. Start Freelance Graphics and begin a new presentation using the steps explained in Unit 1. You've been given your first assignment: create a presentation that Tom Leary will use to introduce the new StreetSmarts line to the Conscious Clothing managers at the next board meeting.

STEPS

1. **In the Welcome to Freelance Graphics dialog box, make sure Create a new presentation is selected; then click OK**
   The Choose a Look for Your Presentation dialog box displays.

2. **Scroll one by one through the SmartMaster list box**
   Each time you click the down scroll arrow in the bottom of the vertical scroll bar, the newly highlighted SmartMaster appears in the preview window.

3. **Press [S]**
   The highlight jumps to the first SmartMaster beginning with the letter S.

4. **Scroll down to skyline.mas, then click the mouse button**
   This SmartMaster, which shows the outline of a city skyline, is an appropriate choice for the clothing line to be introduced in your presentation. See Figure 2-3.

5. **Click OK**
   The Choose a Look for Your Presentation dialog box closes and the Choose Page Layout dialog box displays.

TABLE 2-1: Choosing a SmartMaster to suit your presentation style

IF YOUR PRESENTATION IS...	CONSIDER THIS...	TO MAKE YOUR POINT
Formal	world1.mas	Background world map gives international flavor
Formal	graphlin.mas	Color selection and graph line help show business progress
Informal	notebook.mas	Notebook-like page gives an informal look to text
Informal	present.mas	Easel-style write-on board provides an easy-to-see area for text and charts
Informal	spotlite.mas	Floodlight highlights are for text and graphics
Modern	corporat.mas	Stylish design of curves and lines provide artistic yet professional look
Modern	sketch.mas	Splash of color in bottom right corner adds accent to pages

FIGURE 2-3: Choosing a SmartMaster

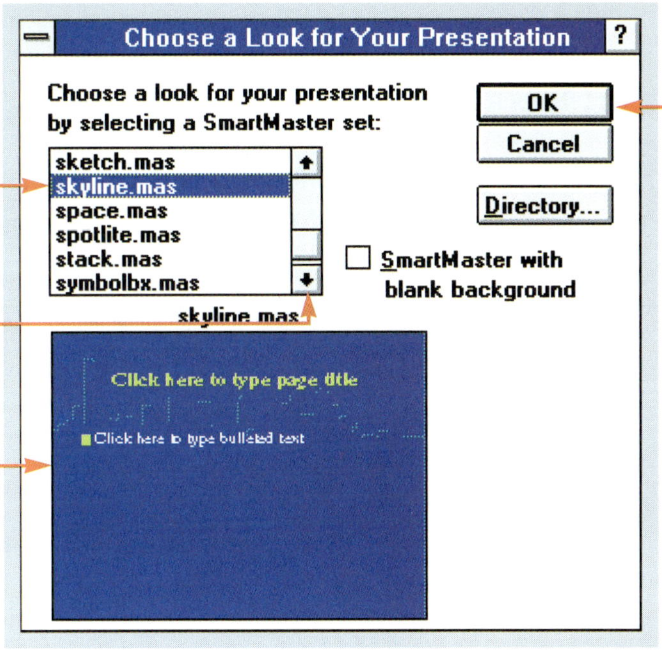

Changing SmartMaster settings

Even though the SmartMaster settings are built into your presentation, you can change them easily at any time by simply choosing a different SmartMaster set. Click Style and then click Choose SmartMaster Set, as shown in Figure 2-4. Now just choose the SmartMaster you want using the steps explained in this lesson.

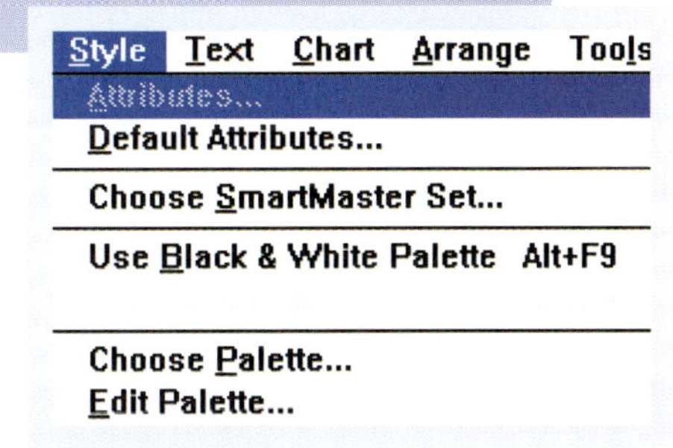

FIGURE 2-4: Style menu

QUICK TIP

Choose the SmartMaster custom.mas if you want to create your own SmartMaster set based on the preset page lay-outs and text formats.

Selecting a page layout

The page layout you select defines the areas where you enter text, create charts, or add graphics. Freelance Graphics provides you with 11 different page layouts from which you can choose, plus one that lets you add a totally blank page. Table 2-2 introduces the most common page layouts. ▶ During the course of creating your presentation, you will be using all of the different page layouts. Familiarize yourself with the various page layouts and then select the Title page layout so you can begin the first page of your presentation. The Choose Page Layout dialog box should be displayed on your screen, as shown in Figure 2-5.

STEPS

1 Click **Bulleted List**

The preview window shows the way the Bulleted List page layout appears. The title of the layout appears above the preview window. Notice that this layout shows the page title and the first bullet entry. You can enter as many items in a bulleted list as you have room for.

2 Click **1 Chart**

The preview window shows a page with a title and room for a chart. You use this page layout when you are presenting chart information that requires no text explanation.

3 Click **Bullets & Symbol**

The preview window shows a page layout in which a title, a bullet entry, and a symbol area are displayed.

4 Click **Basic Layout**

The preview window displays the page with only a title. You will use the basic layout for pages you want to design yourself.

5 Click **[None]**

This time, the preview window displays a blank single-color background. The SmartMaster graphics are removed and no text, chart, or symbol areas are defined. Use [None] when you want to create your own page from scratch, not using the SmartMaster background. Because you are just beginning your presentation, you want to start with a title page.

6 Click **Title**, then click **OK**

Freelance Graphics closes the Choose Page Layout dialog box and displays the first page of your presentation with the Title page layout.

FIGURE 2-5: Choose Page Layout dialog box

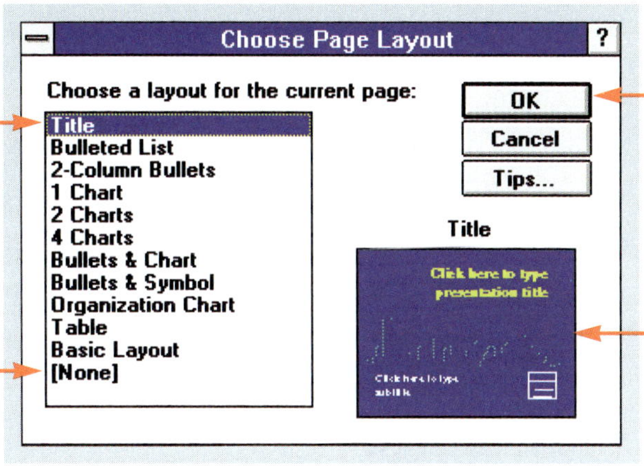

Changing page layout

You can change the page layout even after you add text and other items to the page. Click the Page Layout button Page Layout... in the bottom of the Freelance Graphics work area, as shown in Figure 2-6. The Change Page Layout dialog box opens. Click the layout you want; then click OK.

FIGURE 2-6: Changing page layout

TABLE 2-2: Popular page layouts

PAGE LAYOUT	DESCRIPTION	USE WHEN
Title	Place for title, subtitle, and small symbol	You are creating an opening page or a new section page
Bulleted List	Place for title and bulleted entries	You need to provide text information that can be shown in a series of steps or objectives
1 Chart	Place for title and one chart	You want to call attention to information created in chart form
2 Charts	Place for title and two charts	You need to contrast chart information in two different charts
Bullets & Symbol	Place for title, bulleted text, and symbol	You want to add an illustration or symbol that supports bulleted text
Table	Place for title and table	You need to display text information in a table format

Choosing a color scheme

A **color scheme** is a preassembled palette of colors you can use to quickly create a well-coordinated presentation. The SmartMaster you selected includes a preset color scheme that is applied to all the elements in your presentation. Freelance Graphics allows you to choose a different color scheme and to change individual colors in any scheme. Figure 2-7 shows the different palette items you can change. ▶ If you plan to print hard copies of your presentation pages on a black and white printer, dark backgrounds mean dark printouts. At Conscious Clothing you only have access to a black and white printer; therefore you need to change the color scheme in your presentation to lighten things up. Start with the newly created title page displayed on your monitor.

STEPS

1. **Click Style on the menu bar, then click Choose Palette**
   The Choose Palette dialog box opens. See Figure 2-7. You use this dialog box to select pre-assembled palettes coordinated by the Freelance Graphics designers. You can scroll through the list of choices to see the color options that are available.
2. **Scroll to and click pal2.pal**
   A new palette of colors appears in the Selected palette area. The two elements you are primarily concerned with at this point—background and text—are changed. The background colors have changed from dark to light; the text colors have changed from light to dark.
3. **Position the mouse pointer on Preview; press and hold the mouse button to preview the color selection**
   The Choose Palette dialog box closes and you see a preview of how the selected color scheme will look in your presentation. It's important to press and hold the mouse button; just a quick click won't work.
4. **Release the mouse button**
   The Choose Palette dialog box displays again.
5. **Click pal6.pal, preview it, then click OK**
   The new color scheme is applied to your presentation. This new color scheme is easy on the eyes, and it will produce a more readable printout. Freelance Graphics also gives you another quick option to help you see how your pages will look when printed in black and white.
6. **Locate and click the Color/B&W button in the status bar along the bottom of the screen**
   The page changes from color to black and white display. See Figure 2-8.
7. **Click again**
   The presentation page is displayed once again in color with all its shading intact. Now you can continue working on the file as it will appear when you present it.

FIGURE 2-7: Choose Palette dialog box

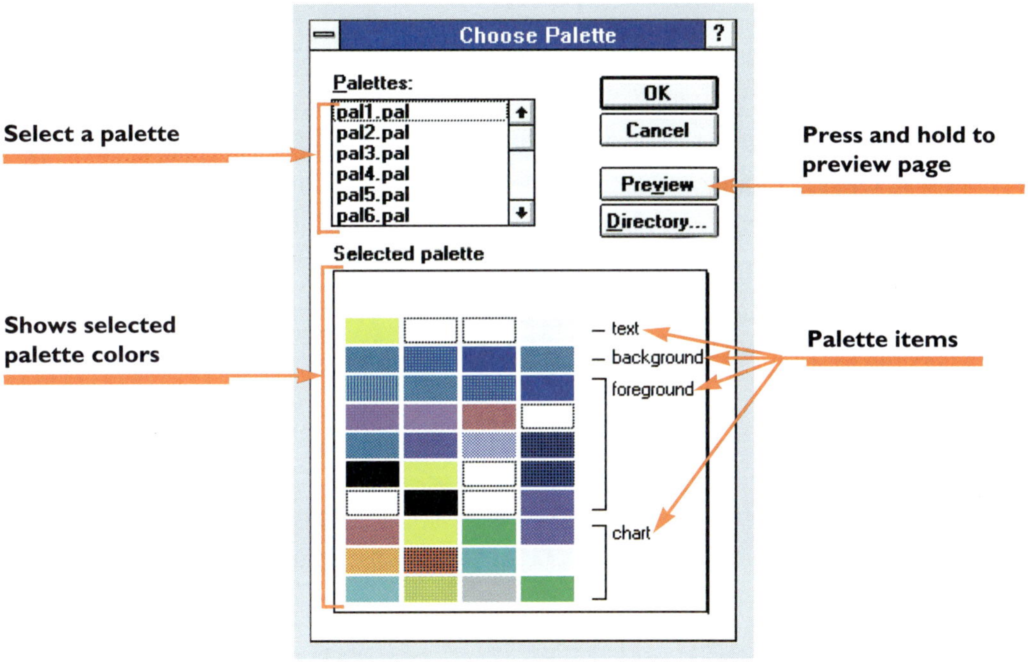

FIGURE 2-8: Display changed to black and white

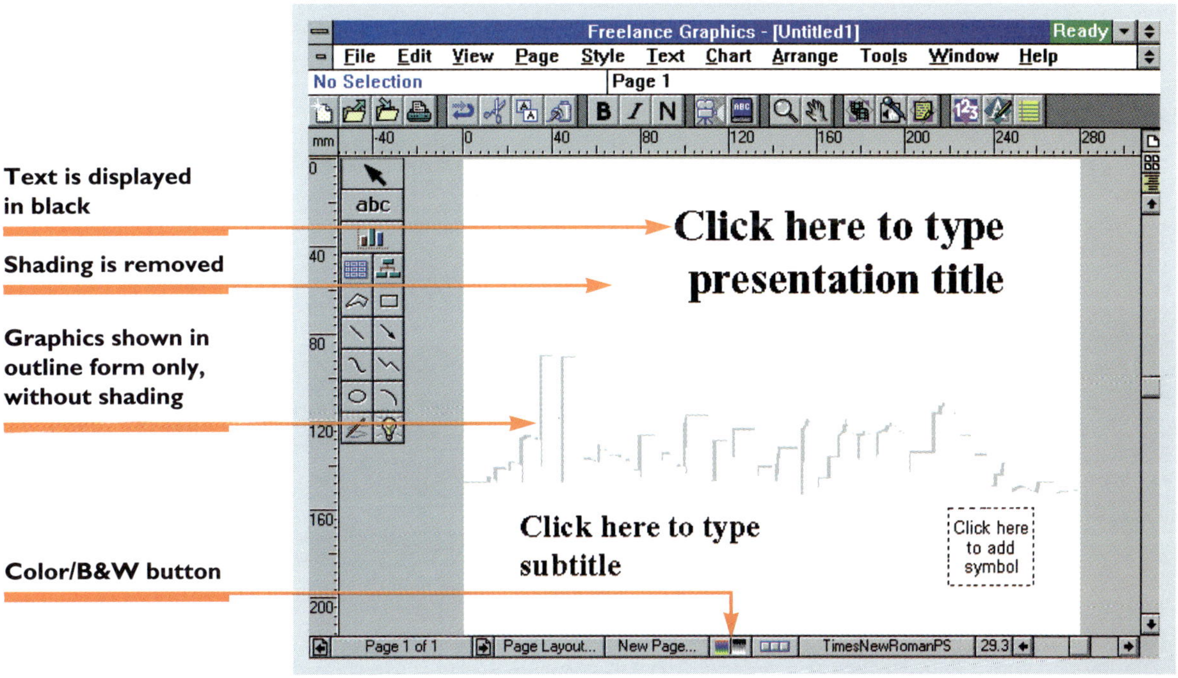

Changing background color

If you want to change only the background colors of your presentation, there's no need to change the entire color scheme. Just click Page, then click Background. In the Page Background dialog box, click the 1st Color and 2nd Color you want; then click OK. (The second color is used only if you select a shaded pattern.)

Replacing prompt text

Freelance Graphics makes it easy for you to enter text in your presentation by providing prompt text on presentation pages. The **prompt text** shows you the font size and style that will be applied to the text you enter. An example of prompt text on the title page layout is Click here to type presentation title. When you click the prompt text, a text entry box appears so that you can type your information. Figure 2-9 introduces the text entry box you will work with. ▶ You are ready to begin entering the text for the presentation you've been planning. Go ahead and enter the title and subtitle for your presentation.

STEPS

1. **Click the prompt text Click here to type presentation title**
   A text entry box displays, with the flashing cursor positioned at the right edge. See Figure 2-9. The text entry box includes the text entry area, the Promote and Demote buttons (which you'll use later when you create bulleted lists in Unit 4), the Tips button, and the OK button.
2. **Click Tips**
   The Text Tips dialog box opens, giving you information about how to enter and indent text.
3. **After reviewing the information, click OK**
   The dialog box closes and the presentation page with the selected text entry box displays again.
4. **Type StreetSmarts, but do not press the Enter key after you type the entry**
   The characters move in from the right as you type. If you make a mistake while typing, press [Backspace]—not the Delete key—to delete incorrect letters and then retype the entry.
5. **Click OK**
   The text entry box closes, but the handles around the edge of the prompt text area show that the box is still selected.
6. **Click the prompt text Click here to type subtitle**
   The text entry area appears, this time with the flashing cursor positioned at the left edge of the box.
7. **Type A new look for a new generation**
   When the text you type fills the box, Freelance Graphics automatically moves text to the next line and enlarges the box. See Figure 2-10.
8. **Click outside the text entry box**
   The text entry box closes and because you clicked outside the box, the text box is no longer selected.

FIGURE 2-9: Text entry box

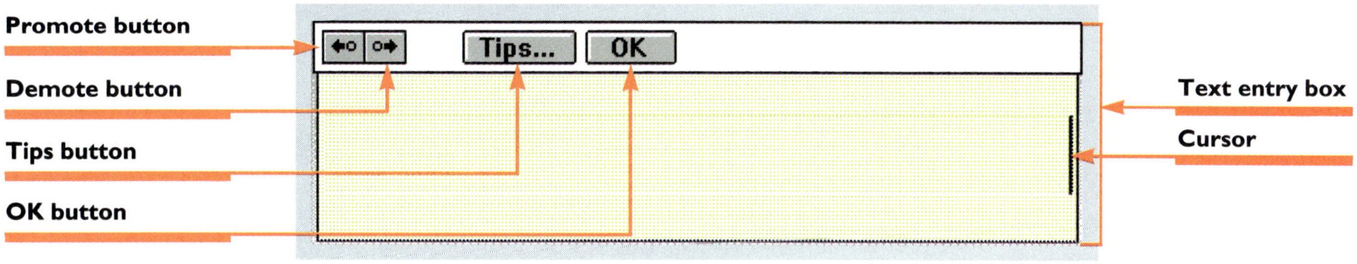

FIGURE 2-10: Entered text

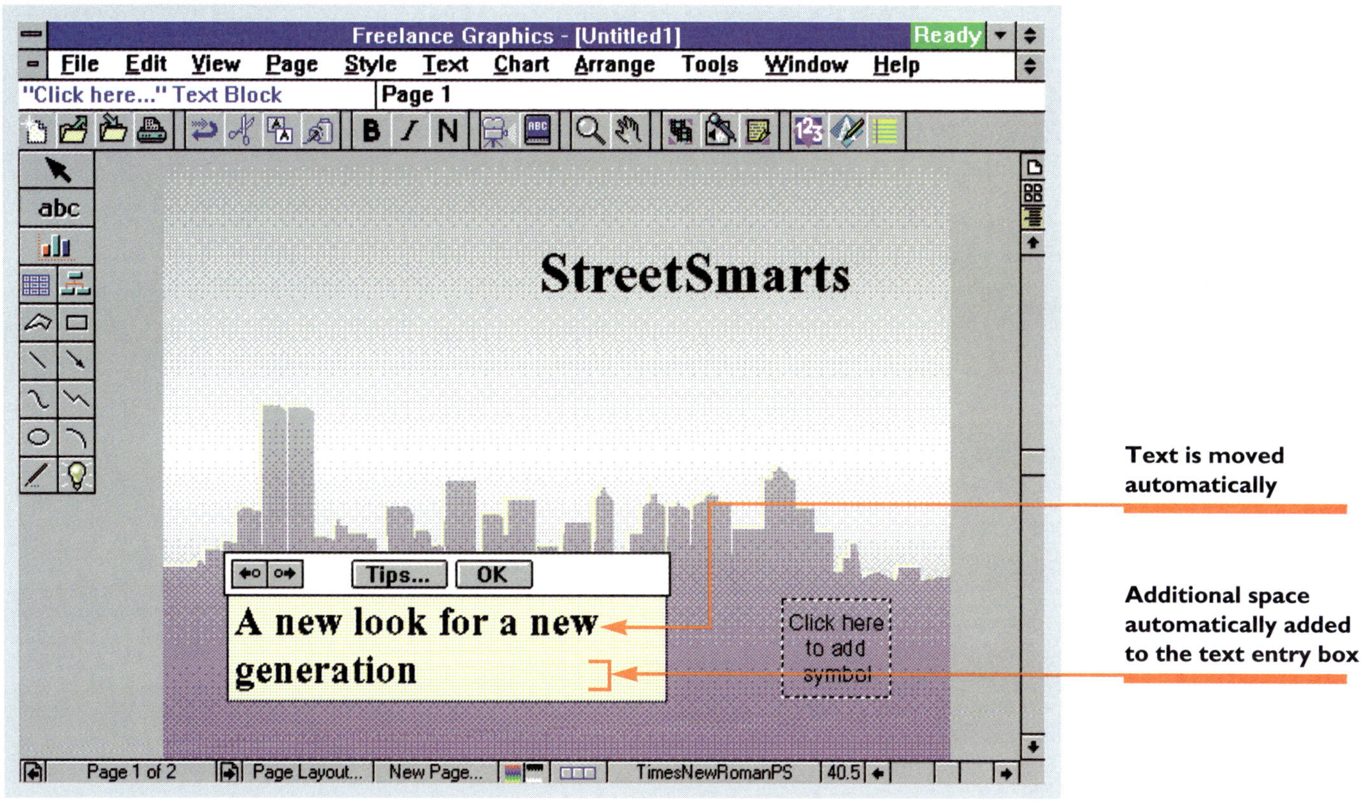

Choosing different text settings

If you don't like the way text looks in the SmartMaster you've selected, you can easily change it. The Text menu contains commands you can use to change the various text settings. First click the text with the settings you want to change, then click Text in the menu bar to display the text options. Then choose the option you want. Some options, such as Italic, work as toggles; others, such as Font, display a dialog box in which you choose the settings you want.

TROUBLE?

If you press the Enter key when you're working in a text entry box, Freelance Graphics adds a blank line. When you're done entering text, click OK.

Viewing the presentation

Freelance Graphics gives you three different ways to view your presentation: Current Page view, Page Sorter view, and Outliner view. Up to this point in the presentation, you've been working in Current Page View. Table 2-3 helps you determine which view to use depending on the task at hand. ▶ Finding out how to use the different Freelance Graphics views now will help you evaluate your presentation in different ways after you add pages. Use the view buttons and the View menu to explore the different views and enter text for a new page in the Outliner.

STEPS

1 Click the **Outliner button**

The Outliner view appears. Instead of a presentation page, you see a screen that resembles a piece of paper from a yellow legal pad. On the first line is the title text you have entered; on the second line is the subtitle. In Unit 3, "Working with Text," you will learn more about working with Outliner features.

2 Click after the word **generation**; then click **Page** on the menu bar and click **New**

This adds a new page in the Outliner. The new page is assigned the number two in the left margin.

3 Type **Credits** and press **[Enter]**, then enter the following text:

- Type **Jim Frye, Marketing Director** and press **[Enter]**
- Type **Tom Leary, Marketing Manager** and press **[Enter]**
- Type **Julie Crowel, Marketing Assistant** and press **[Enter]**
- Type **James Whitmire, Market Research** and press **[Enter]**
- Type **Patrice Moyer, Design Supervisor**

This text completes a full page of bulleted text for Page 2 of the presentation. Compare your screen with the Outliner view shown in Figure 2-11.

4 Click **View** in the menu bar, then click **Page Sorter**

The Page Sorter view appears showing the title page and the newly created bulleted page. See Figure 2-12. Locate the view buttons in the upper-right edge of the presentation window.

5 Click the **Current Page button**

The familiar Current Page view appears, but this time, the new page is displayed.

TABLE 2-3:
Which view should you use?

BUTTON	VIEW	DESCRIPTION	USE WHEN
	Current Page	Displays a page as it will appear in screen show	You are creating your presentation page by page, adding text, charts, and graphics
	Page Sorter view	Displays all presentation pages in reduced size on a single screen	You want to check overall page layout, page order, set screen show effects, or duplicate pages
	Outliner view	Shows only the text in the presentation in outline form	You want to enter, edit, or reorganize the text in your presentation

FIGURE 2-11: Outliner view

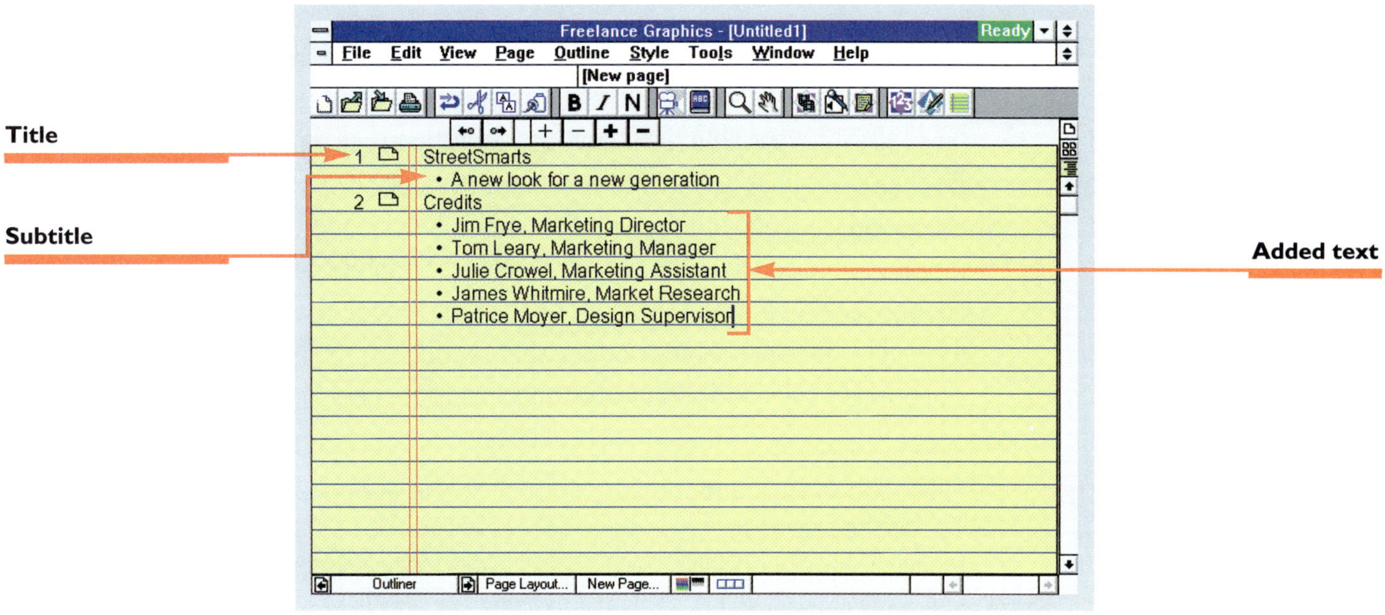

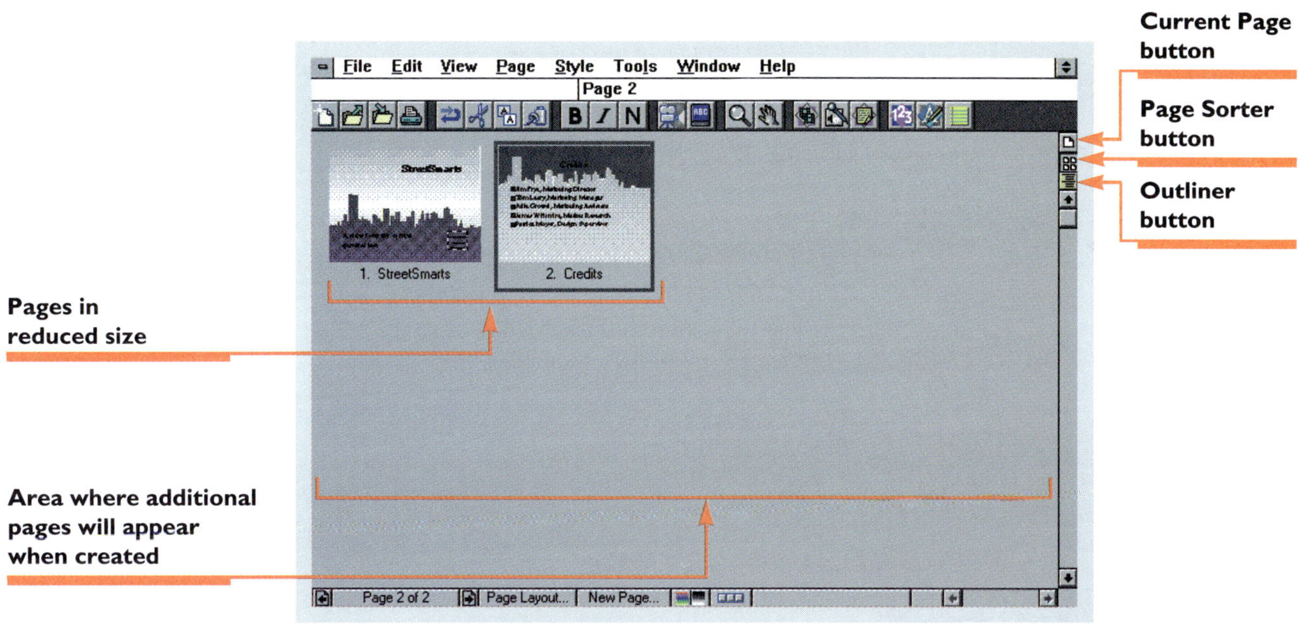

FIGURE 2-12: Page Sorter view

Viewing multiple presentations

You can view more than one presentation in the Freelance Graphics window at one time. Arrange the presentations on the screen by clicking Window in the menu bar and clicking Tile, which places the presentation windows side by side, or Cascade, which overlaps the open presentation windows. Figure 2-13 shows two presentations in tiled view. Return the presentation to full-screen display by clicking the Maximize button in the upper right corner of the window.

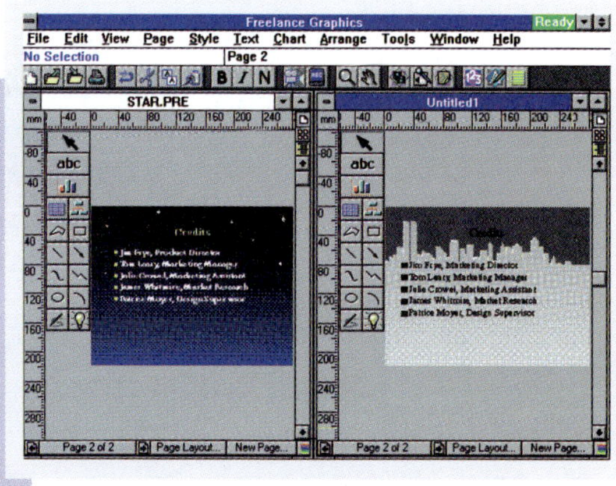

FIGURE 2-13: Tiling window display

Setting display preferences

Many of the Freelance Graphics elements you see on the screen are displayed automatically when you begin working on a new presentation. For example, the toolbox, title bar, presentation window, and SmartIcons all appear by default. Freelance Graphics also includes display preference items that you may want to use as you work on your presentation. Table 2-4 explains the other items you might want to add to enhance your Freelance Graphics display. ▶ As you begin adding elements to your Conscious Clothing presentation, having a ruler along the top and left sides of the presentation window will help you align text boxes and, later, charts. Add a ruler and change the unit of measurement from millimeters to inches.

STEPS

1. **Click View on the menu bar, then click View Preferences**
   The View Preferences dialog box displays, shown in Figure 2-14. The cursor size radio buttons control the size of the pointer, which changes to the crosshair cursor—resembling a plus sign—when you select one of the drawing tools. The checkboxes give you the option of adding different elements to the screen. The Show page borders options let you display a dotted page border so you know how much of your page will print.

2. In the Display area, click **Drawing ruler**
   An X appears in the checkbox.

3. Click **OK**
   The presentation page displays again. Rulers appear along the top and left edge of the presentation window. The letters mm appear in the top left corner of the presentation window telling you that the default measurement is millimeters. Because you are more familiar with inches as a unit of measurement, change the setting to inches.

4. Click **View** on the menu bar, then click **Units & Grids**
   The Units & Grids dialog box opens. Use the Units radio buttons to choose the unit of measurement you want displayed in both the drawing and text block rulers.

5. Click **Inches**, then click **OK**
   Inches is now the standard unit of measurement for your Freelance Graphics presentation. The presentation window reappears with the additional display items in place, as shown in Figure 2-15.

6. Move the mouse pointer across to a point just below the 3" mark in the horizontal ruler, and then down to the 3" mark in the vertical ruler
   A marker in the top ruler line shows the horizontal position of the pointer as you move it. Likewise, a marker in the left ruler line shows you the pointers' vertical position. By using the rulers in this way, you can position text boxes, graphics, and symbols at precise points on your presentation pages.

FIGURE 2-14: View Preferences dialog box

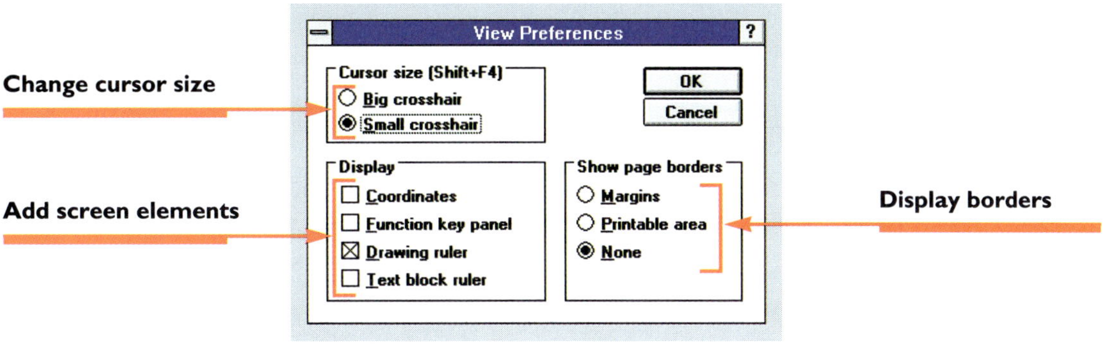

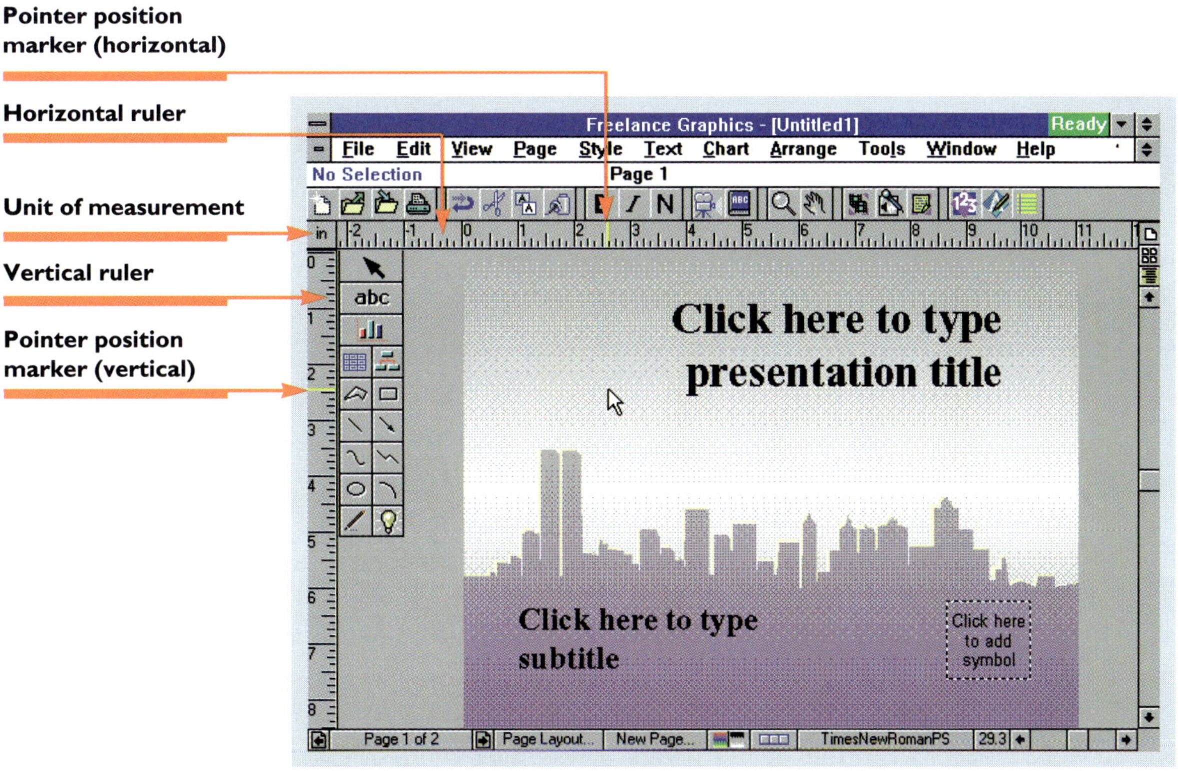

FIGURE 2-15: The enhanced display

TABLE 2-4:
Optional display items

DISPLAY ITEM	WHERE YOU FIND IT	WHAT IT DOES
Coordinates	View, View Preferences	Displays the coordinates of the mouse pointer
Function key panel	View, View Preferences	Displays a panel of function key buttons
Drawing ruler	View, View Preferences	Adds a horizontal ruler and a vertical ruler
Text block ruler	View, View Preferences	Displays a ruler across the top of a selected text block
Grid	View, Units & Grids	Shows a grid of gray dots in the background of the Current Page view so you can accurately align objects such as shapes, lines, and graphics

Saving the presentation

While you are creating your presentation, Freelance Graphics temporarily stores the information in the computer's random-access memory (RAM). When power goes off, all the data in RAM is erased. In order to keep a file so you can use it again later, you must save the file on a disk. You should save your file every 10 to 15 minutes and after each major change to your presentation. Table 2-5 lists the different ways you can save your Freelance Graphics files. ▶ Name and save your presentation to a file on your Student Disk #1. For more information on how to use the Student Disks, refer to the "Read This Before You Begin" page at the beginning of this book.

STEPS

1. **Click File in the menu bar**
   The File menu appears, showing two different file saving commands—Save and Save As.
2. **Click Save As**
   The Save As dialog box opens. See Figure 2-16. In this dialog box, you enter a name for the file, select the file type, and choose the drive and directory on which it will be stored. The cursor is positioned in the File name box.
3. **Click the Drives down arrow**
   The disk drives available on your computer are displayed in the drop-down list.
4. **Click the drive that contains your Student Disk #1**
   In Figure 2-16, the drive is shown as drive A. It may be another drive on your computer.
5. **Click MY_FILES in the Directories box**
   This selects the MY_FILES directory on your Student Disk #1, where you'll store all the presentations you create.
6. **Double click the File name textbox, and type PRESENT1**
   The default entry in the File name box is replaced with the characters you type. You can enter either lowercase or uppercase letters.
7. **Click the File types down arrow**
   The displayed list lets you choose the type of file you want to save. In this case, the default selection, Presentation (PRE), is the type you want. Other file types include SmartMaster Sets (MAS), Symbol files (SYM), and Freelance for OS/2 files (PRS). Freelance Graphics adds the last three characters—called the **file extension**—automatically.
8. **Click the File types down arrow again to close the list**
9. **Click OK**
   The file is saved in the MY_FILES directory on your Student Disk with the name PRESENT1.PRE. The Save As dialog box closes and your presentation file reappears, with the filename displayed in the menu bar.

FIGURE 2-16: Save As dialog box

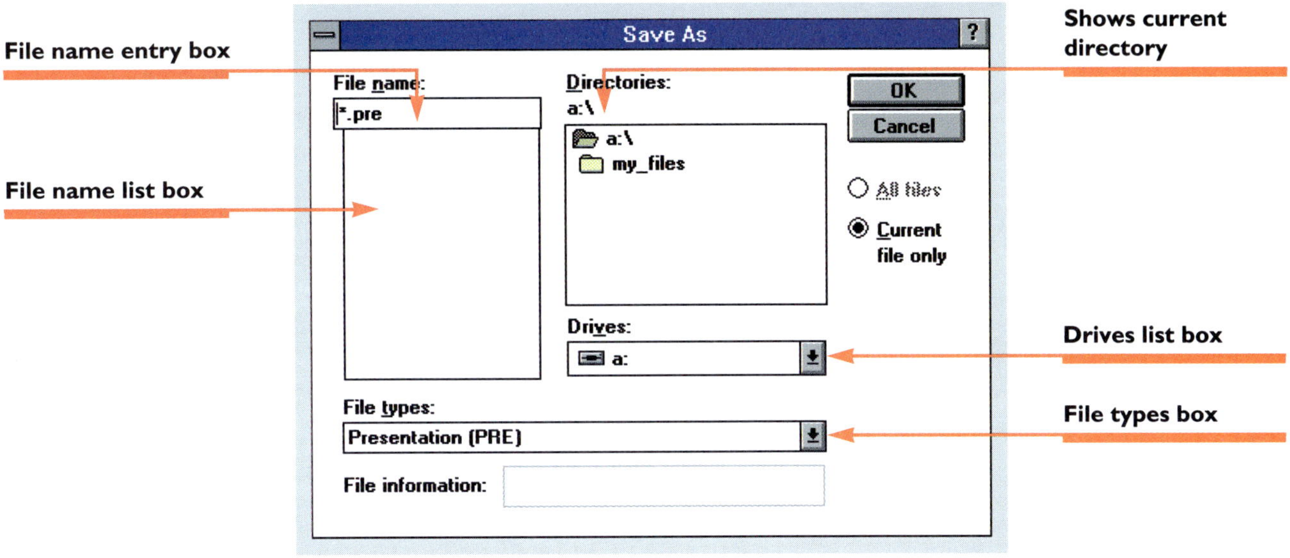

Saving all open files

When you are working with more than one presentation file at a time, you can save all open files by clicking File in the menu bar, clicking Save As, and clicking the All files radio button. When you click OK, Freelance Graphics saves all open files under their original names. If a file has not yet been assigned a name, Freelance Graphics prompts you to provide one.

TABLE 2-5:
Ways to save your file

METHOD	DESCRIPTION	USE WHEN
Save As command	Click File in menu bar; click Save As	You want to save the current file for the first time or you want to save the open file to a different disk
Save command	Click File in menu bar; click Save	You are resaving an existing file
	Click 	You want to save the file for the first time or update an existing file

Printing the presentation

With Freelance Graphics, you can print full pages, audience notes, handouts, speaker notes, and outlines. Don't wait to print until you've finished the entire presentation—a quick printout while you're working can help you catch errors and make improvments along the way. Also, you may want to circulate the print-out among co-workers for feedback on the developing presentation. ▶ Print a copy of your presentation—which currently includes only the first two pages—so Tom Leary can review the design choices you've made so far.

STEPS

1 **Check your printer**
Make sure the printer is connected to the computer, turned on, and supplied with paper. Most printers have a Ready or On-line light that tells you when the printer is ready to print.

2 Click **File** on the menu bar, then click **Print**
The Print File dialog box appears, as shown in Figure 2-17. You will notice there are many print options available. The value in Number of copies is highlighted.

3 In the **Number of copies** box, type **2**
This replaces the default Number of copies entry with the number 2, telling Freelance Graphics you want to print two copies of the presentation.

4 Click **Print**
The Print File dialog box closes and Freelance Graphics displays the Printing Status dialog box to show how the print operation is progressing. If you are using a dot-matrix or ink-jet printer, your printer may begin printing immediately. If you are using a laser printer, the Active light on the printer should begin to flash, showing that your printer is receiving data from the computer. If any printing problems occur, a message alerts you to the problem. See Figure 2-18.

5 Click **File** on the menu bar, then click **Close**
Freelance Graphics closes the PRESENT1.PRE file without asking whether you want to save changes, because you have not made any changes since you last saved the file.

6 Click **File**, then click **Exit**
Freelance Graphics closes, and the Lotus Applications group window displays.

FIGURE 2-17: Print File dialog box

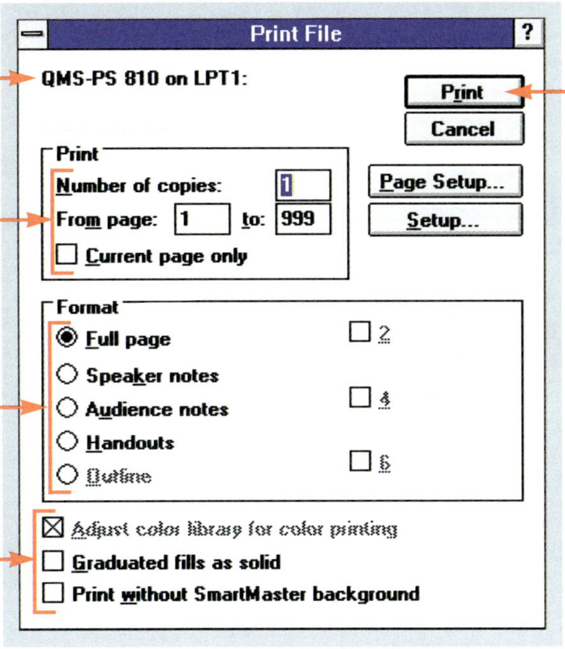

FIGURE 2-18: Sample black and white printout

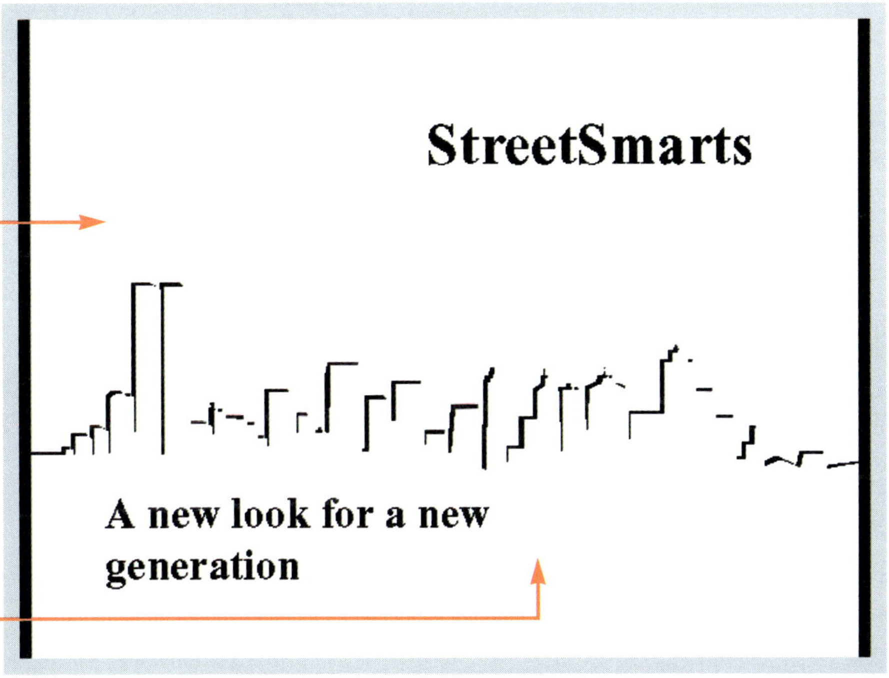

Setting up your printer

Before you can use your printer with Freelance Graphics, you need to make sure it is set up properly. Click File in the menu bar and click Printer Setup. When the Printer Setup dialog box appears, click the printer you want to use in the Printers list. Click OK to close the dialog box and return to the presentation page.

CONCEPTS REVIEW

Label the Freelance Graphics screen items shown in Figure 2-19.

FIGURE 2-19

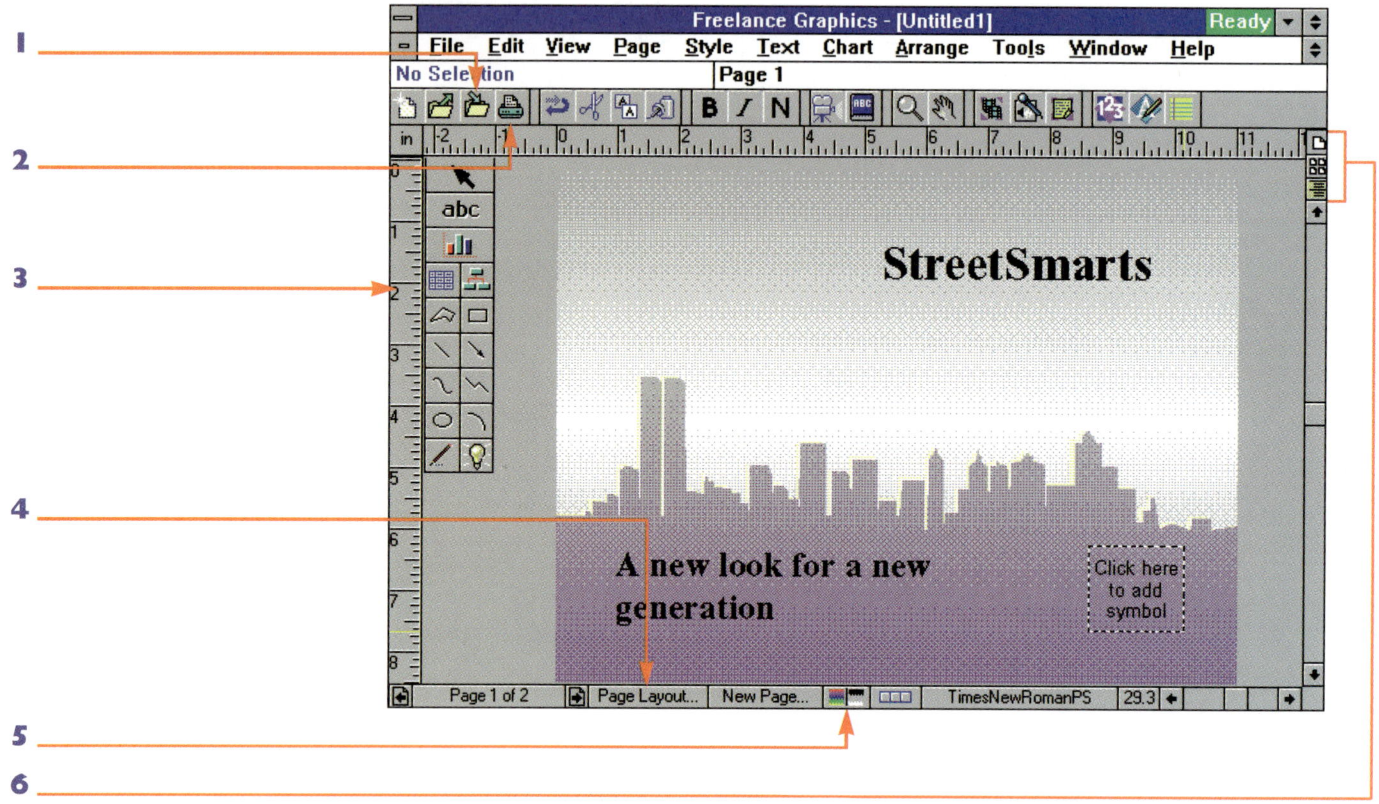

Match each definition with its element.

7 Additional items you can add to the Freelance Graphics display

8 A preset page design with areas for text, charts, and symbols

9 A set of colors Freelance Graphics applies to presentation elements

10 An alternative view in Freelance Graphics that shows all presentation pages reduced to fit on one screen

11 The text area that appears when you click prompt text

a. Page layout

b. Color scheme

c. Display preferences

d. Text entry box

e. Page Sorter

Select the best answer from the list of choices.

12 Which of the following statements best describes the function of a SmartMaster?

a. A SmartMaster helps you design the content of your presentation.

b. A SmartMaster is a preset design you can apply to your presentation.

c. A SmartMaster is a presentation template with pages already in place.

d. A SmartMaster helps you choose the page layout you need.

13 Which page layout should you choose when you want to design your own page?

a. Title

b. Organization Chart

c. Table

d. [None]

14 Which of the following steps accurately describes how to preview a new color palette?

a. Click and hold down the mouse button on the Preview button

b. Click OK

c. Click the Directory button

d. Double-click the Preview button

15 You can view your presentation in each of the following views EXCEPT which one?

a. Current Page view

b. Handout view

c. Page Sorter view

d. Outliner view

16 Which command should you use the first time you save your presentation file?

a. New

b. Close

c. Save As

d. Open

APPLICATIONSREVIEW

1 Begin a new presentation.

a. Start Freelance Graphics for Windows.

b. Select the option for starting a new file.

2 Choose a SmartMaster.

a. Click corporate.mas and watch the preview window. What is the tone of this SmartMaster?

b. Find and preview a SmartMaster design appropriate for an international meeting.

c. Find a SmartMaster design that could be used to communicate environmental issues.

d. Click notebook.mas, a suitable choice for the type of presentation you are creating. Click OK.

3 Choose a page layout.

a. Click Basic Layout. What happens to the page in the preview window?

b. Click [None]. What color is displayed as the page background in the preview window?

c. Click Title. How does the preview change?

d. Click OK.

e. Compare your screen with Figure 2-20

FIGURE 2-20

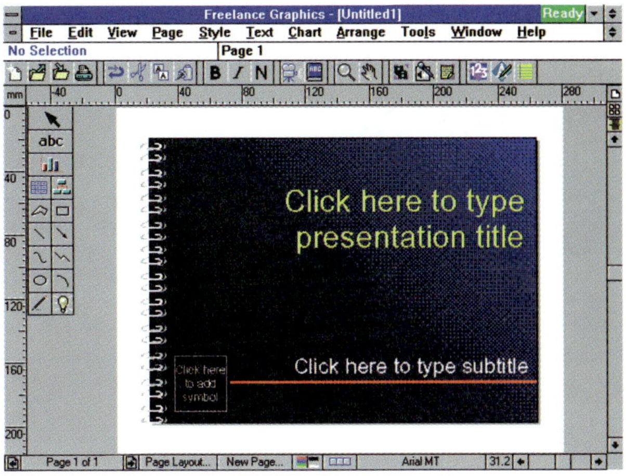

4 Enter text.

a. Click in the top prompt text box. What happens?

b. Type Summer Programs.

c. Click OK. What happens to the text entry area?

d. Click in the lower prompt text box.

e. Type Parks & Recreation.

f. Click outside the text entry area.

5 View the presentation.

a. Click View in the menu bar.

b. Click Page Sorter. What appears on the screen?

c. Locate the view buttons and click the Outliner button.

d. Click View in the menu bar and click Current Page. Compare your screen with Figure 2-21.

FIGURE 2-21

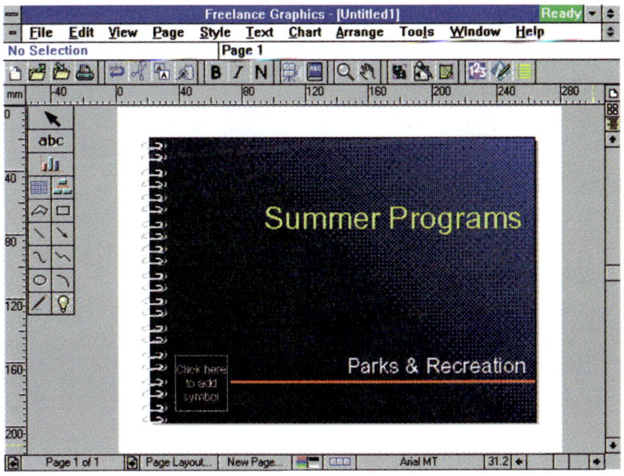

6 Save the presentation.
  a. Click File in the menu bar.
  b. Click Save As. The Save As dialog box appears.
  c. Enter the filename PARKS.
  d. Choose the drive that contains your Student Disk #1.
  e. Select MY_FILES directory.
  f. Click OK.

7 Print the presentation.
  a. Make sure your printer is turned on and ready.
  b. Click File in the menu bar.
  c. Click Print. The Print File dialog box appears.
  d. Click Print. The file prints.

INDEPENDENT CHALLENGE

The Blue Heron Nature Reserve has been part of your community for 50 years. Several affluent neighborhoods are currently under development along the reserve's boundaries, and, understandably, entrepreneurs are wanting to capitalize on this recent growth and supply goods and services.

You and several others in your neighborhood are organizing a campaign to gather support for protecting the reserve. You will design and give presentations to area businesses and community organizations, hoping to get financial, emotional, and political support that will persuade the developers to choose a site that does not endanger the reserve. Your presentation must accomplish the following goals:

- Be visually inviting and interesting
- Convey a serious tone appropriate to the subject matter
- Use colors that are easy for viewers to read near and far
- Produce printed handouts to circulate among attendees

To complete this independent challenge:

1 On paper, create an outline for the presentation. List at least three primary points. A few examples might be:
  - History of Blue Heron
  - Blue Heron Today
  - Blue Heron Tomorrow

2 Within each primary point, list at least two subpoints. For example, the first section might be:
  History of Blue Heron
  - Blue Heron Founders
  - A Blue Heron Timeline

3 On a new sheet of paper, sketch the first five pages of the presentation, showing what page layouts would work best in what order.

4 Start Freelance Graphics and begin a new presentation. Choose a SmartMaster that provides the kind of tone you feel is appropriate for the presentation. A SmartMaster like forest.mas would work well for this presentation.

5 Create the title page for the presentation. Think about an effective attention-getting title (for example, The End of Blue Heron?). Next, consider a subtitle, short and to the point such as: A preserve to be preserved.

6 Save the presentation file as NATURE on your Student Disk #1 in the MY_FILES directory.

7 Print a copy of the presentation's title page.

8 Submit your outline, sketched presentation plan, and printed title page to your instructor.

UNIT 3

OBJECTIVES

- Plan text sections
- Open an existing presentation
- Enter and edit text
- Work with text blocks
- Change text levels
- Select text font, size, and style
- Align text
- Move and resize text boxes
- Use the Outliner

Working WITH TEXT

Now that you've been through the basic process of planning the presentation; choosing SmartMasters, page layouts, and color schemes; and creating, viewing, and printing the first few pages of your presentation, you are ready to begin work on the overall text content. Working with text in Freelance Graphics involves entering, editing, and enhancing the words you'll include in your presentation. You can enter text in both Current Page view and Outliner view. ▶ In a meeting with Tom Leary, you discuss the overall goals of the presentation and show him the sample printouts you created in the last unit. With his approval, you are ready to move on to the next stage: planning, creating, and working with the presentation text. ▶

Planning text sections

Preparing text for a presentation is a process very different from writing a report. In a report, you can take several paragraphs to explain something that in a presentation might be limited to a single bulleted item. In a report, you can assume that your reader can go back and review text sections that are difficult to understand; in a presentation, your words must be clear and carefully chosen so viewers won't be confused. ▶ Because text carries such an important role in your presentation, you should take the time to plan out the text sections you need, to help you create a more carefully crafted presentation. Table 3-1 lists some guidelines for working with presentation text. As you consider the text goals in your presentation, ask yourself these questions:

- **What form will the information take?**
  The answer is important for determining the format of your text. Will you use steps? Lists? Paragraphs? Bulleted lists are ideal for explaining items in a series or steps in a process. For example, the bulleted list you created in Unit 2 lists the names of people involved in the StreetSmarts project. Paragraphs should be short and used only when necessary. Headings should be clear and to the point.

- **Will you be using information from an already-prepared document?**
  You can copy and paste text from other Windows applications if you choose. If you are creating the presentation from a prepared document or if you will be handing out a report to go along with the presentation you deliver, follow the sequence of topics in the report.

- **Is the text necessary?**
  Don't add text just for text's sake. Pages need headings, but explanatory text can distract viewers and dilute your message. If a heading and a colorful chart will communicate your message clearly, there's no need to add a paragraph describing what the chart already shows.

- **Is the text organized logically?**
  In Unit 2, you prepared a rough outline for your presentation pages. You can use that outline to create text, but check it carefully first. Make sure your topics are introduced in a logical order and the page layout you selected originally still works. Don't be afraid to revise or change the plan altogether to suit your evolving presentation.

TABLE 3-1:
Text guidelines

TEXT ITEM	TIP	DESCRIPTION
Title	Use interesting words	Communicate topics clearly but invitingly
	Use parallel headings	Be consistent in the way you word headings (for example, "Introducing StreetSmarts" and "Looking at Objectives" both begin with words that end in "ing")
Bulleted lists	Be concise	Use as few words as possible
	One idea per bullet	Break procedures or ideas into single items, one per bullet
Paragraphs	Use sparingly	Avoid use of paragraphs when bullets will do; too much reading will distract the audience
	Keep short	If a paragraph is longer than 20 words, ask yourself "Is there some other way I could communicate this information?"
All text items	Tailor the layout to the information	Use Page Layout to display the possible layouts you can choose; select bullets for series or sequential information; use concise, clear titles; add paragraphs only when necessary

Reordering pages

You can easily reorder pages at any time in Freelance Graphics. Once you create the basic text content, you can view the pages in Page Sorter by clicking the Page Sorter view button ⊞. Then, if necessary, you can move pages around by simply dragging them to the desired locations. In Unit 4, "Working with presentation pages," you learn more about reordering pages in Freelance Graphics.

Opening an existing presentation

Chances are, you'll often spend more than one work session building a single presentation. You can open an existing presentation when you first start Freelance Graphics—in the Welcome to Freelance Graphics dialog box—or anytime the program is running. Once you open the presentation, you can use the Save As command to save the file under a different name. This process keeps a copy of your original file intact and makes a work file on which you can make changes or enhancements. ▶ In this lesson, start Freelance Graphics and open the presentation file you started in Unit 2. Because you want to preserve a copy of that file for safe-keeping, use Save As to create a new copy of the file under a different name.

STEPS

1 **Double-click the Freelance Graphics program icon**
The Freelance Graphics opening screen appears, followed by the Welcome to Freelance Graphics dialog box.

2 **Click Work on an existing presentation; then click OK**
This tells Freelance Graphics that you want to work on a presentation that is already saved on disk. The Choose Presentation dialog box appears, as shown in Figure 3-1.

3 **Click the Drives list arrow, and, if your Student Disk #1 is in drive A, click a:**
Depending on the drives displayed in your Drives list, you may need to scroll up to locate drive A. A list of files on your Student Disk #1 appears in the File name window. (Note: If your Student Disk is in drive B, click b:.)

4 **In the File name list click UNIT_3-1.PRE, then click OK**
The file UNIT_3-1.PRE opens. Because you need to keep this sample file intact, create a copy of this file and save it under another name.

5 **Click File on the menu bar, then click Save As**
The Save As dialog box opens.

6 **If necessary, click the Drives list arrow and click a; then in the Directories box, double-click MY_FILES**
If your Student Disk #1 is in drive B, click b: instead.

7 **If it's not already highlighted, double-click UNIT_3-1.PRE in the File name list box**
This selects the name of the file you want to save and displays it in the File name text box.

8 **Type text 1**
You can enter the filename in either uppercase or lowercase letters. The text you type replaces the highlighted text.

9 **Click OK**
The Save As dialog box closes. Freelance Graphics automatically adds the three-character extension .PRE to the filename. Now you have two copies of the same file—UNIT_3-1.PRE and TEXT1.PRE—saved on your Student Disk #1. UNIT_3-1.PRE is saved on the root directory of the disk (A:\ or B:\) and TEXT1.PRE is saved in the MY_FILES directory. Changes you make to the presentation in this lesson will be saved in the TEXT1.PRE file.

FIGURE 3-1: Choose Presentation dialog box

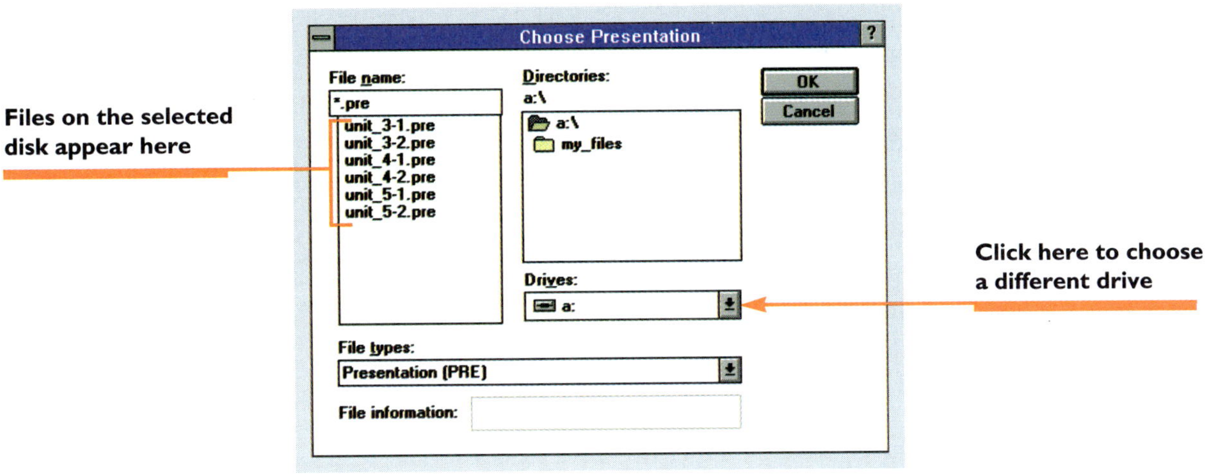

Opening an existing file during a work session

If you are already working in Freelance Graphics and want to open an existing file, you use a slightly different procedure. Click File in the menu bar and then click Open. (You can also use the File Open SmartIcon if you prefer.) When the Open File dialog box appears, as shown in Figure 3-2, choose the drive, directory, and filename of the file you want to open. Click OK to open the file.

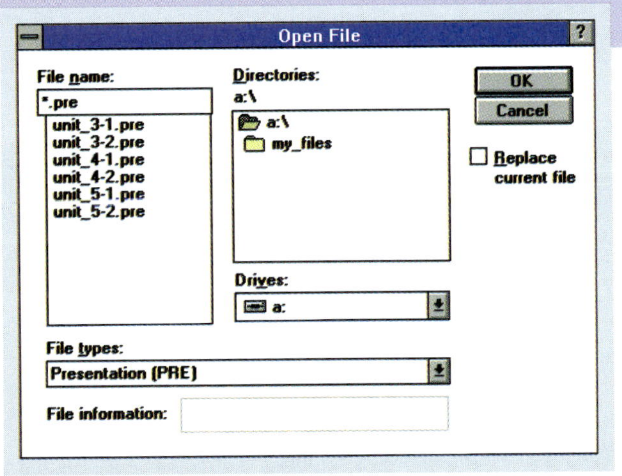

FIGURE 3-2: Open File dialog box

TROUBLE?

For more information about using your Student Disks, read the section at the beginning of this book called "Read This Before You Begin."

Entering and editing text

Freelance Graphics makes it very easy to enter text. You simply follow the instructions in the prompt text boxes to click and type the text you want to add. As your work on the Conscious Clothing presentation will demonstrate, editing is as simple as positioning the cursor and pressing [Backspace] or [Del] and retyping. Table 3-2 explains editing keys you'll use often. ▶ Now that you've opened the presentation you started in Unit 2, you need to begin the process of adding pages and entering and editing text. Start by creating an Objectives page that will introduce the intended goals of your presentation to your audience.

STEPS

1 Click **Page** in the menu bar, then click **New**
The New Page dialog box opens so you can choose another page, as Figure 3-3 shows.

2 Choose **Bulleted List**, then click **OK**
The New Page dialog box closes and the new presentation page, which is Page 3 of your presentation, appears.

3 Click the **Click here to type page title** prompt text and type **Objectives**
The text entry area appears. As you type, the characters appear in the center of the box. This text serves as the title for the third page of your presentation.

4 Click the **Click here to type bulleted text** prompt text and type **To introduce StreetSmarts**
The first bulleted item appears as you type.

5 Press **[Enter]** and type **To introduce our development team**, then click **OK**
This adds the second bullet, as shown in Figure 3-4. For this lesson, you need only two bulleted items.

6 Click **New Page** [New Page...] in the bottom of the window, then select **Bullets & Symbol** and click **OK**
Page 4 of your presentation is a page with room for a title, bullets, and a symbol. For now, you'll enter only the text.

7 Click the **Click here to type page title** prompt text and type **Introducing StreetSmarts**
This step enters the title for Page 4.

8 Click the left prompt text **Click here to type bulleted text** and type **The message of the street in a bold new voice**, then click **OK**
The text is entered as a bullet in the text box on the left side of the page. But before you can continue, Tom Leary stops by to check your progress and asks, "How would it sound if we said 'The message of the street is a bold new voice?'" You need to edit the phrase you just entered, changing the word 'in' to the word 'is'.

9 Click just after the word **in**
The text entry box appears, with the cursor positioned after the word you need to change.

10 Press **[Backspace]** to remove the n, type **[s]**, then click **OK**
This completes the wording change. You have completed the text portion of Page 4 of your presentation. Compare your screen with Figure 3-5.

FIGURE 3-3: The New Page dialog box

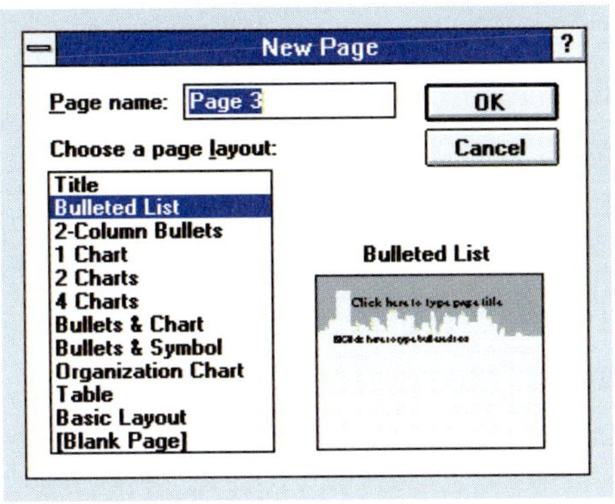

FIGURE 3-4: The Bulleted List page

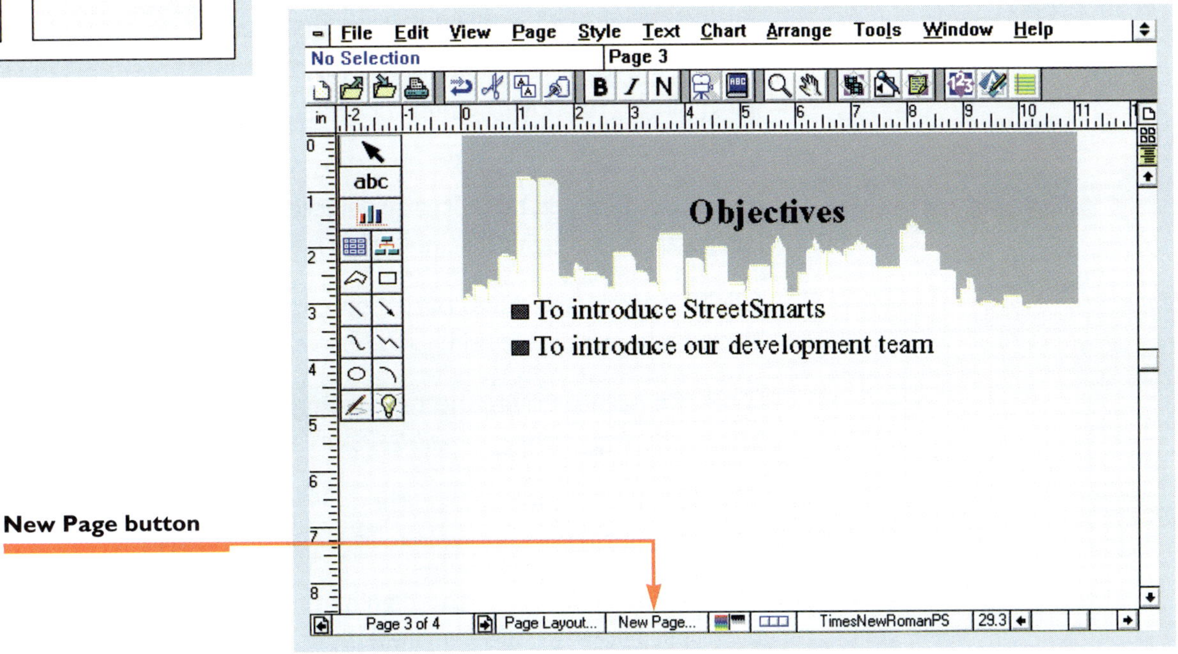

FIGURE 3-5: The Bullets & Symbol page

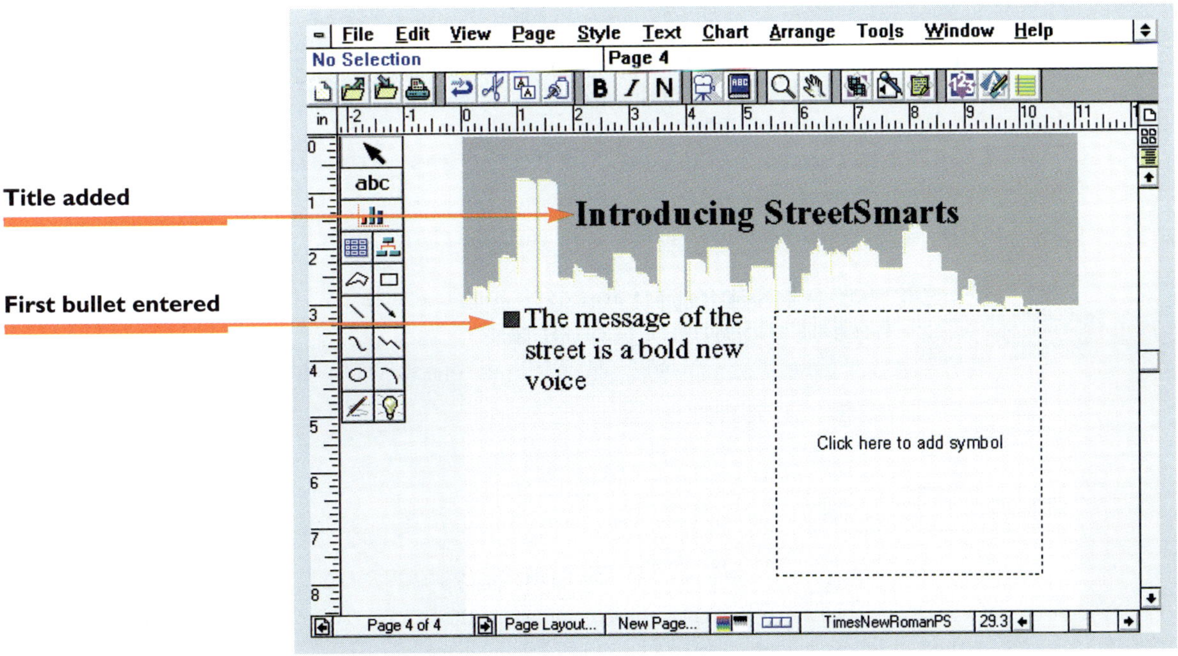

Working with text blocks

Some editing tasks aren't quite as simple as positioning the cursor and pressing [Backspace] or [Delete]. Some editing procedures require that you select the text you want to work with—called a **text block**—before you make any changes. For example, before you can copy a section of text, you must select the text you want to copy. After you click Edit, then click Copy, a copy of the text is placed on the Windows **clipboard**—an unseen area of memory that stores text and graphics you cut, copy, and paste. Table 3-2 lists common block operations. ▶ The second bulleted entry on Page 3 will be similar to the first bulleted entry. You can save time by copying the text and pasting it in the second bullet position. You first need to select a text block to work with, then copy and paste the text block you select.

STEPS

1. **If the text block is not already selected, click the bulleted list text box**
   Handles appear, indicating that the text box is selected.
2. **Click Text in the menu bar, then click Edit**
   The text entry area appears, with the cursor positioned at the end of the text.
3. **Drag the pointer over the text to highlight it**
   Highlighting text selects it as a text block. Compare your screen with Figure 3-6.
4. **Click Edit in the menu bar, then click Copy**
   A copy of the highlighted text is placed on the Windows clipboard.
5. **Click in the space after the highlighted block, then press [Enter]**
   The highlighting is removed from the text, and a new bullet is added.
6. **Click the Paste SmartIcon** 
   The text is pasted from the clipboard to the cursor position.
7. **Double-click the word message, then type wisdom**
   The new word replaces the highlighted word.
8. **Select the text from the word is to the end of the text block, then click the Cut SmartIcon** 
   The highlighted text is removed from the page and placed on the Windows clipboard.
9. **Type worth listening to and click just outside the text area (avoiding the Click here to add symbol prompt text)**
   The text box closes. Compare your screen with the one shown in Figure 3-7.

FIGURE 3-6: Selecting a text block

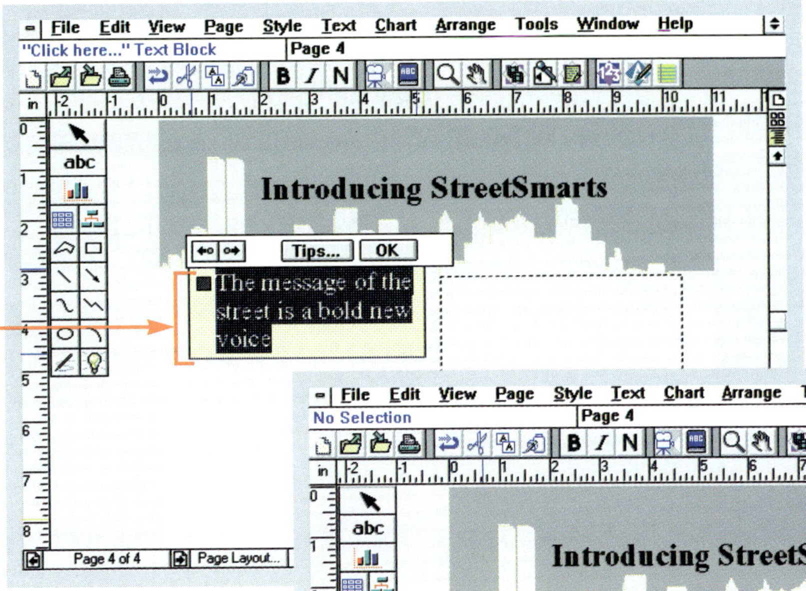

Highlighting text selects it for editing

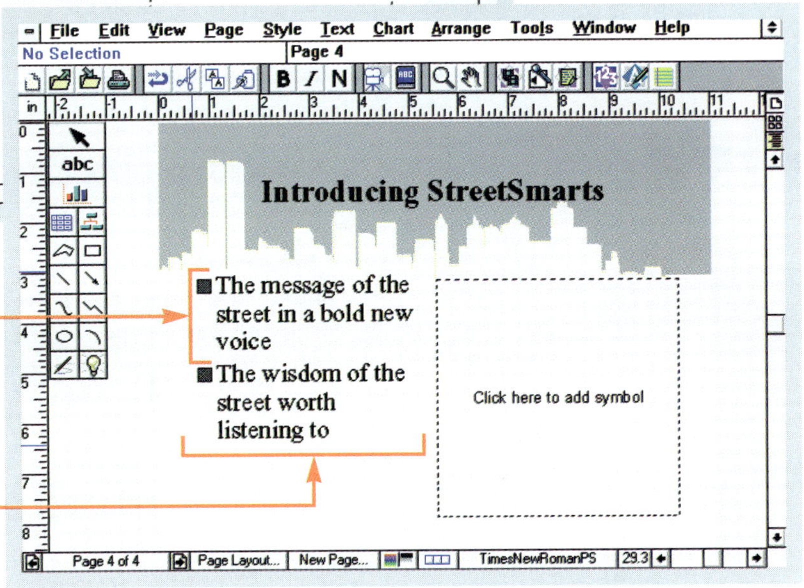

Original text block

Copied, pasted, and edited text block

FIGURE 3-7: A text block that has been copied, pasted, and revised

TABLE 3-2: Common block operations

TO...	DO THIS	OR THIS
Select a block	Click once at the beginning of the block, then press [Shift] and click at the end of the block	Click and drag the mouse over the block
Copy a block	Click Edit, then Copy or use the Copy SmartIcon	[Ctrl] [C]
Move a block	Click Edit, then Cut (or use the Cut SmartIcon); move the cursor to the new location; click Edit, then Paste (or use the Paste SmartIcon)	Press [Ctrl] [X]; move the cursor to the new location; press [Ctrl] [V]
Cut a block	Click Edit, then Cut or use the Cut SmartIcon	[Ctrl] [X]
Paste a block	Click Edit, then Paste or use the Paste SmartIcon	[Ctrl] [V]
Delete a block	Click Edit, then Clear	Press [Del]

QUICK TIP

You can use the Undo command—in the Edit menu—to reverse up to your last nine actions, one by one. Press [Ctrl][Z] or click the Undo SmartIcon to Undo quickly.

Changing text levels

Your presentation text may consist mainly of titles and bulleted lists. Occasionally you'll want to add a paragraph or a note. You can also include bullets within bullets. Every text item in your presentation is assigned to a **text level**. You can use up to three levels of bullets within bullets in Freelance Graphics. Each level has different text settings, or **attributes**, assigned to the level. You can use the Promote and Demote buttons in the text entry boxes to change the level of text. Table 3-3 explains the buttons you can use to change text levels. ▶ You have entered first-level bullets on Page 4 of your presentation. You decide to add three subpoints describing the statements made by this "bold new voice" to help illustrate the tone the clothing will convey. Use the Demote and Promote buttons to find out how they change the look of the text; then add three second-level bullets.

STEPS

1 Click the top text entry in the bullet list box, then click again
The text entry area appears. The cursor is positioned in the middle of the first bulleted entry.

2 Click **Demote**
The bullet character changes from a square to a dash. The text indents and is displayed in a smaller size. In this case, you want to outdent the line once again so you can add three second-level bullets.

3 Click **Promote**
The text moves back out, or shifts left, to its original position. The dash bullet is replaced with the square bullet character. Now you can add the new text.

4 Move the cursor to the end of the first bulleted text item; press [Enter]
A new bullet appears in the same size and shape as the preceding bullet. Here you want to indent the bullet, demoting the text level.

5 Click **Demote**
Again, the bullet character changes from a square bullet to a dash and is indented slightly.

6 Type **Make a statement** and press **[Enter]**
This enters the first bulleted item. The text appears in a smaller text size than the higher-level text. Now, add two more dashes.

7 Type **Make a difference**, press **[Enter]**; type **Make a future** and click **OK**
This finalizes the set of three bulleted entries. Compare your screen to Figure 3-8.

8 Click the **Save SmartIcon** to save your changes
Freelance Graphics saves the changes you made to TEXT1.PRE in the MY_FILES directory of Student Disk #1.

9 Click **File** on the menu bar, then click **Close**
The presentation file closes.

TABLE 3-3: Text level buttons

BUTTON	NAME	DESCRIPTION
	Promote	Shifts a text entry to the left, moving it one level outward toward the left screen margin
	Demote	Indents a text entry one level, moving it one tab inward

FIGURE 3-8: Adding indented text

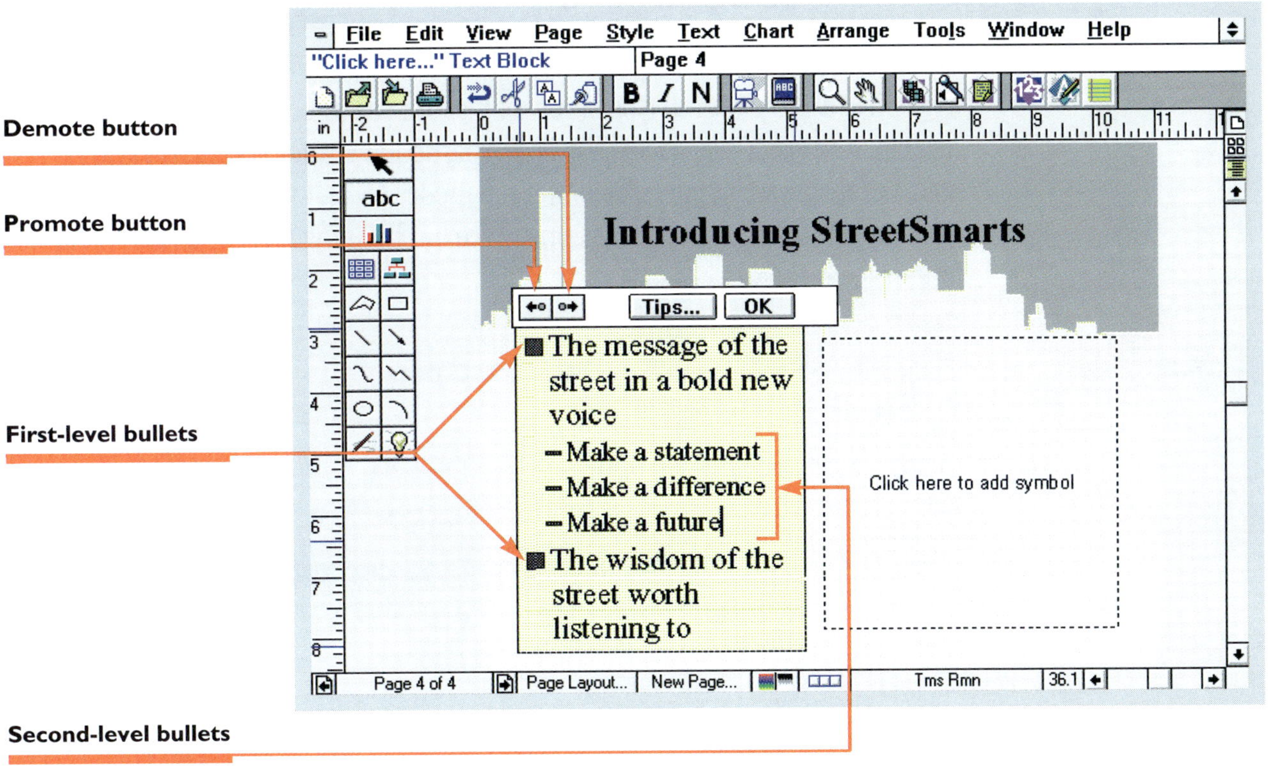

Using Text Tips

When you are first getting used to the promote and demote features, you may have trouble remembering which button you use for which operation. Freelance Graphics includes a Tips button in the text entry area that displays basic instructions for dealing with different text levels. Display the text entry area, then click Tips. A window appears listing the different choices, as shown in Figure 3-9. Review the information and click OK when you're done.

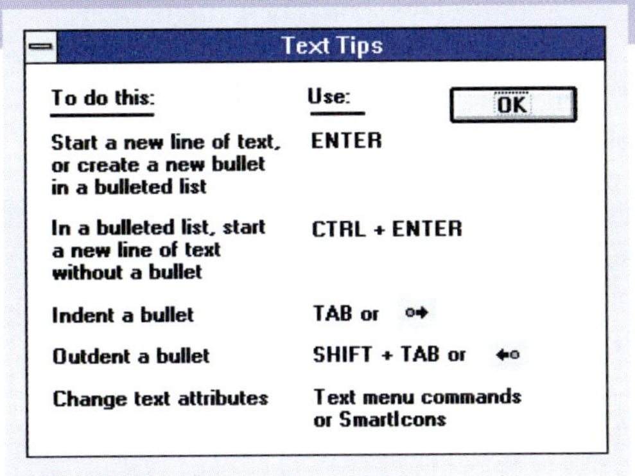

FIGURE 3-9: Text tips

TROUBLE?

If you use the Tab shortcuts shown in the Tips box, be careful not to highlight the text you want to promote or demote, because then the Tab action will replace the text, instead of promote or demote it.

Selecting text font, size, and style

The typeface you choose has a great deal to do with the way your text looks. A **typeface** is the overall type family of the font you choose such as Times Roman. A **font** is one size and style of a particular typeface, such as 10 point bold. ▶Your presentation calls for a more modern look than the font your title page provides. Give the title page a new face by changing the title to a different font, size, and color.

STEPS

1 **Click File on the menu bar, then click Open**
The Open File dialog box appears.

2 **Open UNIT_3-2.PRE on your Student Disk #1**
Make sure that you have selected the drive (A: or B:) containing your Student Disk.

3 **Save the file as TEXT2.PRE in the MY_FILES directory**
This procedure leaves the file UNIT_3-2.PRE intact and gives you a new working file called TEXT2.PRE. The first page of the presentation appears.

4 **Click StreetSmarts**
The text box is selected.

5 **Click Text on the menu bar, then click Font**
The Font dialog box appears, as shown in Figure 3-10. The Font dialog box contains many different text settings. See Figure 3-10.

6 **In the Face area, scroll through the typeface choices, then click Brushscript**
The preview window in the bottom of the Font dialog box shows the sample text in the typeface you choose.

7 **Click the Size down scroll arrow once, to scroll down the list, and click 72**
The size appears selected and is displayed in the Custom text box. The characters are measured in **points**, a typographical measurement that is roughly equivalent to 1/72 of an inch. This means that 72-point letters should be 1" high.

8 **Click the Color down list arrow**
A palette of colors appears.

9 **Click a dark shade of purple that matches the color of the cityscape on the presentation background**
For this example, we selected the purple in the fourth column from the right, fifth row from the bottom of the color palette.

10 **Click OK**
The presentation page appears with the title in the new font and color. Compare your screen to Figure 3-11.

FIGURE 3-10: Font dialog box

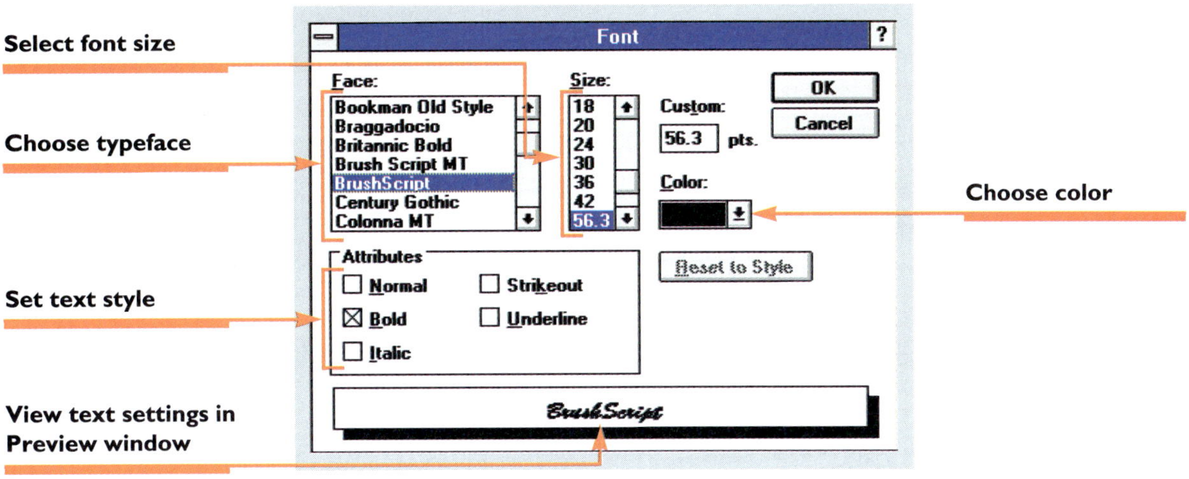

FIGURE 3-11: The revised title page

Choosing typefaces

When you first begin working with different typefaces, you may have trouble deciding which typeface looks right for the presentations you are creating. Times Roman is a traditional book-style font used for easy reading. BrushScript is an artistic font that resembles handwriting, used for special items and emphasis. Helvetica is a common font often used for titles, headings, labels, and notes. Wingdings is a collection of symbols—not alphabetic characters—used for bullets and other special purposes.

QUICK TIP

When you are choosing the font and color of your text, remember to make it readable for your audience. Remember to choose background and text colors that provide a strong contrast so viewers can see the text easily.

Aligning text

In order to change the alignment of text in Freelance Graphics, you use paragraph styles. A **paragraph style** is a group of text settings—such as indent level, font, bullet, and alignment—that affect the text in the selected box. Freelance Graphics allows you to control both the horizontal alignment, simply called **justification**, and the vertical alignment, called **vertical justification**, of the text in your presentation. Table 3-4 explains the different types of justification. ▶ Change the alignment of the bulleted list on Page 3 of your presentation so that the text aligns along the right margin and is centered vertically in the text box.

STEPS

1 Click **Page** [Page 1 of 1] in the lower-left corner of the presentation window
Freelance Graphics takes the page name from the title of each page.

2 Click **4. Introducing StreetSmarts**
Page 4 is displayed.

3 Click anywhere on the bulleted text
Handles appear in the corners and on the sides of the box, indicating that it is selected.

4 Click **Style** on the menu bar, then click **Attributes ["Click here..." text block]**
The Paragraph Styles dialog box appears, as shown in Figure 3-12.

5 In the Justification line, click **Right**
This selects right justification for the text in the selected box.

6 In the Vertical just. line, click **Center**
This selects the text between the top and bottom of the selected text box.

7 Click **OK**, then click outside the text box to deselect the bulleted text box
The presentation page is displayed. Compare your results with those shown in Figure 3-13.

TABLE 3-4: Understanding justification choices

BUTTON	NAME	DESCRIPTION
	Left justify	Aligns text along the left margin
	Center	Centers text between the left and right margins
	Right justify	Aligns text along the right margin
	Full justify	Adds space between characters to force text to align along both the left and right margins
	Top	Aligns text along the top of the text box
	Center	Centers text vertically between the top and bottom edges of the text box
	Bottom	Aligns text along the bottom of the text box

FIGURE 3-12: Paragraph Styles dialog box

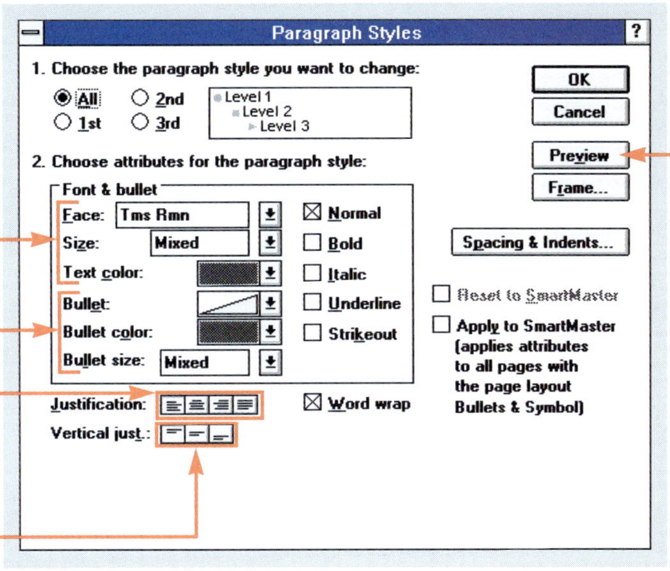

Font attributes

Bullet attributes

Controls horizontal justification

Controls vertical justification

Press and hold to preview changes

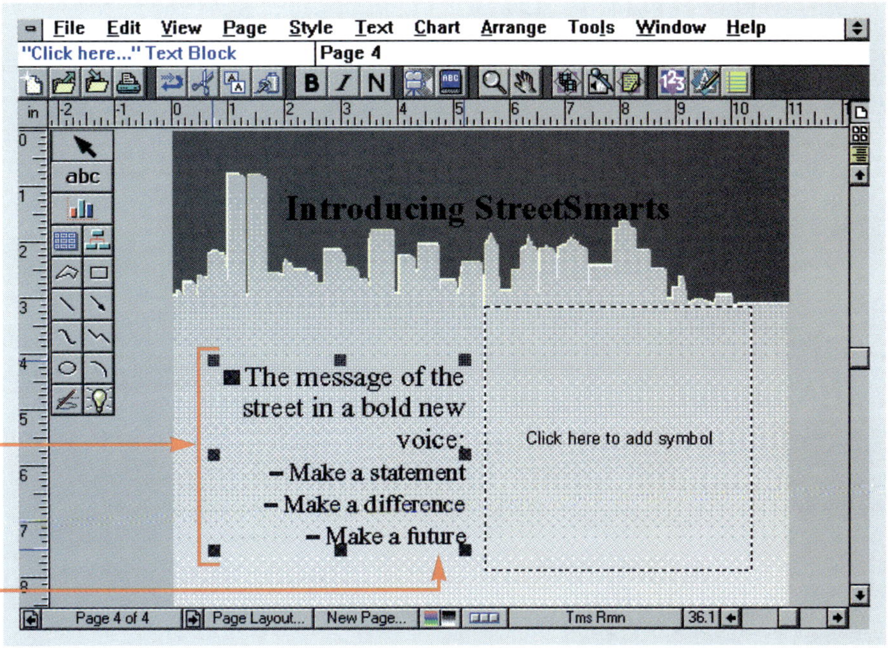

Text is vertically centered in the text box

Text is aligned on the right

FIGURE 3-13: The right justified text

Changing spacing

From within the Paragraph Styles dialog box, you can choose different line and paragraph spacing for the selected text. Click Spacing & Indents. The Spacing & Indents dialog box appears, as shown in Figure 3-14. You can enter new spacing settings for paragraphs, lines, or indents. Click OK to return to the presentation page.

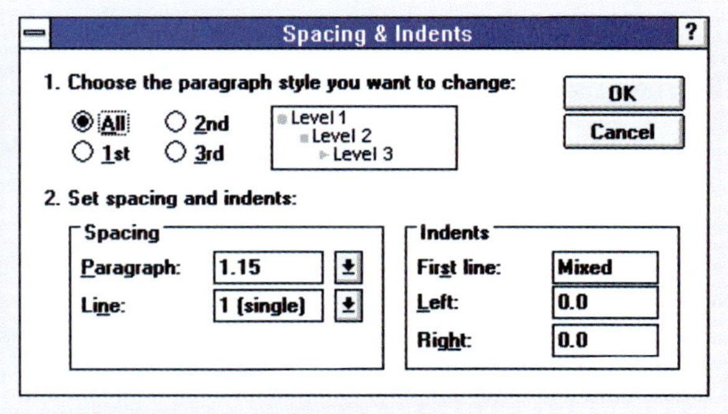

FIGURE 3-14: Spacing & Indents dialog box

Moving and resizing text boxes

When you add other elements to your presentation page, you may need to move or resize an existing text box in order to make room for the new items. This is a simple process that involves only a click and drag of the mouse. Table 3-5 explains where to position the pointer when you are resizing text boxes. ▶ To improve the look of Page 4 of your presentation, try moving and resizing the bulleted text box. First you move the selected text upward on the page; then you resize the box by stretching it to the right.

STEPS

1. Click the **bulleted text box**
   Handles appear in the corners and on the sides of the box.
2. Position the pointer on the box, then press and hold the mouse button, and move the box upward
   Move the box to a position just below the start of the skyline. When you release the mouse button, the box is placed in the new location. See Figure 3-15. Now you are ready to resize the box.
3. Position the pointer on the handle on the right edge of the box
   The pointer changes to a double-headed arrow.
4. Press and hold the mouse button; drag the handle to the right
   The box is resized in the direction you drag the mouse.
5. Release the mouse button
   The text box resizes itself according to your movement. The text inside the box moves to adjust for the resized box. The change shows us that other changes need to be made: center the text and remove the bullet character on the first line to make the text easier to read.
6. Double-click anywhere on the first line of text, then in the Justification line, click **Center**, and click **OK**
   The bulleted text is centered in the selected text box.
7. Click **Text** in the menu bar, then click **Bullet**
   The Bullet dialog box appears.
8. Click **Style**, then click **None**, then click **OK**
   This removes the bullet characters from the text; it cleans things up after the move and resize procedure. The Click here to add symbol prompt text is still visible behind the text, but it will not appear in a slide show or in print. Compare your screen with Figure 3-16.

TABLE 3-5: Resizing rules

TO DO THIS:	DO THIS:
Make the text box shorter or longer	Drag a handle on the top or bottom edge of the box
Make the text box narrower or wider	Drag a handle on the left or right edge of the box
Reduce or enlarge the box proportionally	Drag one of the corner handles inward or outward

FIGURE 3-15: Moving a text box

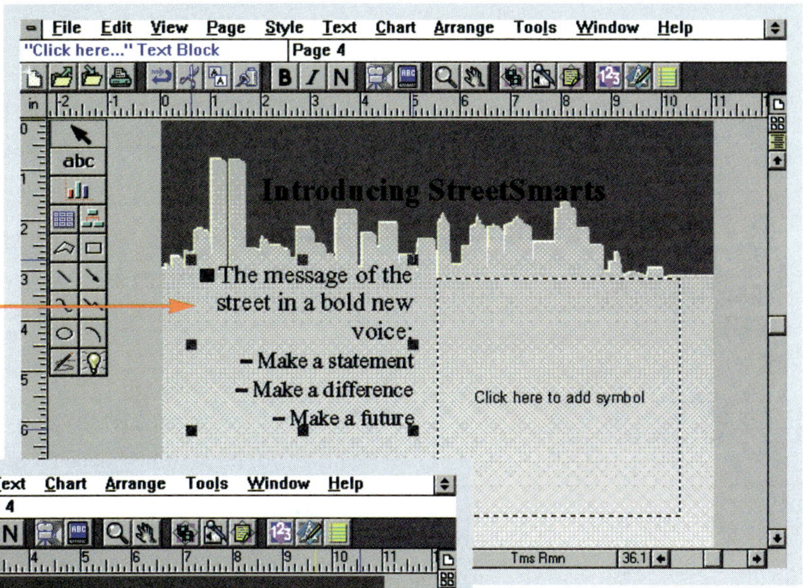

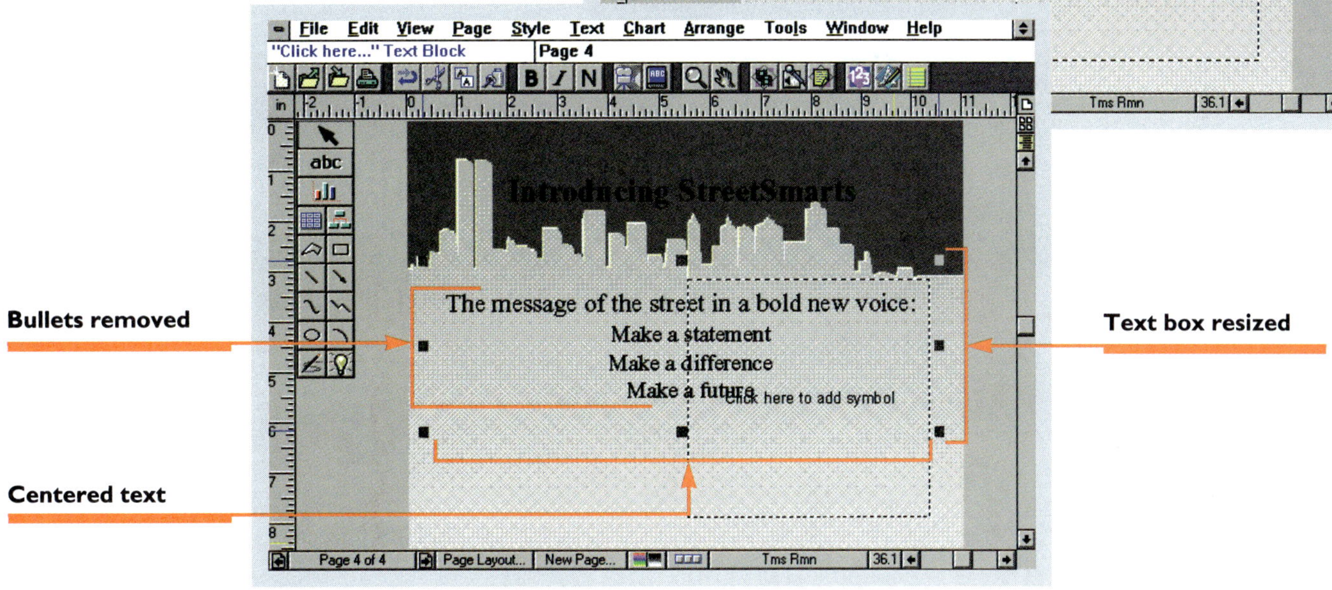

FIGURE 3-16: The modified page

Adding a text box

One task that often necessitates moving or resizing an existing text box is adding a new text box to a page. You'll often find you need to perform this task when you review a presentation and decide to insert additional information. Adding a text box is easy. First, move or resize the existing text box to make room for the new box, click the Text tool abc in the Toolbox. Then move the pointer to the place on screen where you want to add the box; press and hold the mouse button while dragging the box on the screen. After you release the mouse button, the text entry area appears. You can move and resize any text box.

TROUBLE?

If there is too much text to display in a box at its current size, Freelance Graphics will resize the box automatically so that all the text appears. If you need to shrink the box but still keep all the text, put the text in a smaller type size by clicking the Size button 31.2 and choosing a smaller point size.

Using the Outliner

Outliner view shows the text you've entered in an easy-to-understand display, making it easy to revise and add text and formatting. Buttons at the top of the Outliner display allow you to change the information level you're viewing. Table 3-6 explains the Outliner buttons. ▶ As he passes by your office door, Tom leans in and says "Guess what? They told us we could lengthen the presentation by five minutes. Now you can add the marketing and distribution information." Using the Outliner, add the necessary text to the Objectives page you created earlier.

STEPS

1. **Click the [←] button** to the left of the **Page button** [Page 1 of 1] three times
   Page 1 of your presentation appears.
2. Click **Outliner**
   The presentation opens in Outliner view. Compare your screen with Figure 3-17.
3. Click after the word **team** in the second bullet on Page 3, and press **[Enter]**
   The cursor moves to the next line. Another bullet is added.
4. Type **To present our marketing plan** and press **[Enter]**
   This adds another bulleted item to the page and moves the cursor to the next line, adding another bullet.
5. Type **To set distribution goals**
   This adds the final bullet to the page.
6. Click **Collapse Page** [−]
   All bulleted items on the page are hidden; you see only the page title Objectives for this page.
7. Click **Expand Page** [+]
   The full bulleted entries are displayed on the page once again.
8. Click **Current Page**
   Current Page view displays. Figure 3-18 shows the revised page in Current Page view so you can see how the added text fits on the page.

TABLE 3-6: Buttons in the Outliner

BUTTON NAME	DESCRIPTION
Promote	Shifts text one level to the left
Demote	Indents text one level
Expand Page	Shows all levels of current page
Collapse Page	Hides all levels on current page except the title
Expand All	Shows all levels of all pages
Collapse All	Hides all levels of all pages except the title of each page

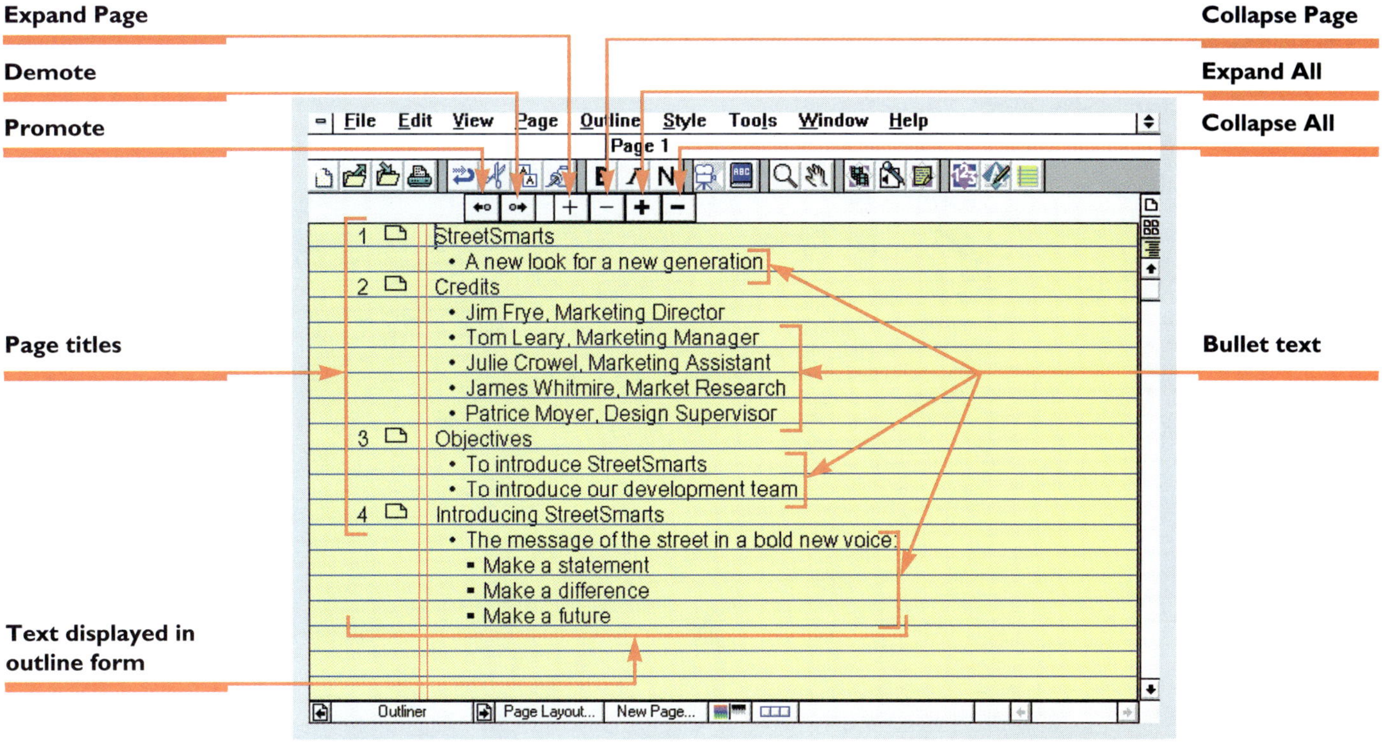

FIGURE 3-17: Displaying the Outliner

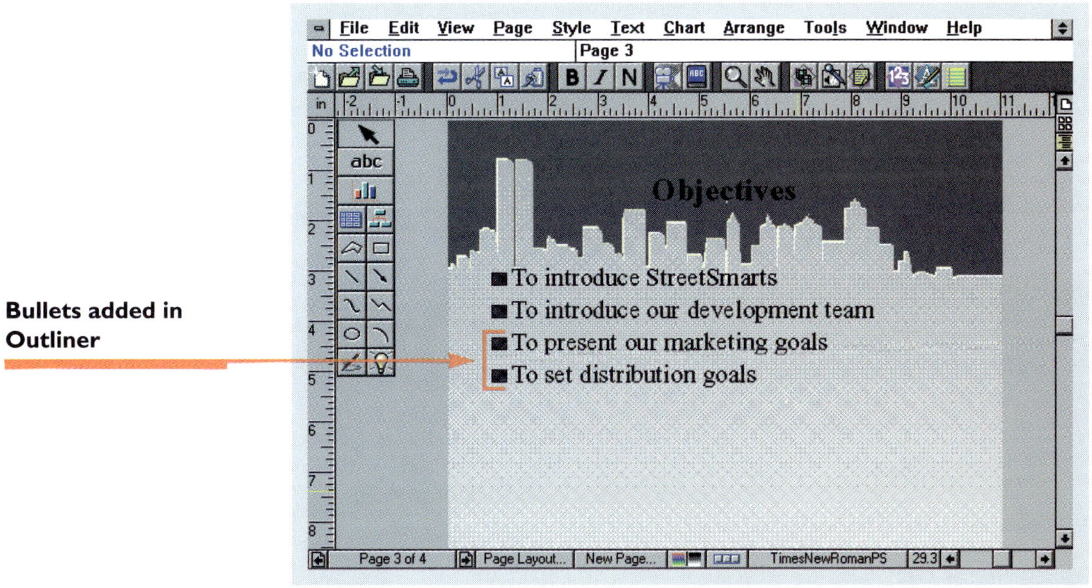

FIGURE 3-18: Page with new bullet entries

Changing to a different page

When you leave the Outliner view and display a different view, the page on which the cursor is positioned becomes the current page. For example, if you click text in Page 2 in the Outliner and then change to Current Page view, Page 2 is the page displayed. If you click Page Sorter view, Page 2 appears highlighted as the current page.

TROUBLE?

Before you start adding text to the Outliner, use Expand All to show all entered text.

CONCEPTSREVIEW

Label the Freelance Graphics screen items shown in Figure 3-19.

FIGURE 3-19

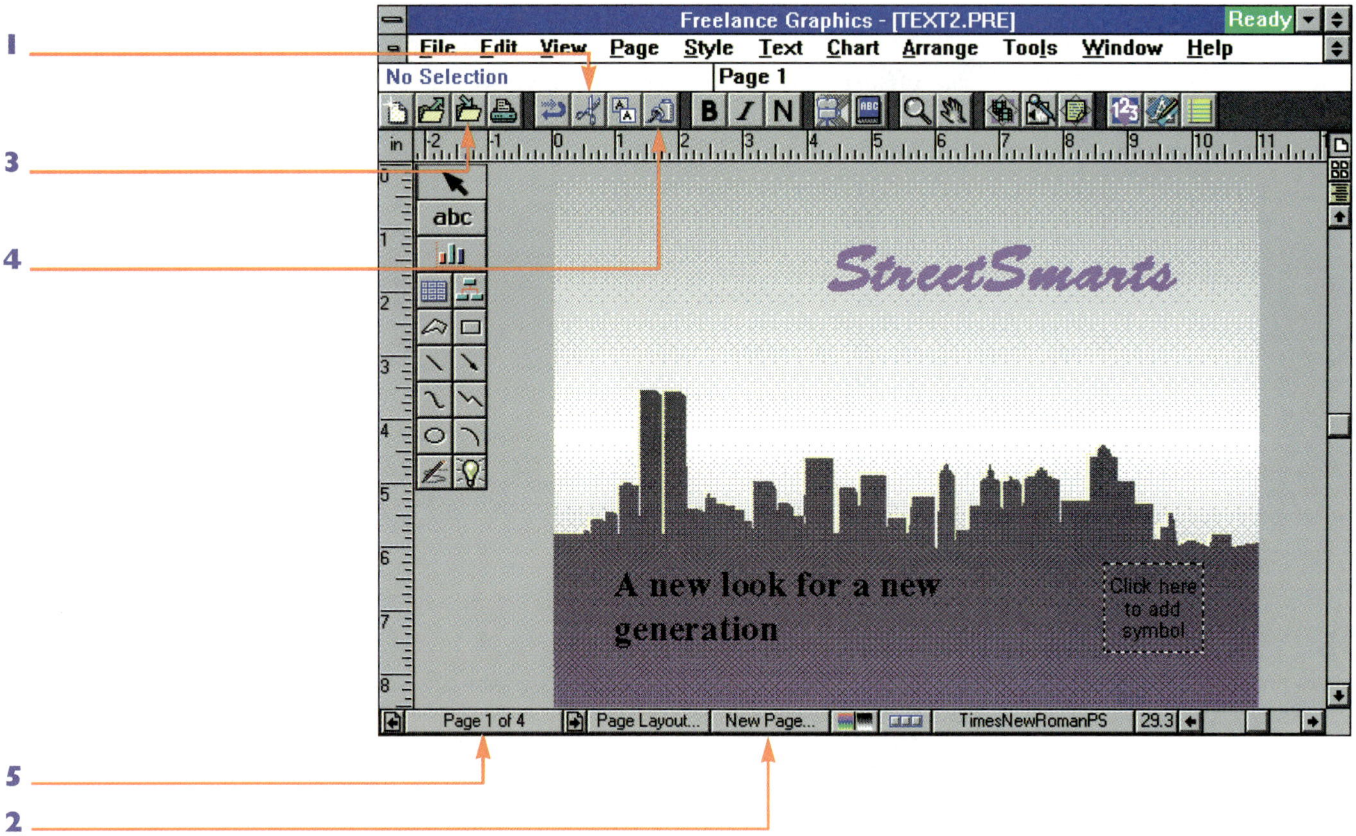

Match each definition with its element.

6 The dialog box that appears when you take the steps needed to work on an existing presentation

7 A highlighted text section

8 One size and style of a typeface

9 A button in the Outliner that shows all text levels on all pages

10 A button in a text entry area that raises the text one level

a. Promote button

b. Expand All button

c. Open File

d. Font

e. Text block

Select the best answer from the list of choices.

11 You can open an existing file using any of the following procedures EXCEPT which one?

a. Click the Open SmartIcon.

b. Click File, then Open.

c. In Program Manager, click File, Run; then type Open and click OK.

d. In the Welcome to Freelance Graphics box, click Work on existing presentation.

12 Which of the following keys deletes the character to the right of the cursor?

a. Backspace

b. Delete

c. Insert

d. All of the above

13 You must highlight a block of text before performing all of the following procedures EXCEPT which one?

a. Changing text font

b. Copying text

c. Clearing text

d. Pasting text

14 Which of the following statements is FALSE?

a. You use Demote to indent text.

b. You can promote text in both Current Page view and Outliner view.

c. Text you add in Outliner view appears only in that view.

d. Paragraph styles control text indent settings.

15 You enter all of the following settings in the Font dialog box EXCEPT which one?

a. Color

b. Typeface

c. Size

d. Spacing

APPLICATIONS REVIEW

1 Create a new presentation in which you will enter two text pages.

a. Open a new presentation file.

b. Choose the buttons.mas SmartMaster; click OK.

c. Choose a Title page layout; click OK.

d. Click the title prompt text and type Welcome To Your PTO.

e. Click the subtitle area and type A 10-Minute Introduction To Your Child's School.

f. Click New Page and choose Bulleted List and click OK.

g. Click the title area and type What Is PTO?

h. Click the bullet area and type Your child's advocate, then press [Enter].

i. Type Your information provider; press [Enter].

j. Type A caring team of parents and teachers.

k. Save the presentation as SCHOOL.PRE in the my_files directory.

2 In the text entry box, mark a block of text, delete it, and restore it.

a. Highlight the second bulleted item.

b. Press [Del].

c. Press [Ctrl][Z].

d. Save your presentation.

3 Modify text settings.

a. Click the text box once so handles appear around the edges of the box.

b. Click the first bulleted entry and click Promote; click outside the box.

c. Click Text, then click Font.

d. Change the font to Helvetica; click OK.

e. Double-click the text box and review the Paragraph Style settings; click OK.

f. Change horizontal justification to Right; click OK.

4 Work in Outliner view.

a. Click the Outliner button.

b. If necessary, click the up arrow in the scroll bar to display the beginning of the presentation text.

c. If necessary, position the cursor in Page 2.

d. Click Collapse Page.

e. Click Expand Page.

f. Change to Current Page view.

INDEPENDENT CHALLENGE

As a new independent video producer, you are trying to develop a new community series for local cable television. Part of your responsibility is to put together a presentation that you can pitch to prospective carriers of your program. You're convinced that with the right mix of humor, music, and topical information, you could reach a unique younger audience.

You've been told that programmers at the local cable station are entertaining the idea of funding a children's show. Your presentation should accomplish the following goals:

- clearly communicate your idea
- explain how your idea is better than other existing programs
- show how the station will benefit by sponsoring your program
- lead viewers through a summary of a sample program
- conclude with a list of highlights that briefly reviews key points in your presentation

To complete this independent challenge:

1 Draw thumbnail sketches of the proposed pages in your presentation. How many pages will you need? How much information will you be able to convey in text, and how much in chart or video? Here are a few guidelines:

- plan to use only four or five pages

- start with a title page that communicates the most important aspect of your idea
- use at least one chart to illustrate financial or ratings information
- conclude with a concise message that is easy to grasp and remember

2 Create a new presentation, choosing a SmartMaster that gives your program the look you want. Consider the color, the text styles, and the background graphics.

3 Create the text pages, with titles, subtitles, and bullets. Edit as you go, correcting any typos and deleting any unnecessary text. Use the text block procedures you learned in this unit to cut and paste text as necessary.

4 Display the text in the Outliner. How does the outline look? Revise the text to better organize your ideas. Print a copy of the outline: click the File Print SmartIcon , click Outline in the Format options, and then click OK.

5 Save your file as CABLETV in the MY_FILES directory on Student Disk #1, and print the entire presentation.

6 Submit your preliminary sketches, the printed outline, and your printed presentation to your instructor.

UNIT 4

OBJECTIVES

- Evaluate page layout and sequence
- Change page layout
- Create build pages
- Change page sequence
- Add pages
- Delete pages

Working WITH PRESENTATION PAGES

After you create a few pages for a presentation, you should review your work and make sure the pages all make sense. Are the pages arranged logically? Are they in the right order? Once you evaluate the basic sequence of the pages, you often find you want to change page layout and order, and add and delete pages. ▶ Tom Leary has reviewed the presentation you've been working on. He thinks that some changes to the organization, layout, and progression of information will improve the flow of the presentation. ▶

Evaluating page layout and sequence

Page Sorter view is the perfect place for seeing the "big picture" of a presentation. Because the presentation pages are all displayed together in a reduced size, you can review the various page layouts you've chosen and check the order of your pages. ▶ In Tom's review of your presentation, he finds that it contains good information, but the pages look too much alike. In this lesson, you use Page Sorter view to evaluate his concerns.

- **Open UNIT_4-1.PRE on Student Disk #1 and save it as PAGES1 in the MY_FILES directory.**
  Next, display your presentation in Page Sorter view, as shown in Figure 4-1, and evaluate the presentation based on the following considerations.

- **Check page layouts.**
  This presentation now includes 12 pages. Is there enough variety in page layouts? Too many of the same kind? Too much text or too little? Eight of the 12 pages in the presentation contain bulleted lists. Ordinarily, this kind of repetition might be a problem, but different formats were used to change the look of the bulleted text. For example, compare Page 3 and Page 4. Both pages contain bulleted lists. In Page 3, the title is moved down to the text area and the bullet characters are changed to checkmarks, as shown in Figure 4-2. Page 4 leaves the title in its original place but removes the bullet characters and centers the text, as shown in Figure 4-3.

- **Check charts.**
  If a presentation includes charts, make sure the charts are placed at logical places in the page sequence. Look for problems like too many charts in a row, too many charts with too little text, or too much text and too few charts. Although you haven't added charts yet, the page layouts show the places where you will be inserting them (you will learn how to add charts to a presentation in Unit 5). Four of the 12 presentation pages include room for charts. Examine Page 5 and Page 6. Both pages contain marketing information, but there is no room for text to reinforce the data presented in the chart. Later in this unit, in "Changing Page Layout," you change the page layout of Page 5 to remedy this problem by making room for explanatory text.

- **Review the text.**
  Have you used bulleted lists effectively? Did you include paragraphs, and if so, are they short and to the point? Could any of your bulleted lists work more effectively in another format? In the presentation shown in Figure 4-1, three of the bulleted lists could be treated as build pages. Pages 7, 8, and 11 all include bulleted lists with several different points that require additional explanation. In "Creating Build Pages," later in this unit, you turn Pages 7 and 11 into builds.

- **Evaluate the overall page progression.**
  Are the topics introduced logically? Do the pages roughly include the same amount of information? (Have you forced several topics on one page and left only one on another?) You can easily reorder pages in Page Sorter and add and delete pages as necessary. In the lessons that follow, you'll make some modifications to the way the pages look and how they are ordered in the presentation.

FIGURE 4-1: Evaluate the presentation in Page Sorter view

Bulleted lists with different format settings

Need more room for text

Potential build pages

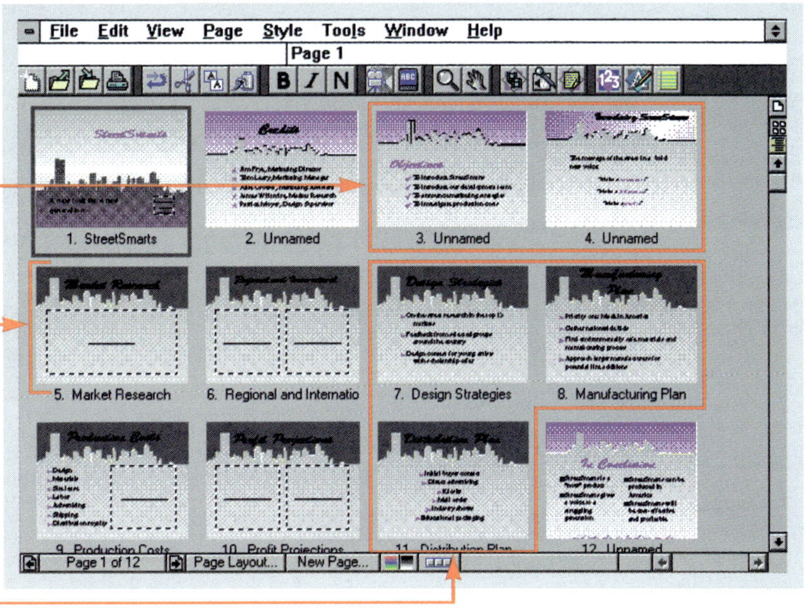

FIGURE 4-2: Bulleted list with new bullet characters

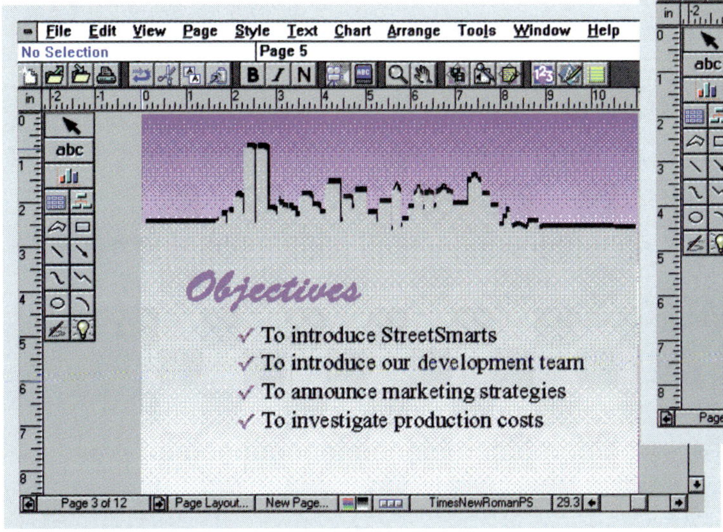

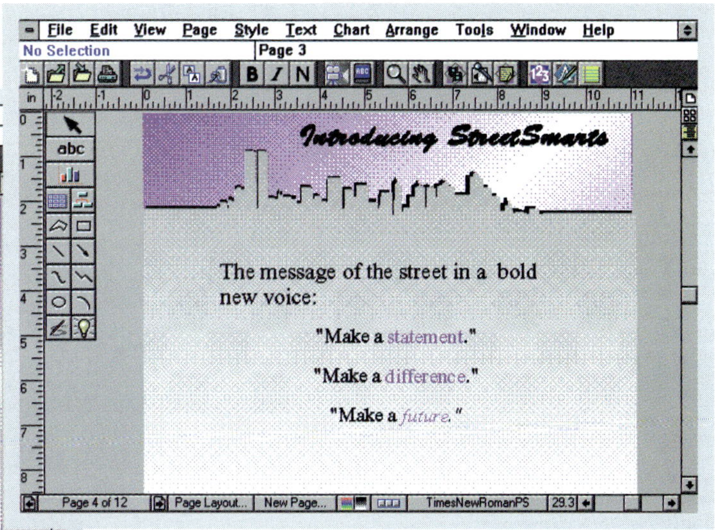

FIGURE 4-3: Bulleted list with no bullets and centered text

How many pages do you need?

When you are thinking about the number of pages to create for a presentation, consider the amount of time you have to present information. On the average, allow 1.5 to 3 minutes for each page that includes text, charts, or both. Introductory pages like title pages or pages showing graphics require only 30 seconds or so. This means that if you've been asked to prepare a short, 15-minute presentation (the length of the Conscious Clothing presentation), you have enough time to show between 5 and 10 pages.

QUICK TIP

When you make changes to the page layout and sequence of a presentation, be sure to save frequently. One way to save quickly is to press [Ctrl][S].

Changing page layout

After you evaluate a presentation, you may find that you need to vary your page choice a little. You can do this by selecting a different layout. Some layout changes are simple—you just choose a new look and Freelance Graphics repositions the text, chart, or graphics for you. Page layout changes can become complicated when the new layout has less room for text. Table 4-1 suggests some layout options to consider when you want to make major layout changes. ▶ Tom Leary suggests you change the layout of Page 5, which is currently a Chart page, to a Bullets & Chart page to allow more room for introductory text. Start with the presentation displayed in Page Sorter view.

STEPS

1 Click **5. Market Research**
A square frame, called the **selection box**, displays around the page.

2 Click **Page Layout** [Page Layout...]
The Choose Page Layout dialog box appears.

3 Click **Bullets & Chart**
A preview of the page with the new layout appears in the preview window in the lower right corner of the dialog box.

4 Click **OK**
The dialog box closes and the page layout is changed, as shown in Figure 4-4. Next, you need to add text to the bulleted list you added.

5 Click the **Outliner button**
Freelance Graphics displays the text of your presentation in Outliner view, positioning the cursor after the title of the Market Research page. Compare your screen with Figure 4-5.

6 Press **[Enter]** and type **Our research shows high interest among buyers and consumers, regionally and nationally**
This explanatory text sets up the charts you will add on Page 5 and Page 6 of the presentation.

7 In the view buttons, click the **Page Sorter button**
Freelance Graphics displays the presentation once again, with Page 5 still selected. The text you entered in the Outliner view appears on the page.

TABLE 4-1:
Layout change options

WHEN YOU WANT TO	TRY THIS
Add text to a chart page	Select the Bullets & Chart layout
Change a bulleted page to a title page	Click Title; delete or move extra text
Add a chart to a bulleted page	Click Bullets & Chart layout; modify text or resize chart
Add the same text—such as a logo or company name—to every page	Click Edit in the menu bar, then click Edit Presentation Pages; add the text on the displayed SmartMaster page
Change a bulleted page to two-column bullets	Click Page Layout, then click 2- Column Bullets; add or move bulleted text as necessary

FIGURE 4-4: The changed page layout

A bulleted text box is added

The chart area is reduced in size

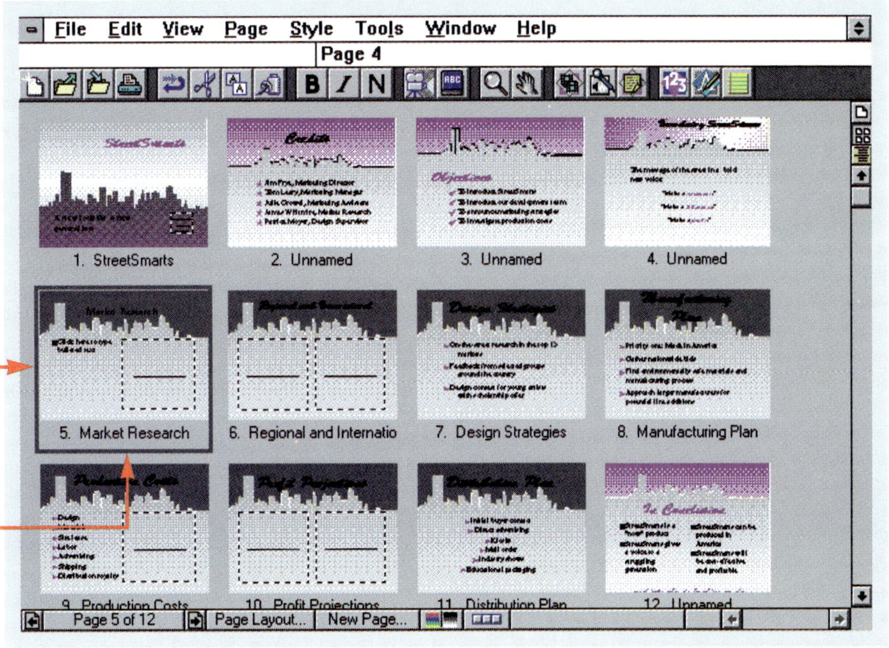

FIGURE 4-5: Adding text for the new layout

Cursor positioned at end of selected page

Press Enter to add a line for bulleted text

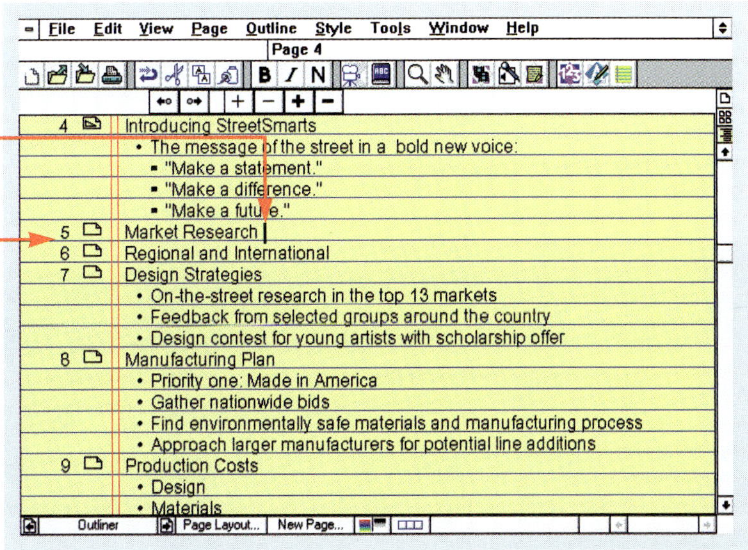

TROUBLE?

You may lose the original font, size, and style settings of text when you choose a new page layout. To make your settings stick, select the desired text, click Style, click Default Attributes, and enter your settings on the Default Paragraph Style dialog box. Then click OK.

Creating build pages

Your slide show will keep the attention of your audience if you turn some of your bulleted lists into builds. A **build** is a bulleted list that displays text items one at a time in a presentation. Each time you click the mouse or press [Enter], the next bulleted item appears. Bulleted items previously displayed are dimmed, so attention is focused on the new entry. ▶ When you turn a bulleted list into a build, Freelance Graphics calculates the number of pages needed to create the build, and then inserts them for you. The original page that includes all the bulleted items is called the **parent page**, and the pages Freelance Graphics adds while building up to the complete list are called **child pages**. ▶ Tom is worried that the Conscious Clothing executives have so much on their minds that they will have a hard time staying focused on your entire presentation. You decide to turn a bulleted list into a build in order to hold their attention.

STEPS

1. Click **7. Design Strategies**
   The selection box moves to that page.
2. Click **Page** on the menu bar, then click **Create Build**
   Freelance Graphics displays a message, telling you that the build is complete, as shown in Figure 4-6. Two new pages were added and the original page (now Page 8) has been renamed.
3. Click **OK**
   The Page Sorter view appears, and you can see the addition of the two build pages. Subsequent pages are renumbered. Compare your screen with Figure 4-7.
4. Click the **Current Page button**
   The page displays in Current Page view. The first two bulleted entries are dimmed, and the last entry appears normally. This page is the final screen in the build, so only the last item is supposed to stand out. See Figure 4-8.
5. Click the arrow to the left of the **Page button** Page 1 of 1
   Page 8, the page preceding the parent page, appears. This is the second of the two child pages, the one with two bulleted entries. Again, only the last bullet appears in full color.
6. Click **File** in the menu bar, then click **Close**
   Freelance Graphics displays the Close Window dialog box, asking whether you want to save the file before closing it.
7. Click **OK**
   The file is saved under the name PAGES1.PRE in the MY_FILES directory on Student Disk #1.

FIGURE 4-6: The completed build

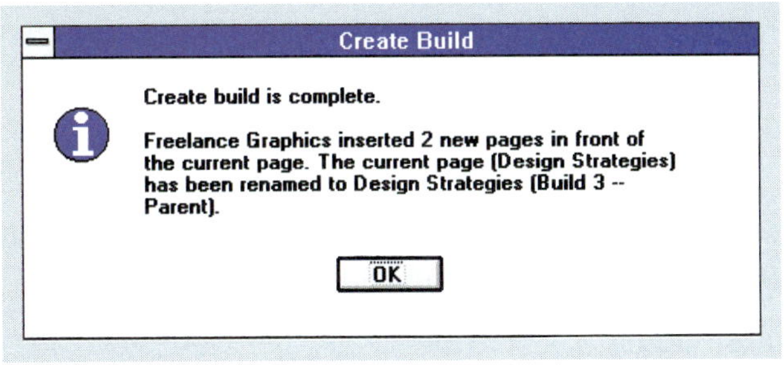

FIGURE 4-7: The new build in Page Sorter view

Build pages

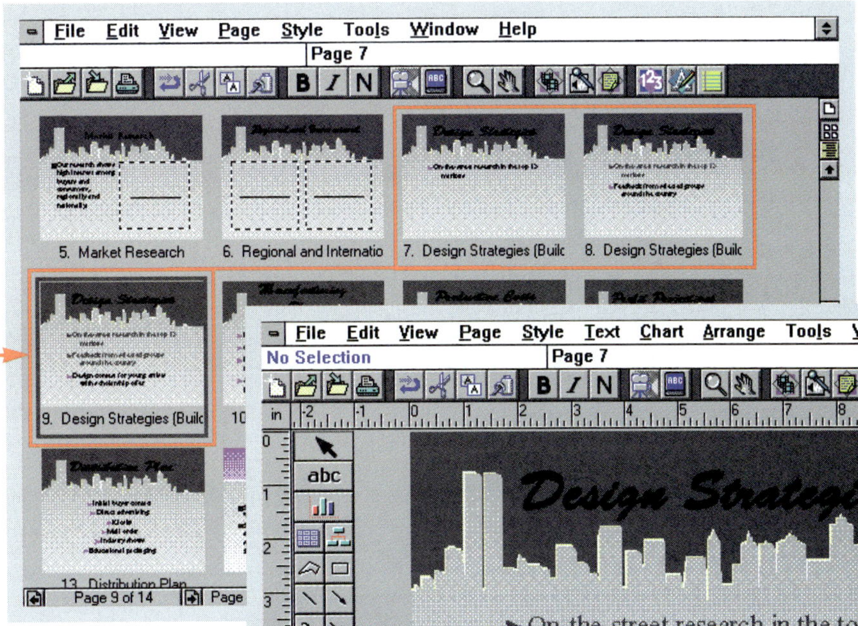

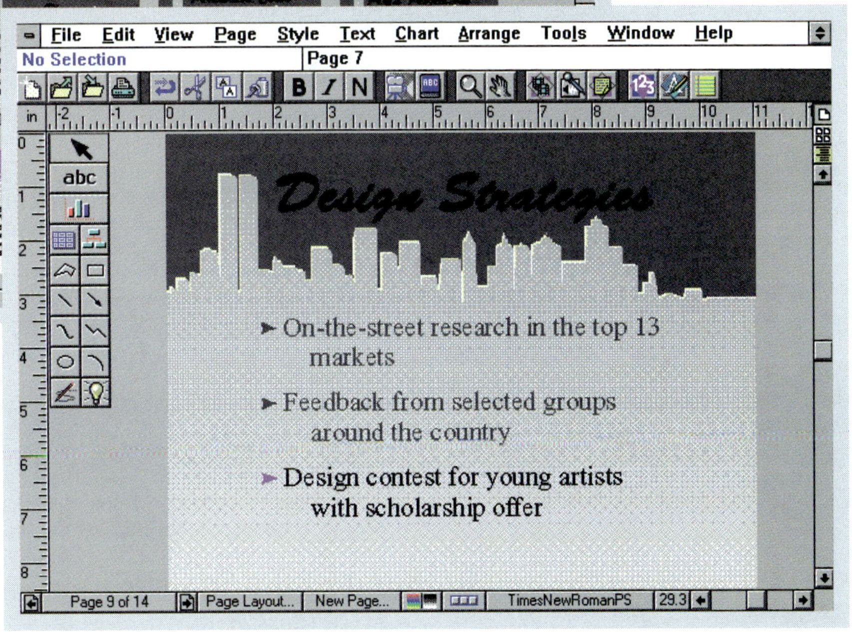

FIGURE 4-8: The last build page

Deleting build pages

Adding build pages to a presentation is a great tool for calling attention to important items. If you use too many build pages, however, they lose their effectiveness. To delete a build, click the parent page, click Page on the menu bar, and click Delete Build. Freelance Graphics tells you how many pages will be deleted and asks for confirmation. Click OK. The build pages turn back into regular bulleted pages, and subsequent pages are renumbered.

QUICK TIP

In Page Sorter view, move to Page 1 quickly by pressing [Home]. Move to the last page in your presentation by pressing [End].

Changing page sequence

Most presentations need some page order adjustment before they are ready to be presented. Freelance Graphics makes it simple to move pages around. You can select and move a single page or multiple pages. Table 4-2 explains the methods you can use to reorder pages. ▶ Tom looks over your shoulder. "Is there a reason why you introduce production costs before you talk about design?" he asks. You look more closely at the sequence of pages and decide to try a different page order.

STEPS

1. **Open UNIT_4-2.PRE and save it in the MY_FILES directory on your Student Disk #1 as PAGES2**

2. **Click 5. Market Research**
   The selection box appears around the page. Now you can drag the page to a new location.

3. **Drag Page 5 on top of 10. Manufacturing Plan**
   As you move Page 5, a vertical bar, called an indicator bar, appears beside the page. This bar helps you place the page where you want it, and should appear to the left of 10. Manufacturing Plan when you release the mouse button. Freelance Graphics places the page in front of Page 10 and renumbers the subsequent pages. Compare your screen to Figure 4-9. Now you're ready to try another method of moving pages.

4. **Click 5. Regional and International**
   Again, the selector box encloses the page. Now move this page by removing it from the presentation and placing it at a new location.

5. **Click Edit in the menu bar, then click Cut**
   Freelance Graphics removes Page 5 from the display. You decide to place it between Page 8, Market Research, and Page 9, Manufacturing Plan.

6. **Click 8. Market Research**
   When you paste pages, always select the page after which you want the page to be inserted. In other words, Freelance Graphics pastes pages in front of the selected pages.

7. **Click Edit in the menu bar, then click Paste**
   Freelance Graphics pastes the page as the new Page 9 and renumbers subsequent pages. Compare your screen to Figure 4-10.

8. **Click the Save SmartIcon, and if necessary, click replace; then close the presentation**
   Freelance Graphics saves the file as PAGES2.PRE in the MY_FILES directory and closes the file.

TABLE 4-2: Ways to change page order

TO MOVE	WITH THE MOUSE	WITH THE KEYBOARD
A single page	Drag the page to the desired location; make sure the indicator bar appears to the left of the page before which you want to place the page	Select the page; press [Ctrl] [X], then move to desired location and press [Ctrl] [V]
Multiple pages	Click the first page you want to move; press and hold [Shift]; click the remaining pages you want to move; drag pages to new location; make sure the indicator bar appears to the left of the page before which you want to place the pages	Move pages one at a time using the procedure described above

FIGURE 4-9: The presentation after a page is moved

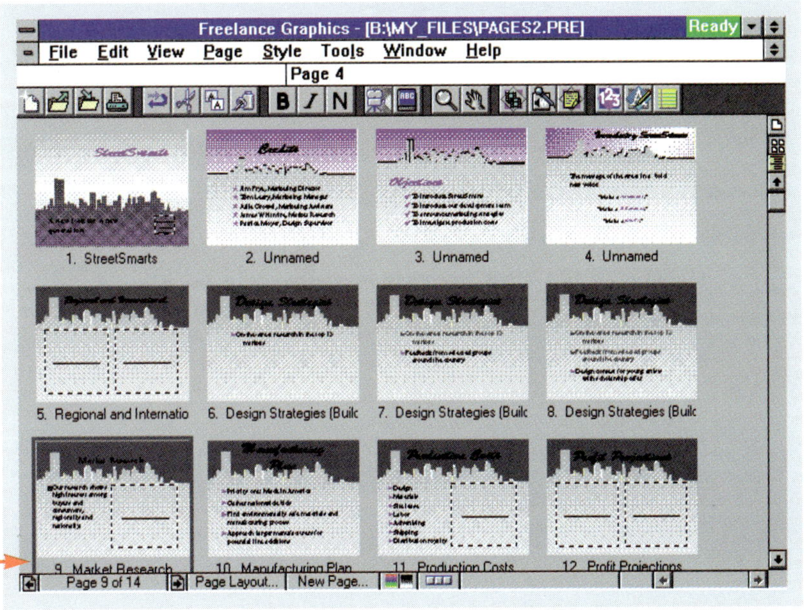

The moved page

FIGURE 4-10: The presentation after a page is cut and pasted

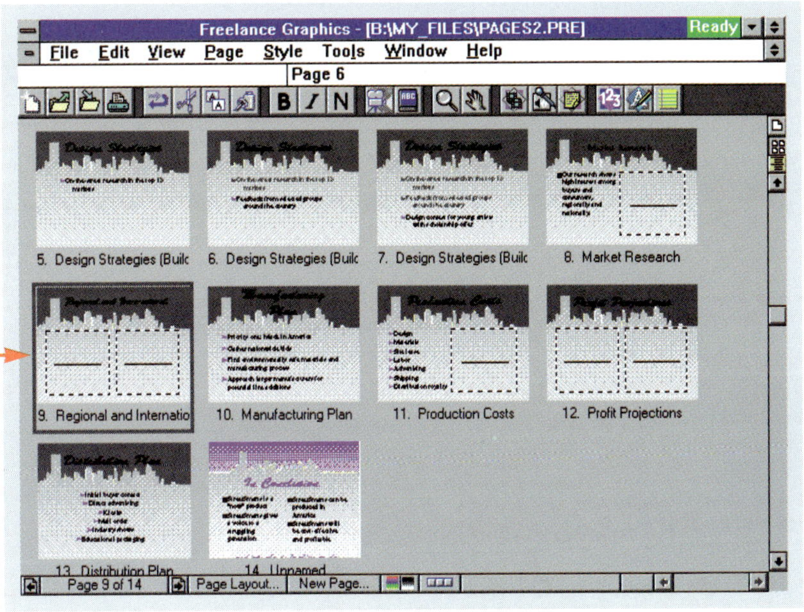

Page moved to this location

Recycling pages

If you think a particular page no longer belongs in your presentation after you evaluate and reorder the pages, don't throw your work away—click Edit, then click Cut to place the page on the Windows clipboard. Then open a new file, paste the page in for use at a later time, and save the file using a descriptive name that will help you remember the contents of the file later.

TROUBLE?

When you move pages, it's easy to get your message jumbled. After making a complex move, check your presentation in the Outliner view to make sure the text still makes sense.

Adding pages

You can add pages in any view in Freelance Graphics—Current Page view, Outliner view, or Page Sorter view. Table 4-3 shows different ways you can add pages. ▶ The number of pages in your presentation is growing rapidly. Tom suggests that adding pages to separate the major sections of the presentation—design, marketing, and manufacturing—would help make the transition between topics more clear. You decide to put title pages before the each of those sections.

STEPS

1. **Open UNIT_4-3.PRE on Student Disk #1 and save it in the MY_FILES directory as PAGES3**
   The presentation appears in Page Sorter view. Page 1, StreetSmarts, is the selected page.
2. Click **4. Introduction**
   The selection box shows the selected page. This is the page after which you want to insert the new page that will mark the beginning of the Design section.
3. Click **New Page** [New Page...], click **Title** page layout, then click **OK**
   The new page appears in Page Sorter view as 5. Unnamed.
4. Click the **Current Page button**, then click the prompt text **Click here to type presentation title**, and type **Part One: Design**; click **OK**
   This displays the new page in Current Page view and adds the section title. You can change the font, size, color, and style of the text later. For now, add another title page at the beginning of a different section. This time, use Current Page view.
5. Click the **Page button** [Page 1 of 1] to display the list of pages, and then click **8. Design Strategies (Build 3_Parent)**
   This selects Page 8 and then displays the page in full-screen view.
6. Press **[F7]**, click the prompt text **Click here to type page title**, and type **Part Two: Marketing**; click **OK**
   Freelance Graphics adds another page—with the same page layout style as the page in Current Page view. The text you type becomes the title for Part Two of your presentation, as shown in Figure 4-11. Use Outliner view to add the title page for your final selection.
7. Click the **Outliner button**
   The Outliner view appears, with the cursor positioned on the new page you added in Current Page view.
8. Click after the last line of text on **13. Regional and International**
   This positions the cursor at the point after which you want to add the final section page.
9. Press **[F7]**, then type **Part Three: Manufacturing**
   Freelance Graphics adds a blank line, which begins the new page. The text you enter becomes the title. Freelance Graphics renumbers subsequent pages.
10. Click the **Save SmartIcon**, then close the presentation
    Freelance Graphics saves the file as PAGES3.PRE in the MY_FILES directory and closes the file.

FIGURE 4-11: Page added in Current Page view

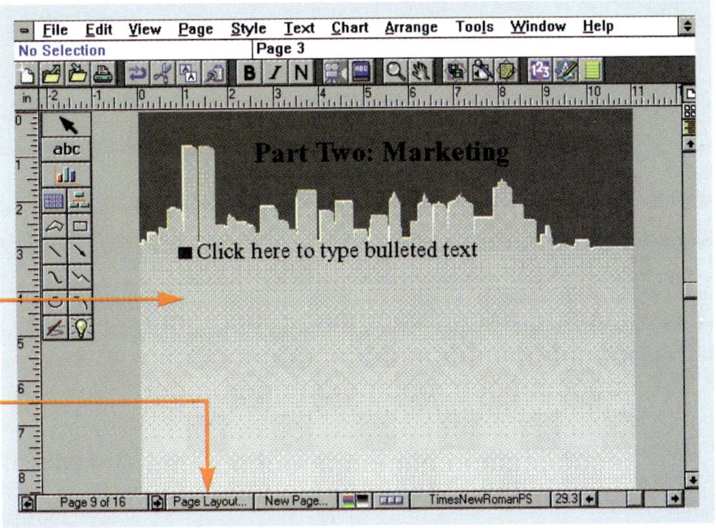

The new page appears in the same format as the previous page

Click here to change the page layout

Naming pages

You can easily name—or rename—a presentation page in either Current Page view or Page Sorter view. Display the desired page (or select it, if you are using Page Sorter), then highlight the page number in the edit line, just above the SmartIcon palette. The edit line changes to show a text-entry area and two buttons: an X and a checkmark, as shown in Figure 4-12. Type the name for the page and click the checkmark to accept the name, or click X to cancel it.

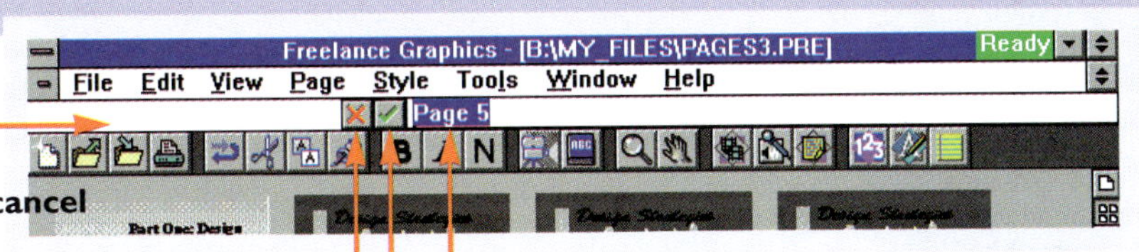

Edit line

Click here to cancel changes

Click here to accept new name

Highlight old name and type new one

FIGURE 4-12: Naming a page in the edit line

TABLE 4-3: Methods of adding pages

METHOD	DESCRIPTION
Click New Page [New Page...]	Displays the New Page dialog box so you can choose the layout you want
Click Page in the menu bar, then New	Displays the New Page dialog box so you can choose the layout you want
Press [F7]	Adds a new page in the same layout as the selected page
Click New Page SmartIcon	Displays the New Page dialog box so you can choose the layout you want; this option is available only if you have added the New Page SmartIcon to the default or displayed palette
Press [Enter], then [Shift] [Tab]	Changes a first-level bullet to a page title and renumbers subsequent pages; available in outliner view only

Deleting pages

It's sometimes possible to "overdo it" as you are adding pages to your presentation. You may find that you've exceeded your time limit—you can't possibly fit 20 pages into a 10-minute presentation! Freelance Graphics allows you to quickly delete unnecessary pages. You can use the Cut, Clear, or Remove commands on the Edit menu to remove pages, or you can simply select the page you want to erase and click the Delete SmartIcon. Table 4-4 explains different deletion methods. ▶ Tom is concerned about the length of the presentation. He suggests you remove the Credits page in order to save some time.

Steps

1 **Open UNIT_4-4.PRE on Student Disk #1 and save it in the MY_FILES directory as PAGES4**
The presentation opens in Current Page view.

2 **Click the Page Sorter button**
All the presentation pages appear in Page Sorter view. Page 1, StreetSmarts, is the selected page.

3 **Click 2. Credits**
The selection box encloses the selected page. This is the page you want to delete.

4 **Click Page in the menu bar, then click Remove**
See Figure 4-13. This deletes the page and renumbers the rest of the pages in the presentation.

5 **Click File in the menu bar, then click Close**
Freelance Graphics displays the Close Window dialog box, asking whether you want to save the file before you close it.

6 **Click OK**
Freelance Graphics saves the file under the name PAGES4.PRE in the MY_FILES directory.

FIGURE 4-13: Using Remove

Remove is available only in Page Sorter view and Current Page view

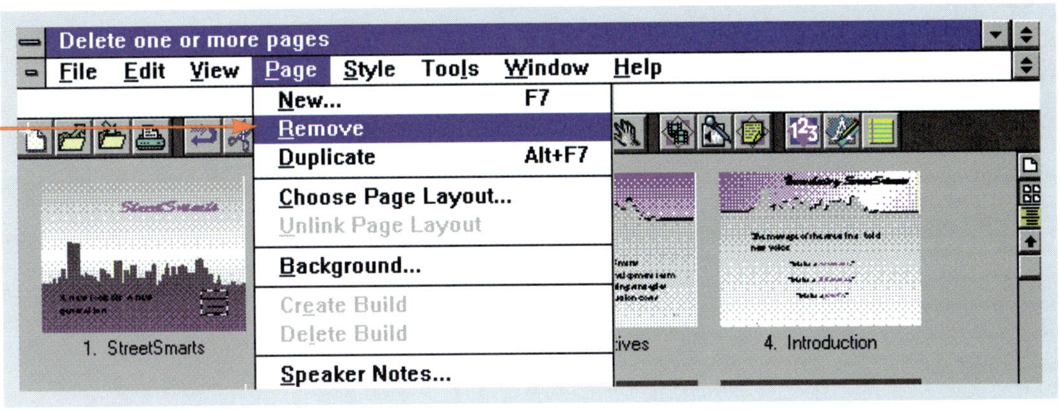

Preserving data

In some cases, you may be undecided about whether or not to delete a page. Do you really need the information the page contains? To find out how the presentation looks without a page, move the page to the end of the presentation. Now review the presentation to see whether the page will be missed. If not, delete it. If so, move the page to the point where it will be most effective.

TABLE 4-4:
Methods of deleting pages

METHOD	AVAILABLE IN	DESCRIPTION
Click Page in the menu bar, then Remove	Current Page view Page Sorter view	Deletes the selected page or pages
Click Edit, then Cut	Page Sorter view	Removes selected page (this option is available in Outliner view only if page text is highlighted)
Click Edit, then Clear	Page Sorter view	Removes selected page (this option is available in Outliner view only if page text is highlighted)
Click Delete SmartIcon	Page Sorter view	Deletes the selected page (this option is available only if you have added the SmartIcon to the displayed palette)
Press [Backspace] to delete page text	Outliner view	Erases text and renumbers subsequent pages
Click page to select; then press [Del]	Page Sorter view Outliner view	Deletes the selected page; in Outliner view, an entire page must be enclosed in a selection box or order to delete it

CONCEPTS REVIEW

Label the Freelance Graphics screen items shown in Figure 4-14.

FIGURE 4-14

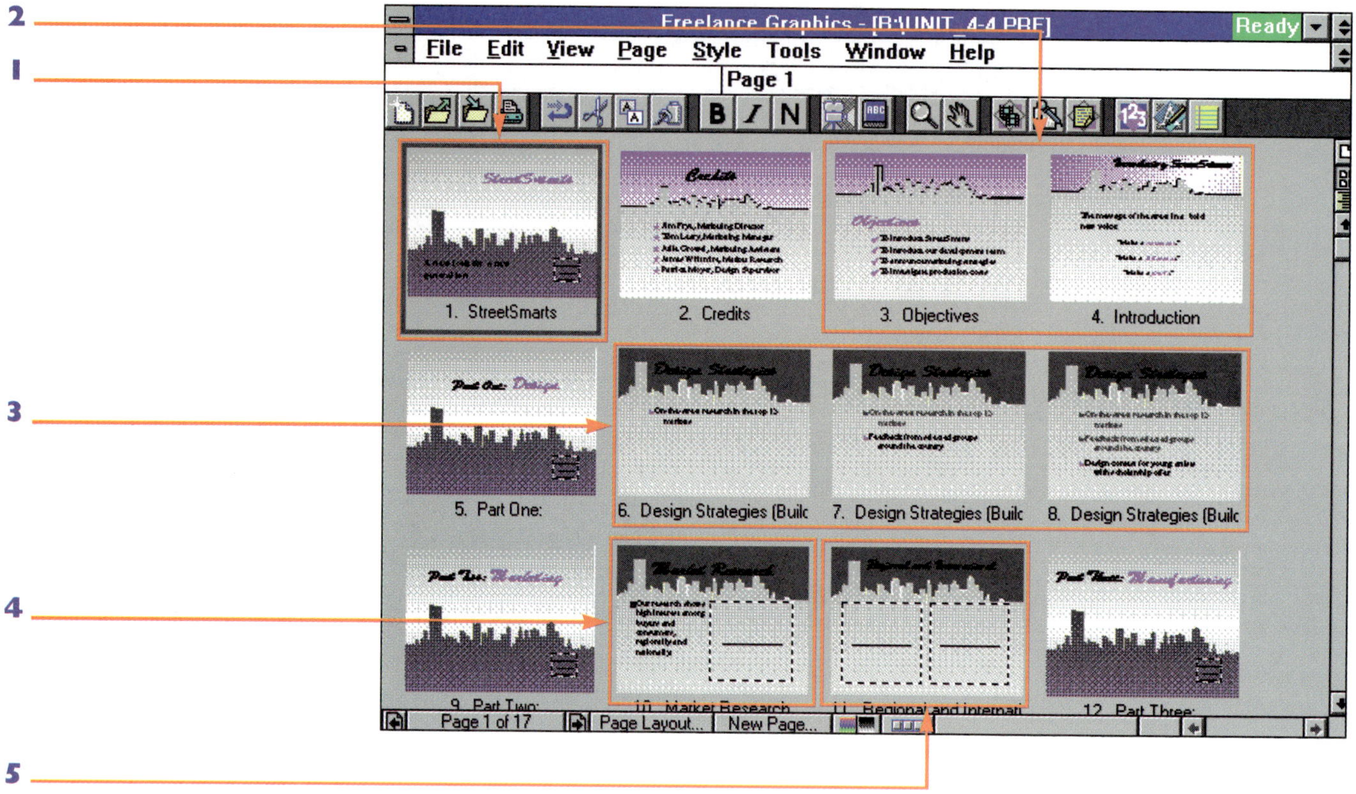

Match each definition with its element.

6 The original bulleted list from which Freelance Graphics creates build pages

7 A command in the Page menu that deletes pages in Page Sorter view or Current Page view

8 A build page created automatically by Freelance Graphics to show a new bullet added in a series

9 A command in the Page menu that creates an exact copy of the selected page

10 A feature of Freelance Graphics that, in a screen show, adds one bullet at a time, dimming previous bullets and calling attention to the new bullet

a. Child
b. Build
c. Duplicate
d. Parent
e. Remove

Select the best answer from the list of choices.

11 Which one of the following items should NOT be a concern when you evaluate pages in Page Sorter view?

a. The variety of page layouts
b. The way topics are presented
c. The number of bulleted lists used
d. The spelling of entered text

12 Which one of the following statements describes the way you remove a bullet character?

a. Press [Backspace]
b. Display the Bullet dialog box; click None
c. Click the Promote button
d. None of the above

13 Which one of the following statements describes how to add a page?

a. Click Page Layout, then choose page

b. Press [Ctrl] [F7]

c. Click Page, then click New

d. All of the above

14 Which one of the following statements is FALSE?

a. Press [F7] to add a page in Current Page view.

b. The New Page dialog box does not appear when you press [F7] in Outliner.

c. A page you add in Outliner does not appear in Current Page view or Page Sorter view until you enter text.

d. Press [Alt] [F7] to duplicate the selected page.

15 Which one of the following methods describes the way you can delete a page in Page Sorter view?

a. Click the Delete SmartIcon

b. Click Edit, click Cut

c. Click Page, click Remove

d. All of the above

APPLICATIONS REVIEW

1 Start a new presentation.

a. Open a new presentation file.

b. Choose the pillar.mas SmartMaster; click OK.

2 Create three new pages.

a. Select the Title page layout; click OK.

b. Click the title area and type Time-Away Timeshares, Inc.

c. Click New Page and choose Bulleted List; click OK.

d. Click the title area and type What Do We Offer?

e. Click the bulleted text area and enter the text shown in Table 4-5.

TABLE 4-5

BULLET	ENTER THIS TEXT
◆	Complete management services
◆	On-site security
◆	Monthly reports
◆	Full bookkeeping services
◆	Peace of mind for owners

f. Press [F7]. This step adds another page.

g. Click the title area and type Who Are Our Clients?

h. Save your presentation on the Student Disk #1 in the MY_FILES directory as TIMEAWAY.

3 Evaluate the presentation.

a. Display the presentation in Page Sorter view.

b. Identify any changes you want to make. Consider the order of the topics and the types of layouts you've chosen.

c. Compare your screen with Figure 4-15.

FIGURE 4-15

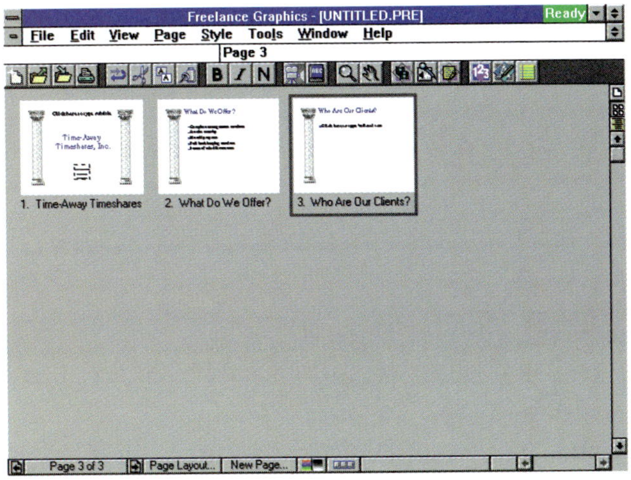

4 Change the page layout.

a. Make sure 3. Who Are Our Clients? is selected.

b. Click the Page Layout button [Page Layout...]. The Choose Page Layout dialog box appears.

c. Click Bullets & Chart; click OK. The page layout of Page 3 changes accordingly.

5 Change the order of pages.

a. Make sure 3. Who Are Our Clients? is still selected.

b. Position the pointer on Page 3.

c. Drag Page 3 on top of 2. What Do We Offer? Make sure the indicator bar appears to the left of Page 2.

d. Release the mouse button. Page 3 becomes Page 2 and remains selected.

6 Create a build.

a. Click 3. What Do We Offer?

b. Click Page in the menu bar, then click Create Build. Freelance Graphics displays a message that four build pages have been added.

c. Click OK.

d. Compare your screen to Figure 4-16.

FIGURE 4-16

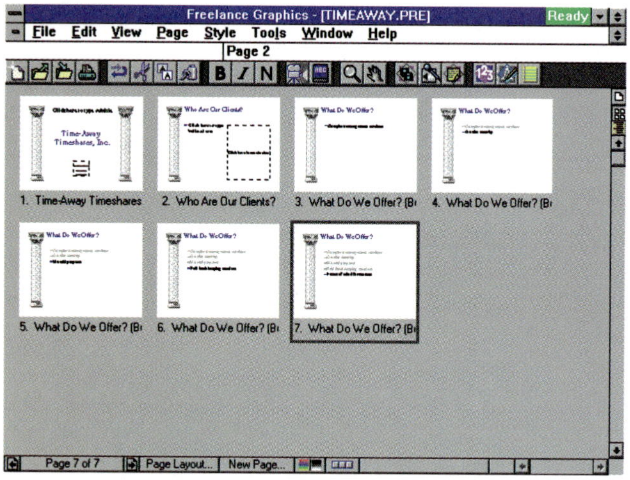

7 Add two new pages.

a. Click Page 2. Who Are Our Clients?

b. Click Page in the menu bar, then click New. The New Page dialog box appears.

c. Click 2 Charts, then click OK. The new page is added in the specified format.

d. Click 8. What Do We Offer? and press [F7]. Freelance Graphics automatically adds a new page.

8 Delete and restore a page.

a. Click Page 3, the unnamed page in 2 Charts format.

b. Click Page in the menu bar, then click Remove.

c. Click Edit in the menu bar, then click Undo Delete Page(s).

d. Close your presentation, saving your changes.

INDEPENDENT CHALLENGE

The Safe Kids Festival is a big event in your town. One of your friends is a medical student who is going to be working in a booth sponsored by the local health department, to raise awareness about child immunizations. She has asked you to create a 10-minute presentation that she can show to interested on-lookers who visit her booth during the festival. She also needs handouts to give to parents and educators that list various vaccinations, provide a projected schedule for inoculations, and tell people where they can go for immunizations at no charge.

Your presentation should accomplish the following goals:

- provide information in a professional manner
- include the health department name and phone number on every page
- use page layouts that can be seen easily by an audience of 10 to 12 people
- invite viewers to get involved with the program
- present the entire presentation in 10 minutes or less
- allow presenters to hand out printed slides that viewers can review later

To complete this independent challenge:

1 Think about the overall tone for the presentation. Your audience will be varied—teachers, mothers, fathers, grandparents, children. What look will appeal to the largest group of people? Choose a SmartMaster that reflects the style and tone you choose. (Hint: The SmartMaster medical.mas shows a medical symbol and uses a light color palette, providing a serious—but not too serious—tone.) Start the presentation by choosing a SmartMaster and creating a title page.

2 Plan five pages based on the information in Table 4-6, choosing the appropriate layout for each page. Draw a thumbnail sketch of your planned pages.

TABLE 4-6

PAGE	EXPLAIN
1	What services you're offering (free vaccinations)
2	Why you're offering the service (for child health and safety)
3	What benefits your service brings (fewer childhood illnesses, reduced risk of serious disease)
4	How they can take advantage of the offer (come to local health department or call for an appointment)
5	How they can help your program (contributions of time or money are appreciated)

3 Create the pages in your presentation file, entering the page titles and text. Keep titles brief and use a font that is easy to read.

4 Display the presentation in Page Sorter view and evaluate your work. You need to add a page that gives a brief history of the health organization. Where would it fit best?

5 Add the new page in a Bullets & Chart format. Type a title for the page and a one-sentence history or slogan. Come up with your own or use Serving our community for over 50 years.

6 Save the presentation file as MEDICAL in the MY_FILES directory of Student Disk #1.

7 Print your presentation.

8 Submit your sketch and your printed presentation to your instructor.

UNIT 5

OBJECTIVES

- Plan a chart
- Create a basic chart
- Add a legend
- Modify a chart
- Add chart headings and notes
- Enhance a chart
- Create an organizational chart
- Create a table

Creating CHARTS AND TABLES

Charts can communicate in a glance what might take you pages to describe. Want to see how your project fared in a recent sales promotion? A chart can tell you quickly. Need to compare your income this year with the amount you made last year? Displaying information in a chart puts it in a colorful, understandable form. Freelance Graphics makes creating, editing, and enhancing charts a simple process, no matter what type of chart you envision. ▶ Some of the information you need to include in your presentation for Tom Leary just can't be communicated with text. For example, your market research information makes a strong point when displayed in a chart; otherwise, the numbers and explanatory text may be lost on your viewers. ▶

Planning a chart

Most spreadsheet programs offer a chart feature that helps you create charts based on numeric data in a spreadsheet. As you probably have discovered for yourself, numbers are easier to understand when they are presented in visual form. You can easily see the data relationships—like how one product compares to another product—in a chart, and you can easily understand the point being made. Charts provide an easy way to communicate financial information in a presentation without overwhelming viewers with dry numeric comparisons. Freelance Graphics includes a number of different chart types and chart options that help you display data in just the right way. Table 5-1 introduces a few of the most common chart types. ▶ Before you begin creating a chart, take a few minutes to think about how you want it to turn out. In planning the chart, consider these items:

- **What will the chart communicate?**
  Are you showing the results of a sales competition, the projections for the fiscal year, or the number of employees hired? For your Conscious Clothing presentation, you need to relate the results of a market survey of both clothing buyers and consumers. In your survey, you asked clothing buyers and consumers to look at a series of products and tell you whether they would or would not be interested in such a product. You divided the responses according to the age group of the participants. Figure 5-1 summarizes the results of the research findings.

- **What is the best type of chart to show this information?**
  Some charts communicate information better than others, depending on the task. A **pie chart**, for example, is a good way to show how a particular item (or slice) compares to a whole (the pie). You might, for example, use a pie chart to show how one age group responded to your survey compared to how the entire group responded. For this presentation, a **bar chart** works best. The data items shown in a bar chart (one for Buyers and one for Consumers) can be displayed side-by-side, making it easy for viewers to understand the comparison.

- **What data will be used in the chart?**
  Is your data printed on a sheet you need to enter, or is it saved in a spreadsheet file in Lotus 1-2-3 for Windows? If you plan on using data that is saved in a file, you may be able to cut and paste the information into the Chart Data & Titles dialog box when you begin to create your chart. See the next lesson, "Creating a Basic Chart" for more information. The chart you create in this presentation is based on data in a printed report, so you need to type it in yourself.

- **What is the best way to display the data in the chart?**
  The basic Freelance Graphics charts—bar, line, area, pie, XY, radar, and scatter—all have a variety of styles and options from which you can choose. Would your chart make sense if the bars were displayed sideways? Should you use two pie charts instead of one? Freelance Graphics helps you find a chart style that suits your needs. A simple bar chart with default settings will serve the purpose in the Conscious Clothing presentation for your first chart. Later in this unit, however, you'll work with more sophisticated chart types.

TABLE 5-1:
Common chart types

CHART	NAME	DESCRIPTION
	Bar	Displays data series as bars set next to each other for easy comparison
	Line	Shows data series as points on a line; good for showing results that occurred over time
	Single Pie	Shows data series as slices of a pie; good for displaying how segments relate to a whole
	Area	Displays data as layered areas; good for illustrating contrasting data
	XY (Scatter)	Displays data series as independent points; good for contrasting two or more data sets to see whether there is a correlation between the sets
	Radar	Shows each data series as a line connecting in a hexagon shape; use to plot several related data sets, like products sold over a specific period of time
	High-Low-Close-Open	Displays a range of items for each data set displayed, including high value, low value, opening value, and closing value; use to show stock price changes, temperature changes, or other items that show a fluctuation in value during a specific period of time

FIGURE 5-1: The results of the marketing research

Report: Market Research

In preparing data analysis for the StreetSmarts line, we surveyed 100 buyers and consumers in each of the following age groups:

* 26 to 35 years old
* 36 to 45 years old
* 46 and older

We asked them to review prototype products for teens and young adults. These products included T-shirts, sweatshirts, hats, and jackets. Then, we interviewed each person and asked whether he/she would make a positive purchasing decision for such a product. Here are the results of our findings:

In the Buyer category, 34 out of 100 people aged 26 to 35 years old responded favorably. In the 36-45 age group, 42 out of 100 said yes, and 14 out of 100 people in the 46 and above age group answered positively. In future testing, we expect the demographics of our study to vary greatly from region to region.

In the Consumer category, 82 out of 100 people in the 26-35 age group responded positively, while 65 people in the 36-45 year-old category and 43 people of the 46 and above age group were favorably interested in our prototype products.

TROUBLE?

Need help to start charting? Take the Create a Chart lesson in the QuickStart.

Creating a basic chart

When you are ready to create a chart, you have two options: you can add a new page with an area blocked out for a chart, or you can add a chart to an existing page by clicking the Chart tool in the Toolbox. You can also choose whether you want to specify your own style settings for the chart or use the **default settings**, those settings already programmed into the Freelance Graphics chart feature. Table 5-2 explains the different chart elements you'll work with as you create Freelance Graphics charts. ▶ Tom Leary wants to see a chart that compares the responses of buyers and consumers in the different age groups. Because this is your first chart, use the default chart settings to create the chart quickly.

STEPS

1 Open UNIT_5-1.PRE on Student Disk #2 and save it in your MY_FILES directory as CHART1.
This creates a working copy of the presentation file. If you have not yet created a MY_FILES directory on Student Disk #2 you will need to refer back to the Working with Windows section. Read the lesson entitled, "Using File Manager."

2 Click the **Page button** Page 1 of 1 and click **10. Market Research**
Freelance Graphics displays Page 10 in full-screen view. Notice that Freelance Graphics reserves an area on the right side of the screen for the chart you're going to create.

3 Click the prompt text **Click here to create chart**
The New Chart Gallery dialog box appears, as shown in Figure 5-2.

4 Click **Use Default Chart**
The Chart Data & Titles window appears. This is the area in which you enter the labels and data you want to display in your chart. Surrounding the space, or **cell**, where column A and row 1 meet—called **cell A1**—is a square frame. This frame is called the **cell pointer**. If there is a value in the selected cell, the value is displayed in the Freelance Graphics edit line.

5 Press **[Left Arrow]** so the cell pointer highlights the cell just to the left of cell A1, then type **26-35**
The information you type appears in the cell.

6 Press **[Right Arrow]** so the cell pointer highlights cell A1, and type **34**; press **[Right Arrow]** again to move to cell B1, and type **82**
This completes the first line of data in the Chart Data & Titles window. Using the arrow keys, move the cell pointer and enter lines 2 and 3, as shown here:

36-45	42	65
46 and above	14	43

Compare your screen with Figure 5-3.

7 Click **Preview** and hold down the mouse button
Freelance Graphics applies its default chart settings to the data you entered. The chart appears on the screen in the chart area.

8 Release the mouse button to return to the dialog box, then click **OK**
The Chart Data & Titles dialog box closes, and Freelance Graphics displays the chart in Current Page view.

9 Click the **File Save SmartIcon**, then click **Replace** if necessary
Freelance Graphics saves your changes in the file CHART1.PRE in the MY_FILES directory.

FIGURE 5-2: New Chart Gallery

Displays available chart types

Click to use default Freelance Graphics style settings for the selected chart type

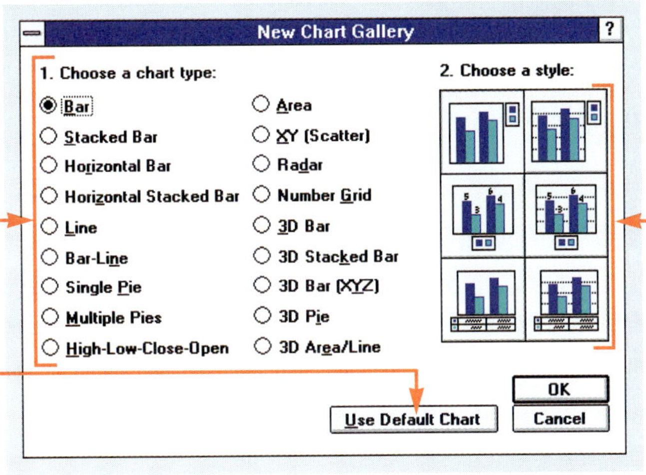

Lets you choose a chart style for the selected chart type

FIGURE 5-3: Entering chart data

Row labels

Press and hold to preview chart

Numeric data to be charted

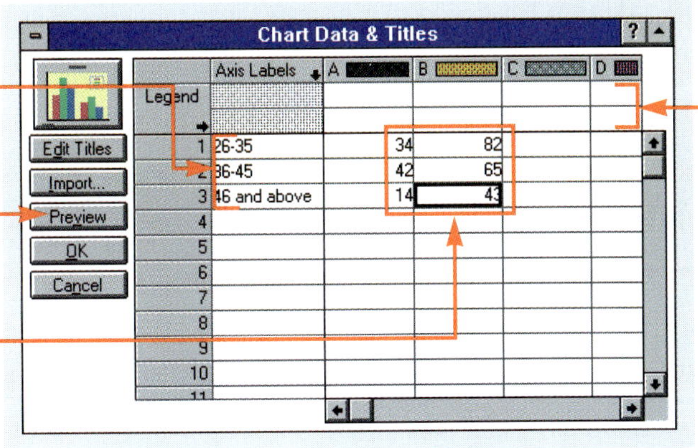

Column label area

TABLE 5-2: Chart elements

Gridlines	Horizontal lines that help viewers determine data values
Y axis	The vertical axis along which data items are measured
Data series	An individual item (or group) of data being charted
Legend	The key to help viewers identify the data series
X axis	The horizontal axis on which data items are displayed

Using existing data and charts

If you have an existing worksheet that you created in another program, such as Lotus 1-2-3 for Windows, you can copy and paste the data right into the Chart Data & Titles dialog box. In the worksheet, select the information and copy it to the Windows clipboard. When you display the Chart Data & Titles dialog box in Freelance Graphics, click the cell in which you want to paste the data, click Edit in the menu bar, and then click Paste. Or you can import the entire chart by clicking File in the menu bar, clicking Import Chart, selecting the chart's filename, and clicking OK.

Adding a legend

The legend for a chart is like the key of a map. For example, if your chart is a bar chart, the legend shows you which data is represented by which color bar. After you add a legend—accomplished in the Chart Data & Titles dialog box—you can change its color, font, position, or size. You can even control whether it is placed inside or outside of the chart area. ▶ Tom likes the bar chart, but he thinks it might be difficult for viewers to identify which bars represent consumers and which bars represent buyers. Add a legend to your chart and move it inside the chart area, displaying it in a portion of the chart that will not interfere with the data being shown.

STEPS

1 **Double-click an open area of the chart**
The Chart Data & Titles dialog box appears. Note: If you click one of the bars, lines, or labels, the Attributes dialog box opens. If you display this box accidentally, click Cancel to return to the chart, position the pointer on an open area (such as the blank space between gridlines) and double-click.

2 Click the cell just above A1, in the column label area for column A, then type **Buyers**; press **[Right Arrow]** and type **Consumers**
This enters the two column labels that will be used in the legend for the chart.

3 Click **OK**
The chart appears, but what happened? Freelance Graphics reduced the chart to make room for the legend. Now the chart is too small.

4 Click **Chart** in the menu bar, then click **Legend**
The Chart Legend dialog box displays. See Figure 5-4. Here you can choose the font, style, color, and placement of the legend text. You can even hide the legend.

5 In the Location options, click **Top** and **Inside**
This tells Freelance Graphics to put the legend inside the chart itself, at the top of the chart.

6 Click **OK**
Now the legend appears without causing the chart to be resized. Compare your screen with Figure 5-5.

FIGURE 5-4: Chart Legend dialog box

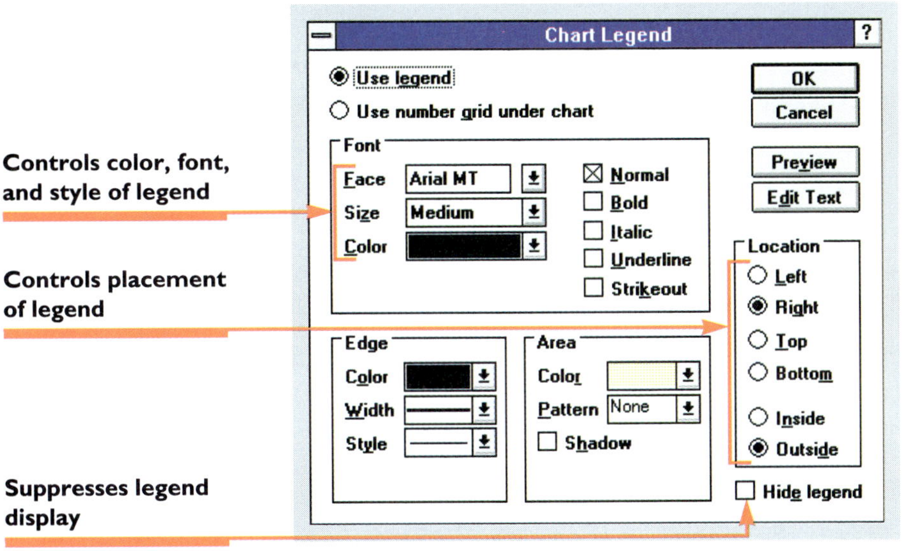

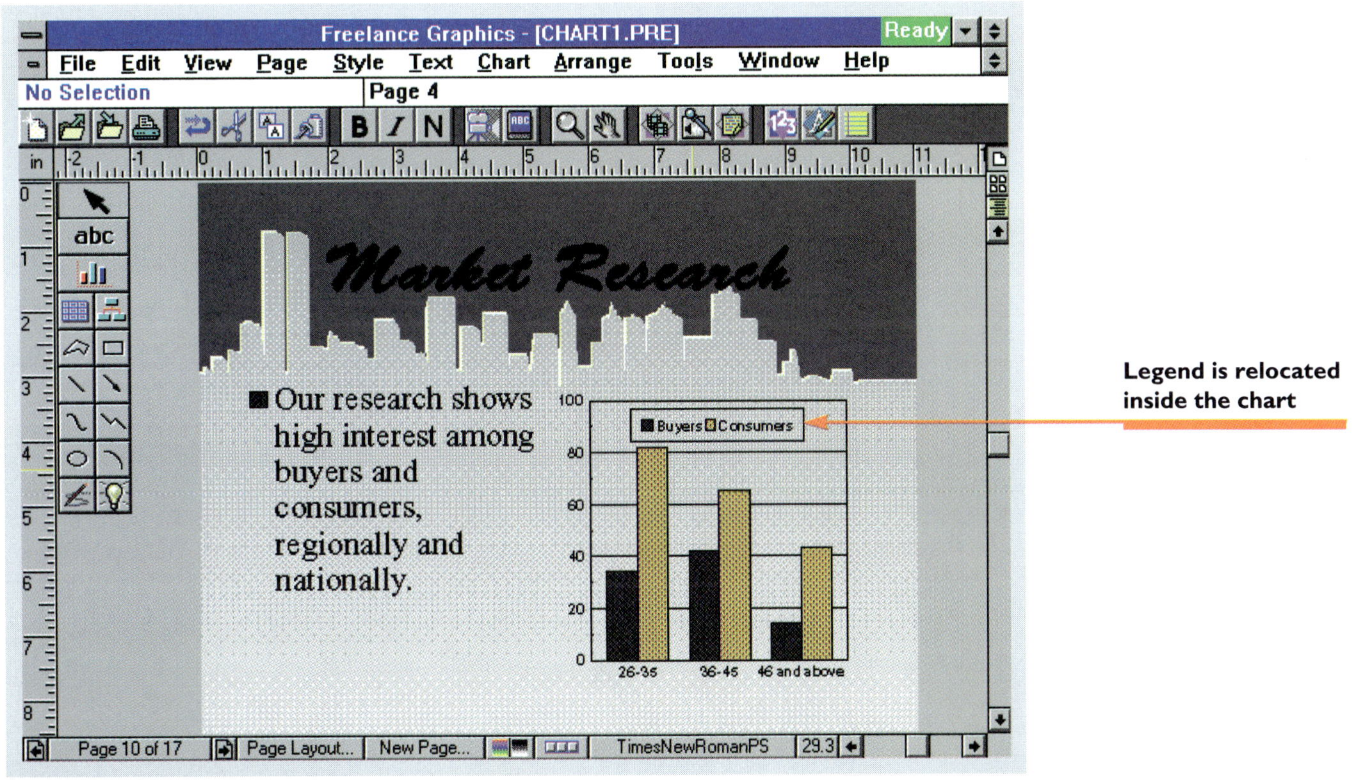

FIGURE 5-5: The added legend

Hiding the legend

Depending on the type of data you are presenting, you might not need the legend. To suppress the display of a legend, click Chart, click Legend, and click the Hide Legend checkbox; then click OK.

TROUBLE?

If you need to adjust the font size of legend text, open the chart legend dialog box and select a different font size.

Modifying a chart

Modifying a chart is a simple process, and all of the commands you use to modify other parts of a presentation—like Cut, Paste, and Spell Check—can be used on charts, too. ▶ When you got to work this morning, there was a note from Tom on your keyboard: "Please add a chart to the presentation that compares buyers and consumers in the middle age range, so we can easily show who our primary purchasers will be." You decide to copy the bar chart you already created so that you can use the same data entered in the Chart Data & Titles dialog box and then change the chart type to a multiple pie chart to contrast the information.

STEPS

1. **If necessary, click the chart to select it**
   Handles appear on the sides and corners of the chart area, showing you that it is selected.
2. **Click Edit in the menu bar, then click Copy**
   A copy of the chart is placed on the Windows clipboard.
3. **Click the arrow located to the right of the Page button** 

   Page 11, Regional and International, appears. This page includes two chart areas.
4. **In the menu bar click Edit, then click Paste**
   Freelance Graphics pastes the chart into the chart area on the right, as shown in Figure 5-6. The prompt text Click here to create chart is still visible, but will not appear when you print.
5. **Make sure the chart is still selected, then click Chart in the menu bar and click Type**
   A cascading menu of chart options appears beside the Chart menu display.
6. **Click Multiple Pies**
   Freelance Graphics redisplays the chart data in pie chart form. The legend is automatically modified to reflect the change. You decide to separate, or **explode**, a section of the pie to focus attention on the mid-range purchasers.
7. **Position the mouse pointer on the largest section of the pie chart on the left, then double-click the mouse button**
   The Pie Chart Attributes dialog box opens, as shown in Figure 5-7. Here you can change the color, style, angle, and effects of the current pie slice.
8. **Click Explode this slice, then click OK**
   The presentation page redisplays with the modified chart. See Figure 5-8.
9. **Click File in the menu bar, then click Close, saving the file when prompted**
   The file is saved under the name CHART1.PRE in the MY_FILES directory on Student Disk #2.

FIGURE 5-6: The pasted chart

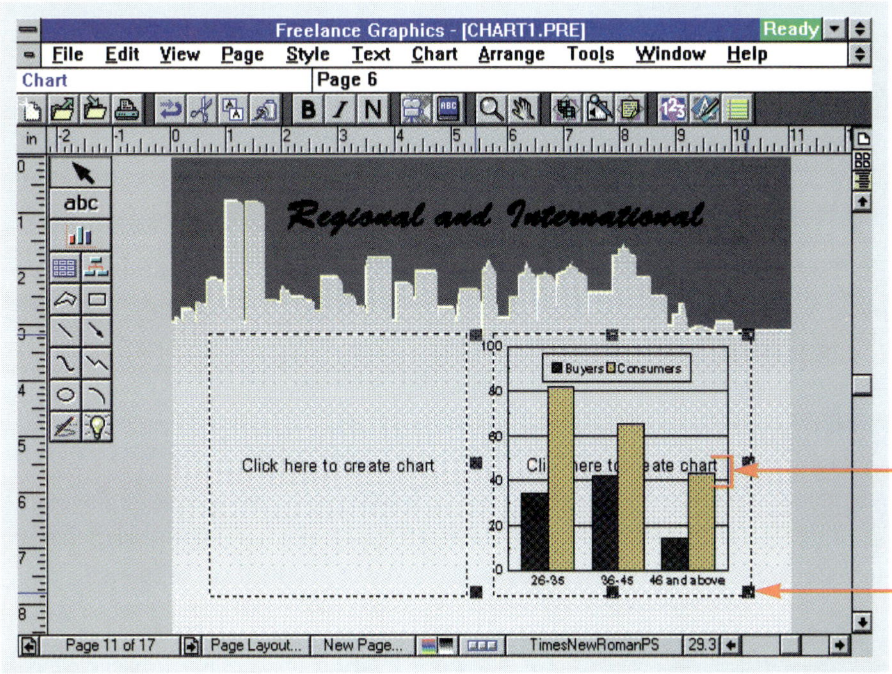

Prompt text does not appear in a slide show or when you print

Chart is pasted automatically over a chart area

FIGURE 5-7: Pie Chart Attributes dialog box

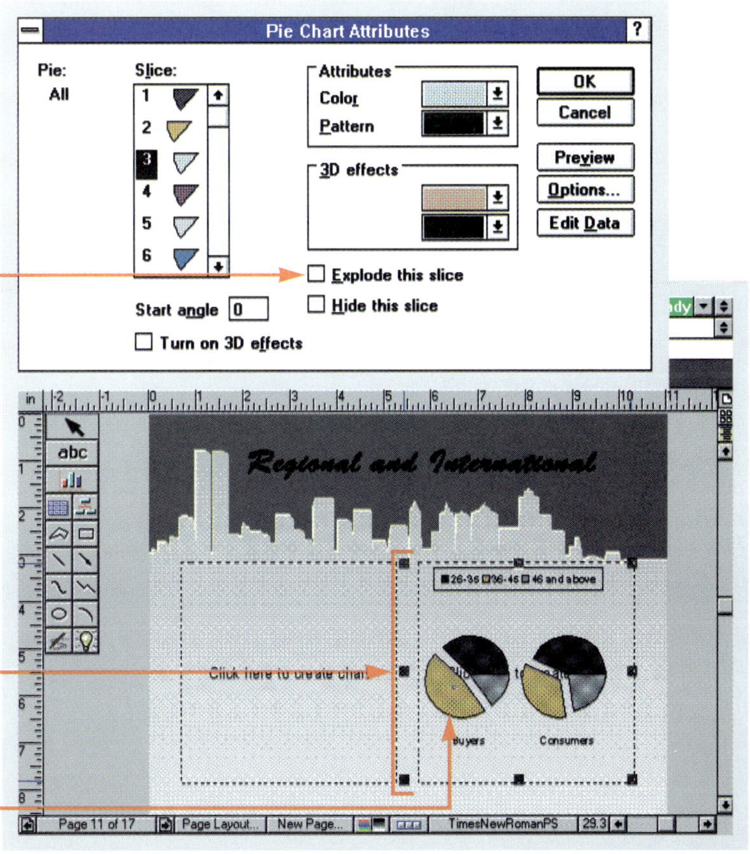

Click here to explode selected data series

Bar chart data used to create multiple pie charts

Double-click slice to display attributes

FIGURE 5-8: The modified chart

QUICK TIP

If you plan to create several charts of the same style, you can save an existing chart's settings as the new default settings by clicking Charts, then Replace Defaults.

Adding chart headings and notes

A **chart heading** is text used as a **title** on a chart. A **note** is a short sentence or caption, usually placed below the chart, that helps call attention to, or clarify, chart information. Other text items, called **axis titles**, allow you to affix a title to the X axis or Y axis of your chart. Table 5-3 lists the various text items you can add to charts. ▶ Because you have a limited amount of room in your presentation to include text that describes the Conscious Clothing research findings, the title, note, and axis titles are particularly important to include. Add these text items to your chart now.

STEPS

1. **Open UNIT_5-2.PRE on Student Disk #2 and save it in the MY_FILES directory as CHART2**
   The presentation opens in Current Page view. An area chart has been added to the multiple pie chart page, Page 11. The name of the page has been modified to more accurately reflect the marketing information displayed. Now the name is Purchasers and Products, as shown in Figure 5-9.
2. **Click the area chart to select it, then Chart, in the menu bar, then click Edit**
   The Chart Data & Titles window opens.
3. **Click Edit Titles**
   A second Chart Data & Titles window, known as **Edit Titles view**, opens providing you with space for entering headings, notes, and axis titles. The first line in Headings is highlighted. See Figure 5-10.
4. **Type Product Comparison by Prototype, then click Notes text box and type Rated on an average test of 100 scorers per product**
   This enters a heading and the first line in the Notes section.
5. **In the Axis Titles section, click the X text box and type Products, then click the Y text box and type Positive Responses**
   These entries add labels to the X and Y axes.
6. **Click OK**
   Current Page view redisplays, along with the text you have added to the chart. Compare your screen to Figure 5-11.

TABLE 5-3: Adding chart text

TEXT ITEM	DESCRIPTION	WHERE YOU ADD IT
Labels	Text that identifies data series	Chart Data & Titles window (Data)
Heading	Chart title	Chart Data & Titles window (Edit Titles view)
Note	Text that explains chart features	Chart Data & Titles window (Edit Titles view)
X axis title	Text that identifies the X axis	Chart Data & Titles window (Edit Titles view)
Y axis title	Text that identifies the Y axis	Chart Data & Titles window (Edit Titles view)

FIGURE 5-9: The modified page with additional chart

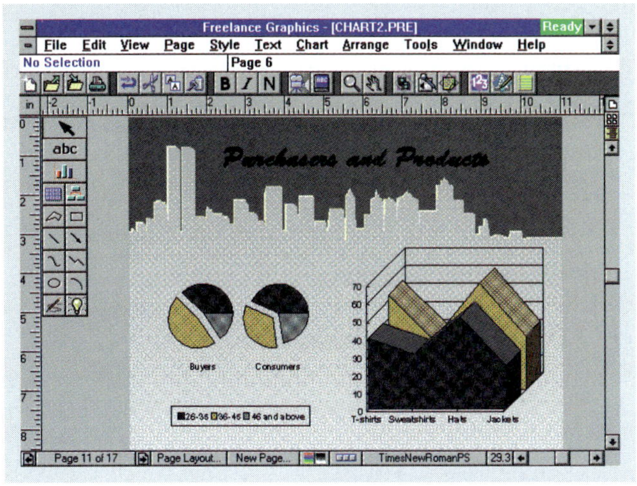

FIGURE 5-10: The Edit Titles view of the Chart Data & Titles window

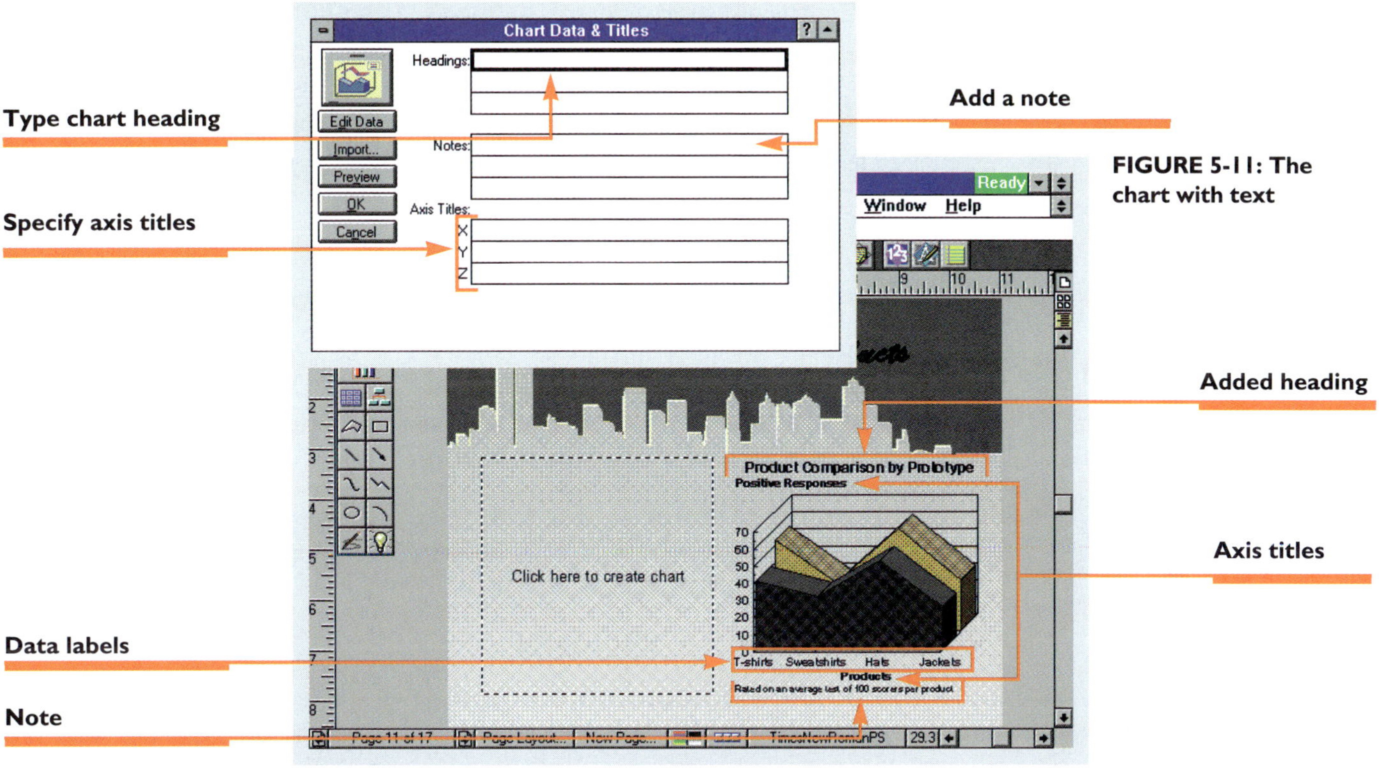

FIGURE 5-11: The chart with text

Aligning headings and notes

You can control the way your headings and notes look—and the way they are positioned on the chart—by clicking Charts, then clicking Headings & Notes, or you can double-click the heading or note you want to change. When the Headings & Notes dialog box appears, click the heading or note you want to work with, then choose the font and alignment settings you want and click OK. See Figure 5-12.

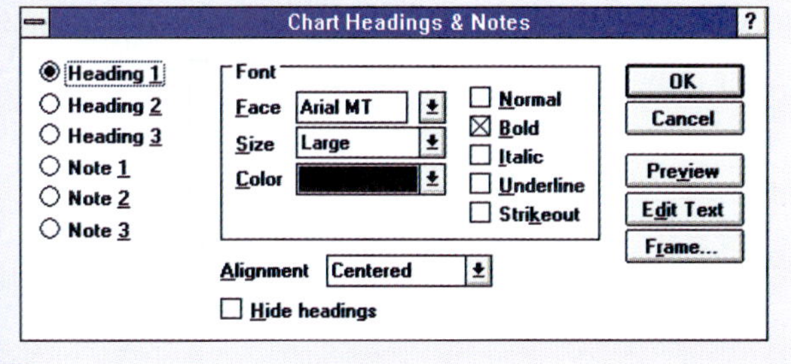

FIGURE 5-12: Headings & Notes dialog box

Enhancing a chart

Freelance Graphics provides a number of options you can use to make a chart stand out. You can change the color of the chart background, turn it into a 3D chart, add a grid or frame, or change the way the text looks. Table 5-4 lists different enhancement options you can try on your charts. ▶ Tom suggests you add a background to the bar chart on Page 10 to make it stand out against the page. You decide to further enhance the chart by adding 3D effects.

STEPS

1. **Click the left arrow beside the Page button** Page 1 of 1
   Page 10, Market Research, displays as the current page.

2. **Click the chart**
   The chart appears selected, with handles on the sides and corners of the chart area.

3. **Click Chart, then click Background**
   The Chart Background dialog box appears, as shown in Figure 5-13. Here you set the different area and edge colors for the background. Freelance Graphics has already chosen a contrasting color for the background—shown in 1st Color and 2nd Color. (If you choose a pattern, these colors are mixed to create the pattern.) The background is not displayed behind the chart until you click the Display checkbox.

4. **Click Display and click OK**
   Freelance Graphics displays the background of the chart area. Now turn the chart into a 3D chart.

5. **Click Chart, then click Attributes**
   The Chart Attributes dialog box appears. Here you can choose the data set, color, and 3D display options for your data. (Note: If you're working with another type of chart, like a line chart, the Attributes dialog box appears different from the one shown here.)

6. **Click Turn on 3D Effects, click OK**
   Freelance Graphics returns you to the chart on the presentation page. The 3D effect has been added to the bars in the chart, as shown in Figure 5-14.

7. **Save your changes and close the file**

TABLE 5-4: Chart enhancement ideas

WHAT TO CHANGE	HOW TO CHANGE IT
Font	Click Chart, then click Change All Chart Text
Background color	Click Chart, then click Background
Add or remove grid	Click Chart, then click Grid
Add or remove frame	Click Chart, then click Frame
Change data set color or style	Click Chart, then click Attributes
Change title alignment, style, or color	Click Chart, then click Headings & Notes

FIGURE 5-13: Chart Background dialog box

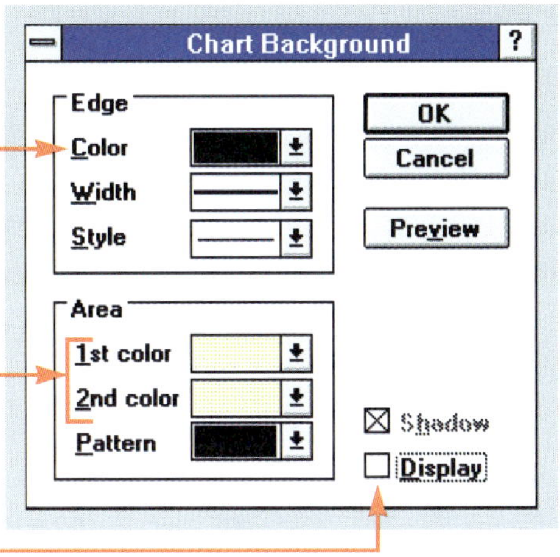

Use these colors or choose your own

Click Display to display the background

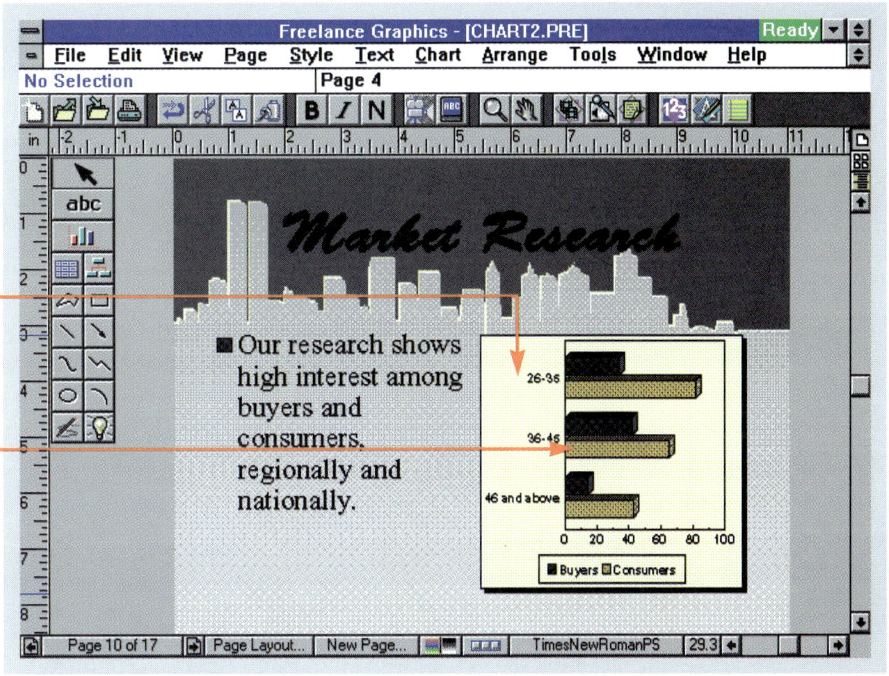

Added background

Bars appear in 3D

FIGURE 5-14: Chart with background and 3D effects

Creating a chart SmartIcon set

In Unit 1, you learned about SmartIcons, the on-screen buttons that help you select often-used commands easily. Freelance Graphics includes a number of SmartIcons for working with charts—you can create a SmartIcon set with just the chart SmartIcons for times when you are creating or editing charts. Display the SmartIcon dialog box, then drag all the chart SmartIcons from the Available Icons list to the center list. Drag any unwanted icons in the middle list outside the dialog box; that way, Freelance Graphics knows to exclude them. Finally, click Save Set and type Charts when prompted for a name. After you click OK, the new chart SmartIcon set is displayed at the top of your work area.

QUICK TIP

When you want to change a chart element, double-click the item you want to change. If the wrong dialog box displays, click Cancel to close the box then try again.

Creating an organizational chart

Organizational charts show relationships between people or groups of people. When you create an organizational chart, you have two choices: you can use the Organizational chart tool to add a chart to an existing page, or you can add a new page with an organizational chart area blocked out. ▶ Add a new page to your presentation showing an organizational chart of the StreetSmarts research and development team. This page will appear near the end of your presentation.

Steps

1. Open the file UNIT_5-3.PRE on Student Disk #2 and save it as CHART3 in the MY_FILES directory
   This creates a working copy of the unit presentation file. The presentation appears in Page Sorter view.

2. Click **Page 16, Distribution Plan**, then click the **New Page button** New Page..., then click **Organization Chart**, then click **OK**
   Freelance Graphics adds the new page in Page Sorter view. The new page has room for an organizational chart and a title.

3. Click the **Current Page button**, then click the prompt text **Click here to create organizational chart**
   The Organization Chart Gallery dialog box opens. See Figure 5-15.

4. In the style area, click the second style in the top row
   This selects the style of the boxes used to display the text you enter.

5. In the chart level area, click **Laddered list**, and click **OK**
   The display changes to show how the lowest level will appear in your chart. After you click OK, the Organization Chart Entry List appears. The cursor is positioned on the first line of the entry area.

6. Type **Jim Frye**, press **[Enter]**, type **Product Director**, and press **[Enter]** twice
   Freelance Graphics skips one line and displays an automatically indented bullet on the next line. Refer to Table 5-5 for help on indenting and outdenting text.

7. Type **Tom Leary**, press **[Enter]**, type **Marketing Manager**, press **[Enter]** twice, then press **[Tab]**
   This enters the second chart entry and indents the cursor for the next item.

8. Type the following two entries, pressing **[Enter]** once after each name and twice after each entry:

Julie Crowel	Marketing Assistant
James Whitmire	Market Research Specialist

9. Press **[Shift][Tab]** to shift the cursor to the left and type **Patrice Moyer**; press **[Enter]**, then type **Design Supervisor**
   This completes the data entry for the organizational chart. Compare your screen with Figure 5-16.

10. Click **OK**
    Freelance Graphics creates the organizational chart and displays it in Current Page view, as shown in Figure 5-17.

Click chart type

Click low-level display

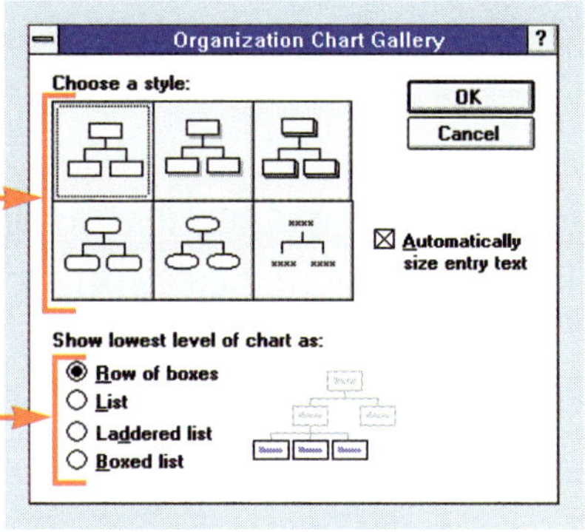

FIGURE 5-15: Organization Chart Gallery

FIGURE 5-16: Organization Chart Entry List

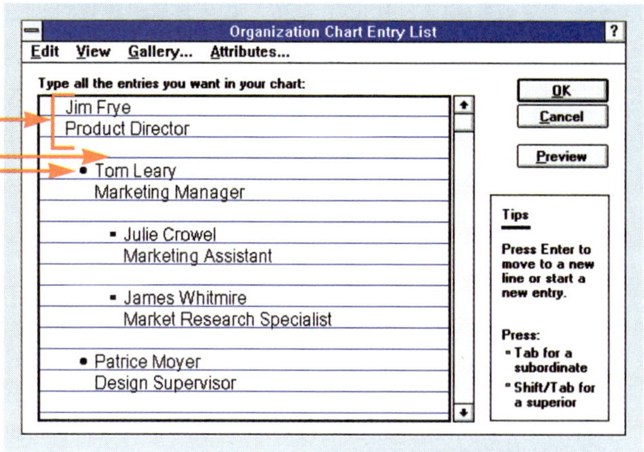

Press Tab to indent

Press Enter twice

Type entry

FIGURE 5-17: The created organizational chart

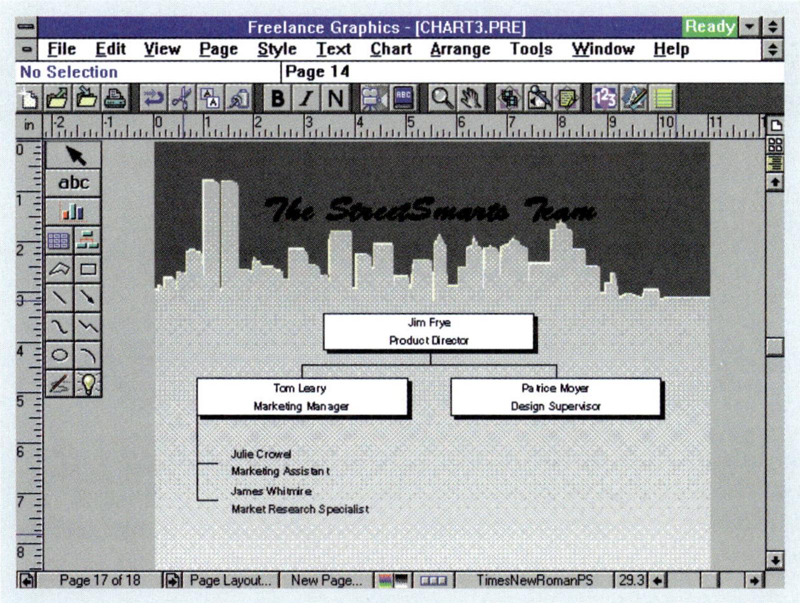

TABLE 5-5:
Keys used in Organizational Chart Entry List

KEYPRESS	DESCRIPTION
[Enter]	Starts a new line
[Enter] [Enter]	Begins a new entry
[Tab]	Indents entry
[Shift] [Tab]	Outdents entry
[Backspace]	Deletes the character preceding the cursor position

Creating a table

A table is nothing more than text aligned in columns and rows. Freelance Graphics allows you to create tables in a variety of styles and sizes—you decide how many rows and columns you want. You create a table by creating a new page with a Title layout or by clicking the Table tool from the Toolbox and adding the table to the current page. Table 5-6 explains the Table options available when you click Table in the Chart menu. ▶ Add a new table page and create a table to show how Buyers and Consumers rank the importance of three different product issues: price, message, and materials.

STEPS

1. Click the **Page Sorter button**; then click **11. Purchasers and Products**
   After seeing the presentation in Page Sorter view, you decide to insert a table page after Page 11 to explain some of the market research information you've gathered.
2. Click the **New Page button** New Page..., then click **Table** and **OK**
   A new page appears with a spot mapped out for a table.
3. Click the **Current Page button**
   The new page displays in full-page view.
4. Click the prompt text **Click here to create table**
   The Table Gallery appears, as shown in Figure 5-18. In this dialog box, you can choose a table type, select a shadow, and specify the number of columns and rows you want to include in the table.
5. In the table style area, click the middle table in the bottom row, then click the **Drop shadow** down scroll arrow and click **Bottom Right**
   This chooses the style of the table and tells Freelance Graphics where to place a shadow.
6. In the rows and columns area, choose three columns by clicking the left arrow next to **Columns** once, then click **OK**
   This reduces the number of columns from four to three, closes the dialog box, and displays the basic table.
7. Click inside the table
   A data-entry area opens.
8. Position the cursor, if necessary, in the upper-left corner of the table, and then enter the following data, pressing **[Tab]** after each entry:

	Buyers	Consumers
Most important	Price	Message
Important	Message	Price
Least important	Materials	Materials

9. Drag the mouse pointer over all the text to highlight it, then click the **Size button** 31.2, and choose **24.0**
   This reduces the size of the text in the table. Compare your results with Figure 5-19.
10. Save and close your presentation file

FIGURE 5-18: Table Gallery

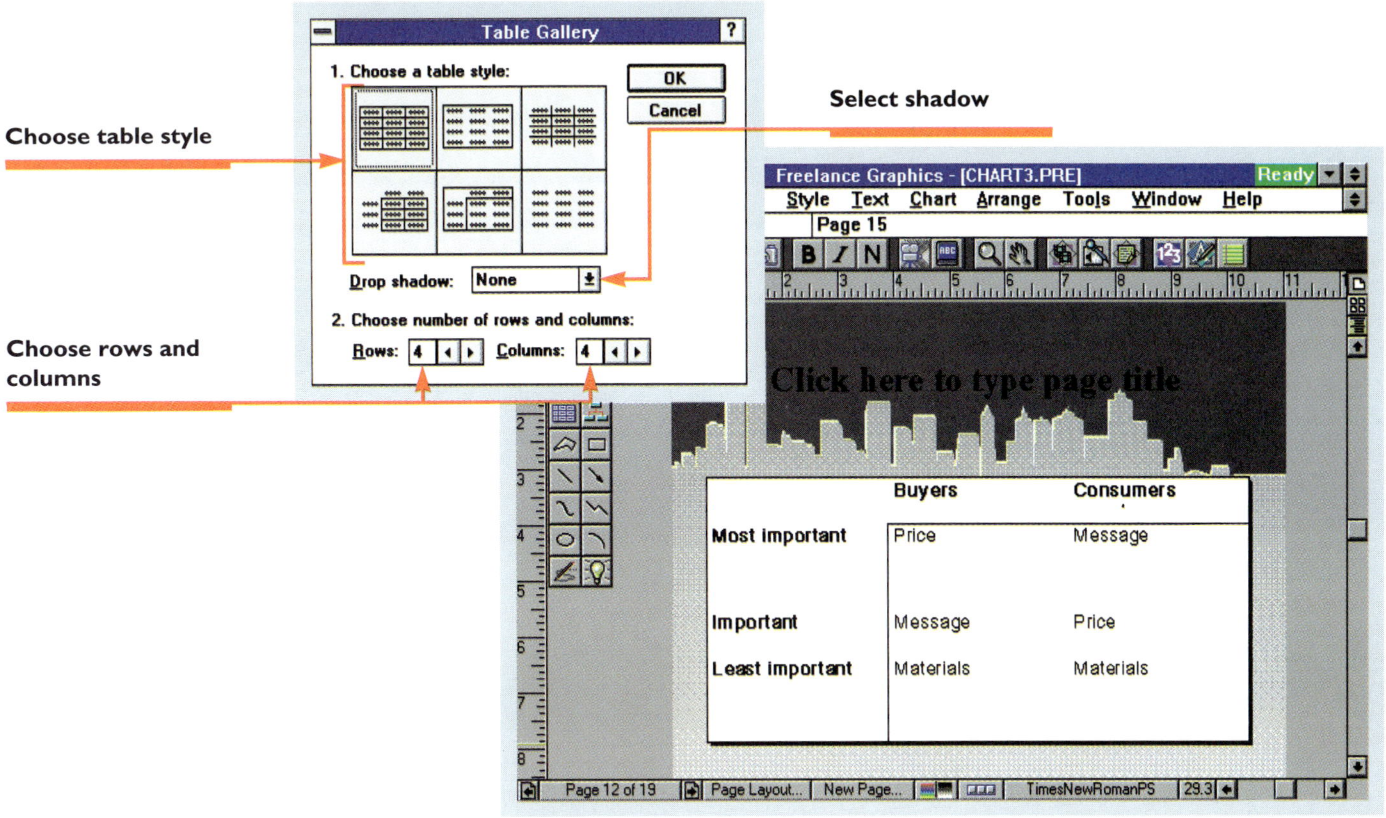

FIGURE 5-19: The added table

Modifying tables

You can easily add, delete, resize, and move rows and columns from the table you have created. First, select the table. Then click Chart in the menu bar, then click Table. A menu of Table options opens. Click the option you want and Freelance Graphics makes the change.

TABLE 5-6:
Table options

OPTION	DESCRIPTION
Insert Column/Row	Adds a column or row after the cursor
Delete Column/Row	Deletes the selected column or row
Size Column/Row	Lets you control the height and width of columns and rows
Move Column/Row	Allows you to move the selected column or row to a new position

QUICK TIP

To change the style of a table quickly, click the table, click the Table tool, click Change table style, click OK, and choose the new style you want.

CONCEPTS REVIEW

Label the Freelance Graphics screen items shown in Figure 5-20.

FIGURE 5-20

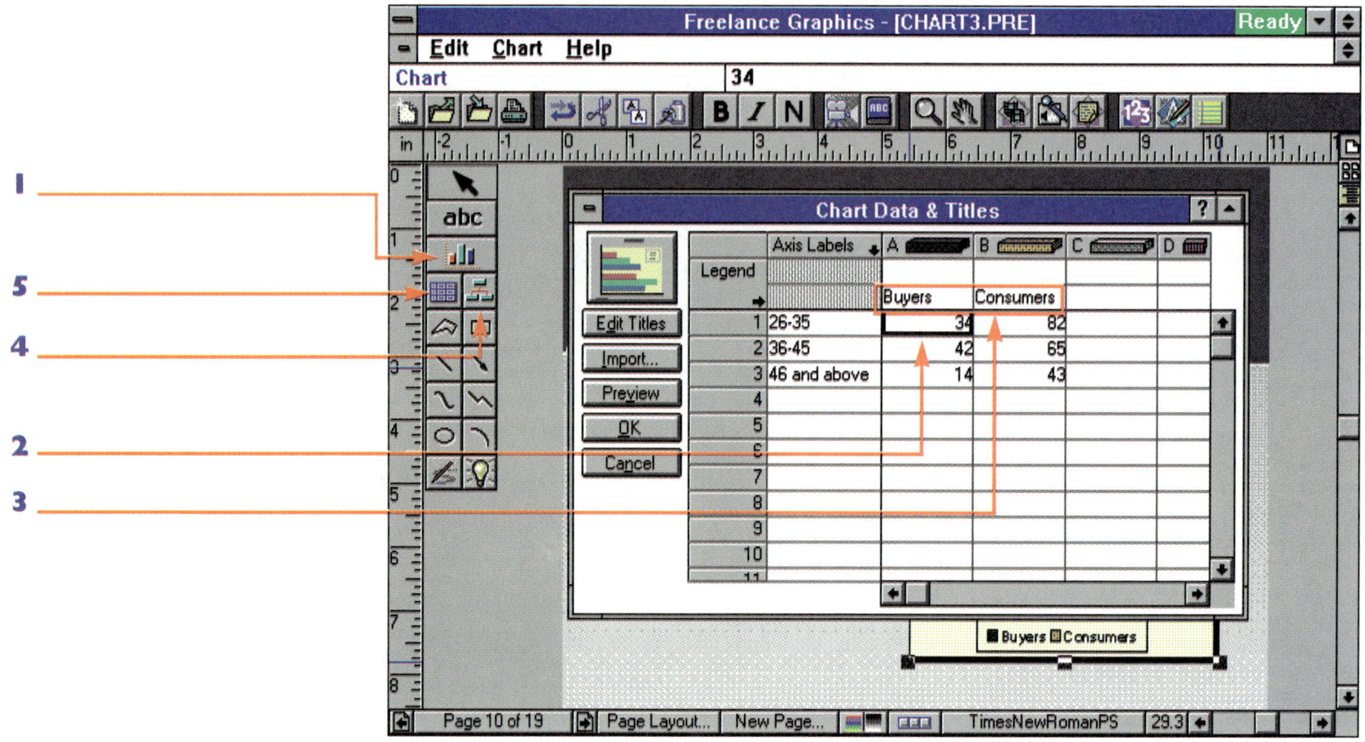

Match each definition with its element.

6 A chart that shows data as points on a line

7 The intersection of a column and row in the Chart Data & Titles dialog box

8 A chart that shows how sections relate to a whole

9 Preset chart settings saved byFreelance Graphics

10 The horizontal line along which items are charted

a. Pie chart
b. Default settings
c. Line chart
d. Cell
e. X axis

Select the best answer from the list of choices.

11 How can you add a chart to your presentation?

a. Click the Chart tool
b. Click the prompt text Click here to create chart text
c. Import the chart from another program
d. All of the above

12 In which of the following situations would a bar chart be most appropriate?

a. When you want to show the percentage of buyers under 30
b. When you want to show the average time it took buyers to respond to your survey
c. When you want to compare the responses of the 26-35 and 36-45 age groups
d. None of the above

13 Which one of the following statements describes the function of a legend?

a. Totals the data displayed

b. Explains the use of the X and Y axes

c. Displays the chart title

d. Shows which data sets go with which color or pattern

14 Which one of the following statements describes the function of a chart heading?

a. Displays the legend

b. Provides the page number and department name

c. Titles the chart

d. Adds note text beneath the chart area

15 Which one of the following statements best describes an organizational chart?

a. A chart that lists text items

b. A chart displaying small boxes of data

c. A chart that shows relationships among people

d. None of the above

APPLICATIONS REVIEW

1 Start a new presentation.

a. Open a new presentation file.

b. Choose the dotline1.mas SmartMaster; click OK.

2 Create two new pages.

a. Select the Title page layout; click OK.

b. Click the title area and type Macadamia Mania.

c. Click the subtitle area and type A chocolate-covered success.

d. Click New Page and choose 1 Chart, then click OK.

e. Click the title area and type Quarterly Sales.

f. Save your presentation as NUTS in the MY_FILES directory of your Student Disk #2.

3 Create the chart.

a. Click the prompt text Click here to create chart. The New Chart Gallery appears.

b. Click Use Default Chart. The Chart Data & Titles window appears.

c. Enter the data as shown in Table 5-7.

d. Click OK. The page is displayed with the chart in place.

e. Compare your screen with Figure 5-21.

TABLE 5-7

	QTR1	QTR2	QTR3	QTR4
Plain	1250	1370	1420	1400
Salted	1300	1000	1420	1350
Chocolate	1800	2100	2000	2150

FIGURE 5-21

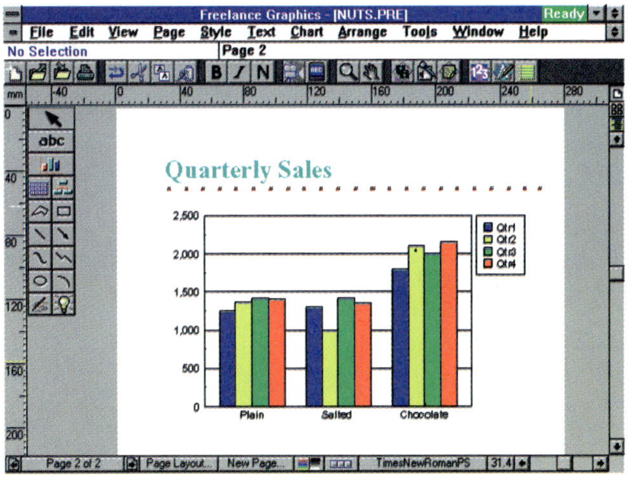

4 Add a chart heading and note.

a. Double-click an open area of the chart. The Chart Data & Titles window appears.

b. Click Edit Titles. A second window of Chart Data & Titles appears.

c. In the Headings box, type Nuts about Nuts!

d. Click Notes and type Based on year-end averages.

e. Click OK.

5 Create an organizational chart.

a. Click the New Page button New Page... .

b. Choose Organizational Chart page layout; click OK.

c. Click the title area and type It's nutty at the top!

d. Click the prompt text Click here to create organization chart. The Organization Chart Gallery opens. To accept the default style, click OK. The Organization Chart Entry List appears.

e. Type Elizabeth Snow, press [Enter], type President, press [Enter] twice.

f. Type Kristy VanCleeve, press [Enter], type Vice President, Operations, press [Enter] twice.

g. Type Phil Wilson, press [Enter], type Vice President, Production, press [Enter].

h. Click OK and compare your screen to Figure 5-22.

i. Save and close the presentation.

FIGURE 5-22

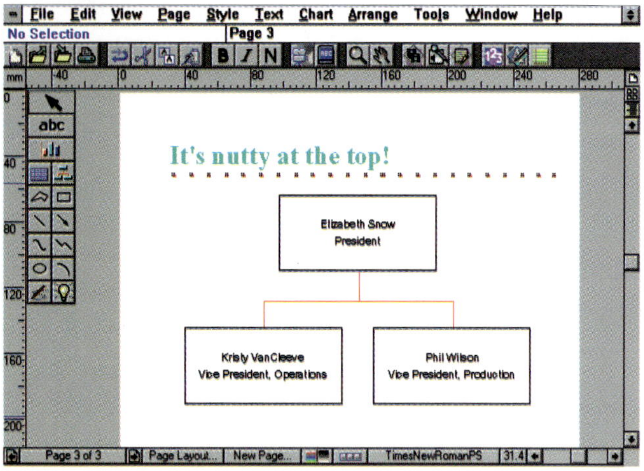

TABLE 5-8: Tutor chart summaries

SAMPLE DATA

Test Scores		Qtr1	Qtr2	Qtr 3	Qtr4
	Before	43	46	52	45
	After	52	62	68	73
Enrollment		Qtr1	Qtr2	Qtr 3	Qtr4
	Attend	67	85	112	123
	Enrolled	99	114	153	164
Gang Activity		Qtr1	Qtr2	Qtr 3	Qtr4
	Before	45	54	50	53
	After	41	40	38	32

INDEPENDENT CHALLENGE 1

HomeTutors is a special educational service that provides at-risk and latch-key children with access to licensed teachers during after school hours. As one of the founders of HomeTutors, you are presenting an informational meeting for members of the local school board. They will decide whether to invest a small amount of their public funding to pay the salaries of teachers for this extra-curricular involvement.

In the two years since its inception, HomeTutors has been used by over 200 children in surrounding counties. You are extremely proud of the program and feel that, with the right support, it could spread throughout the state. As part of your presentation, you will be presenting numeric information—test scores that have increased dramatically, the percentage of children enrolled compared to the percentage who actually participate, and the dropping rate of gang involvement in areas where latch-key programs are utilized.

Your presentation should accomplish the following goals:

- use a SmartMaster that meets the tone and personality of HomeTutors, as well as meets audience expectations
- communicate text information clearly and succinctly
- portray chart information effectively in a variety of styles
- include three charts in a 10-page presentation: one showing test scores, one showing involvement rate, and one showing local gang involvement. Use a 3D area chart for representing test scores. To show enrollment, use a pie chart with an exploding slice for active participants. Use a bar chart to represent gang activity.
  Table 5-8 provides the data for these charts.
- persuade the school board to consider your proposal
- be presented in under 15 minutes

1. Consider how many pages you'll need in the presentation, given the amount of time available.
2. Plan out the types of charts you will use.
3. Draw a thumbnail sketch of the each of the charts in your presentation, showing the chart type and the way in which data will be displayed.
4. Create the presentation in Freelance Graphics, choosing a SmartMaster that offers the right tone for your audience. Enter the page titles and subtitles, if necessary.
5. Create the basic charts, using the information in Table 5-8.
6. Review the charts and make modifications or enhancements as necessary.
7. Save the presentation as TUTORS in the MY_FILES directory on your Student Disk #2.
8. Print the presentation.
9. Submit your sketches and printed presentation to your instructor.

UNIT 6

OBJECTIVES

- Plan graphics
- Add symbols
- Move, resize, and align graphics
- Use drawing tools
- Edit graphics
- Layer and group graphics

Adding GRAPHICS

The graphics in a presentation have a different purpose than the numerical data you communicate in a visual form, like a chart, or the theme of your message, communicated with text. Instead, you use graphics to reinforce ideas and help make your presentation more interesting and entertaining for viewers. ▶ Your presentation for Conscious Clothing includes a number of opportunities to use graphics. You need to add something visual to the new section pages, plus, as Tom points out, adding graphics will help call attention to several key points in the presentation. ▶

Planning graphics

Freelance Graphics includes over 100 pieces of professionally created graphics—called **symbols**—that you can easily add to your presentation pages. You can also create your own graphics using the drawing tools in Freelance Graphics. In addition to using symbols and hand-drawn graphics, you can use graphics you create in other programs (a procedure known as **importing** graphics). Table 6-1 lists the various kinds of graphics you can use in your presentations. ▶ Before you add graphics to your presentation, you look over the handwritten notes Tom Leary left on your desk. "Don't forget about the section pages," he wrote on one note. "What about adding a graphic here?" he wrote on another. Open UNIT_6-1.PRE on your Student Disk #2. Look at your presentation in Page Sorter view and determine which pages need graphics—and what kinds of graphics you want to add. Figure 6-1 shows the pages on which Tom Leary made his suggestions. Consider these questions as you plan your graphics:

- **What are the goals of the graphics?**
  What you plan to do with the graphics affects the way you create them. If you want to entertain or provide a break for viewers, you may find a symbol in the Symbol Gallery to suit your needs. If you need to illustrate a specific item—such as the design of a line of T-shirts—you probably need to draw the item yourself using the drawing tools in Freelance Graphics.

- **What kinds of graphics will you use?**
  The kinds and number of graphics you use in a presentation may vary. You might use a freehand drawing on one page, a symbol on another, a box to highlight a chart note on a different page, and a logo on yet another. You can even add movie files that automatically play during your presentation.

- **Will the graphics repeat from page to page?**
  In the Conscious Clothing presentation, there is already a graphic element that repeats from page to page. The skyline in the SmartMaster you are using is actually a piece of art that appears on the background of every page in the presentation. You can add an additional graphic to the background if you want it to repeat in your presentation, or you can copy and paste graphics to selected pages. For example, you might add a company logo to every page that helps viewers recognize your company more easily.

FIGURE 6-1: Planning graphics

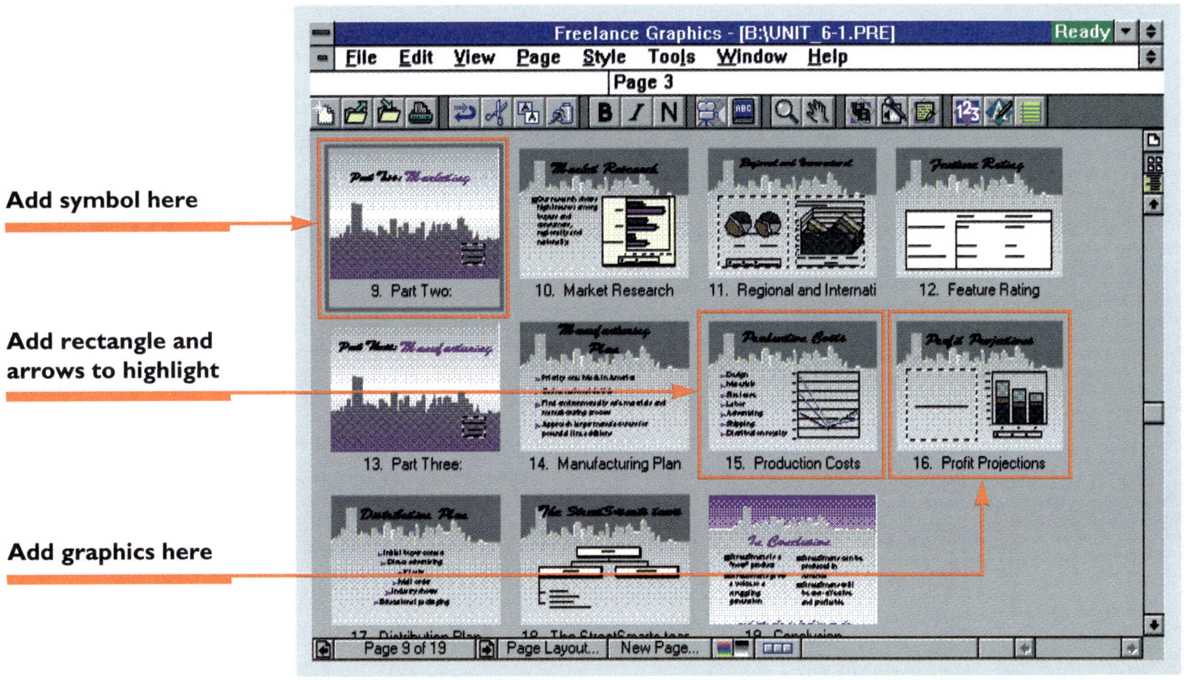

TABLE 6-1: Graphics choices

GRAPHIC	DESCRIPTION	USE FOR
Symbols	Predrawn art objects included with Freelance Graphics	Page illustrations; logos; bullets; page background art; buttons
Clip art	Predrawn art included with other programs or purchased independently	Page illustrations; logos; bullets; page background art; buttons
Shapes and lines	Shapes and lines drawn with the Freelance Graphics drawing tools	Lines to call attention to specific items in a chart or table; boxes to enclose titles or other objects
Custom graphics	A collection of objects you group together to form a specific art object	A special illustration or chart that requires individualized art or a logo
Imported graphics	A graphic you create in another program and open and use in your Freelance Graphics presentation	Page illustrations; screen shots; other presentation pages; scanned photographs
Movie files	A segment of a movie saved in a file that you can run during a presentation screen show	Calling attention to a special program feature; providing real video footage of customer interviews

Adding symbols

The easiest way to add graphics to your presentation is to use Freelance Graphics' symbol files. The **Symbol Gallery** contains ready-to-use symbol files you can add to your presentation pages. The Gallery divides the symbols into a number of different categories—animals, shapes, people, business, finance, etc.—so you can easily locate the symbols you need. ▶ Tom Leary wants you to add something visual to at least one of the section pages. He also asks you to add a graphic to Page 16 to balance out that page, which has only a single chart.

STEPS

1 UNIT_6-1.PRE is already open from your evaluation in Lesson 1; save the file in the MY_FILES directory of your Student Disk #2 as GRAPHICS
The presentation is currently in Page Sorter view, with Page 9 marked as the current page.

2 Click the **Current Page button**
Page 9 opens in full-screen size.

3 Click the **Click here to add symbol** prompt text in the lower-right corner of the page
The Add Symbol to Page dialog box appears, as shown in Figure 6-2. If you accidentally clicked the text box, click outside the box to remove the selection handles, and then click the symbol prompt again to open this dialog box.

4 Press **[P]**
This moves the highlight to the first symbol category starting with the letter P, in this case, people.sym. Assume this is the category you want. In the Choose a symbol area, below, the first symbol of the six available is appropriate. It is already selected, as indicated by the gray lines framing the top and left edge of the image.

5 Click **OK**
Freelance Graphics adds the symbol to the symbol box on the page in the size of the original Click here to add symbol prompt text box. Now you are ready to add a symbol in a different location.

6 Click the **Page button** Page 1 of 1, then click **16. Profit Projections**
Page 16 appears in full-screen size. Although this page has plenty of room for a symbol, the prompt box is for a chart. You can still add a symbol, however. When you add a symbol, it automatically fills the chart area.

7 In the Toolbox on the left side of the work area, click **Symbol**
Again, the Add Symbol to Page dialog box opens.

8 Press **[F]**, then click **finance.sym**, if necessary
A set of financial symbols appears in the lower portion of the dialog box.

9 Click the last symbol (4 of 4) and click **OK**
The symbol showing stacks of coins is added to your page, as shown in Figure 6-3.

10 Click the **File Save SmartIcon** to save the file
If necessary, click Yes to replace the existing GRAPHICS.PRE file.

FIGURE 6-2: Add Symbol to Page dialog box

Scroll through symbol categories

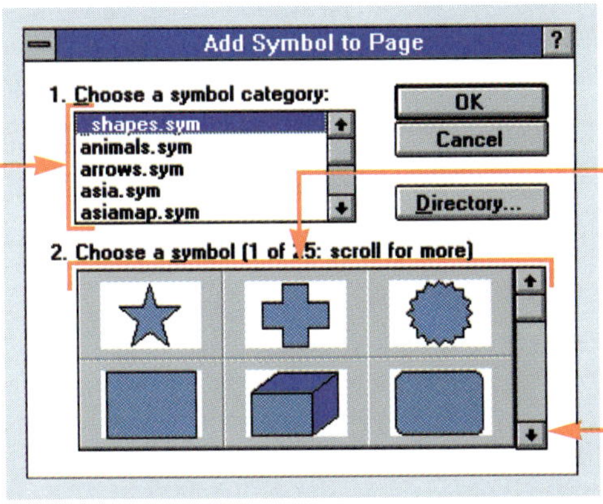

Choose displayed symbol

Scroll to display additional symbols

FIGURE 6-3: The added symbol

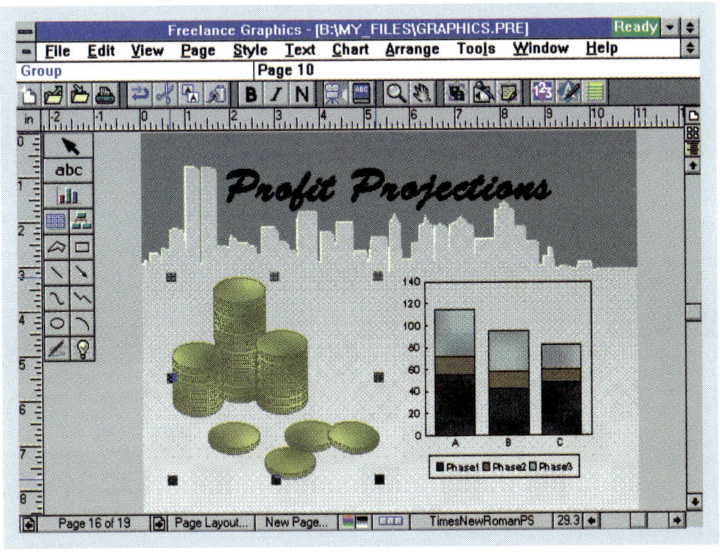

Creating your own symbols

After you learn how to create your own graphics or import graphics from other programs, you may decide that you'd like to save a graphic as a symbol file so you can use it again in Freelance Graphics whenever you want. Just click the graphic, click Tools in the menu bar, and click Add to Symbol Library. Next, click custom.sym and click OK. The symbol file is saved so the next time you want to use it, you can select it from the custom.sym file in the Add Symbol to Page dialog box, as shown in Figure 6-4.

Choose custom.sym for your own symbols

When you want to use the symbol, select it in the Add Symbol to Page dialog box

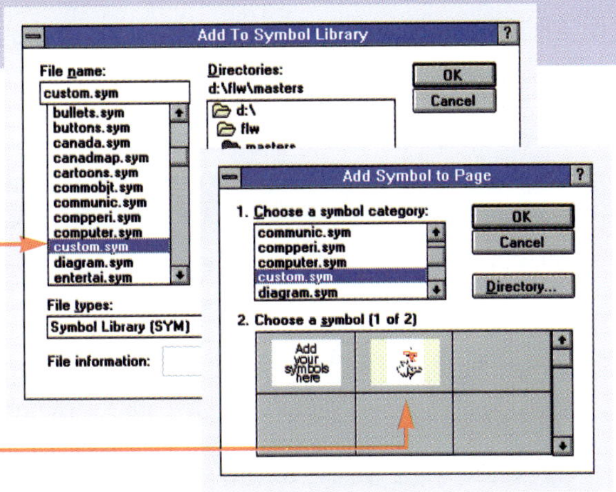

FIGURE 6-4: Saving a symbol file

TROUBLE?

If you accidentally add the wrong symbol, click it and press [Del].

Moving, resizing, and aligning graphics

Placing graphics where you want them is a fairly simple process. You can move a graphic with the mouse by dragging it to the desired location. What do you do when you need to turn an object sideways? Or flip it upside-down? And depending on the number of objects on your page, having one or two graphics that don't align properly with the other screen elements can distract your audience. Table 6-2 lists the various ways you can move and resize graphics in your presentation. ▶ After adding the symbol to Page 9 in the Conscious Clothing presentation, you can see that it is too small for the page. Before you show your work to Tom, you want to move and resize the symbol. After closer scrutiny, you also decide to horizontally flip the symbol you added to Page 16 to create a more balanced look for the page.

STEPS

1 Click the **Page button** [Page 1 of 1] and choose **9. Part Two:** from the displayed list

The page on which you added the people symbol appears in Current Page view. The symbol is still selected. First, move the symbol up and in toward the center of the page.

2 Position the mouse pointer on the symbol; press and hold the mouse button while dragging the symbol up and to the left; release the mouse button

The symbol is moved to the new location. Now you are ready to enlarge it.

3 Move the pointer to the lower-right corner of the symbol, where it changes from a single arrow to a double-headed arrow, then press and hold the mouse button while you drag the symbol corner down and to the right

The symbol enlarges as you drag the mouse. See Figure 6-5.

4 Release the mouse button, move the pointer outside the symbol area, and click

The handles are removed from the symbol. Now you're finished resizing and moving the object.

5 Click [Page 1 of 1] and choose **16. Profit Projections**

The page appears in Current Page view.

6 If it is not already selected, click the coins symbol you added in the previous lesson

Handles appear around the edges and corners of the object.

7 Click **Arrange** in the menu bar, then click **Flip**

A menu is displayed. Choosing one of the commands on this menu tells Freelance Graphics that you want to flip the selected graphic horizontally left to right or vertically top to bottom.

8 Click **Left to Right**

The graphic flips from left to right, as shown in Figure 6-6. The symbol and the chart balance each other better now, with their tallest points positioned in the center of the page.

9 Click the **File Save SmartIcon** to save the file

If necessary, click Yes to replace the existing GRAPHICS.PRE file.

FIGURE 6-5: Resizing an object

The double-headed arrow means you can resize the object

TABLE 6-2:
Move and resize choices

WHEN YOU WANT TO	USE THIS SMARTICON:	FOLLOW THESE STEPS:
Resize an object	[none available]	Drag object handle inward or outward
Move an object	[none available]	Drag selected object in the direction you want
Rotate an object	Rotate	Click a corner of the selected object and drag to rotate
Flip an object	Flip Top to Bottom Flip Left to Right	Select object; then click SmartIcon to flip (or choose Arrange, Flip)
Align objects	Align Left Align Right Align Top Align Bottom	Select objects to be aligned; click SmartIcon (or choose Arrange, Align)

FIGURE 6-6: The flipped graphic

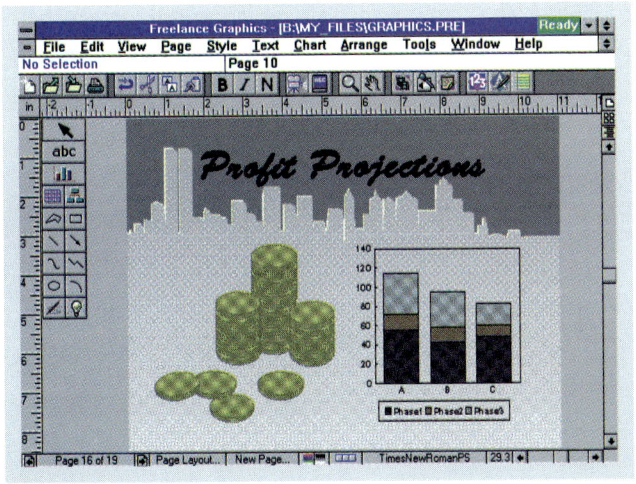

TROUBLE?

If you move or resize an object and it covers up part of another object, press [F8] to move the selected object backward one layer.

Using drawing tools

With Freelance Graphics, you don't have to be an artist to add custom shapes and graphics to your presentation pages. The set of drawing tools displayed in the Toolbox to the left of the work area gives you everything you need for assembling your own custom graphics. The Toolbox includes drawing tools for eight different shapes and also gives you a freehand tool for those times when you're drawing something that isn't a defined shape. ▶ In his notes regarding your printed presentation, Tom suggested adding shaded boxes and arrows leading from the text and pointing to the chart on Page 15 to help viewers see which line on the line chart represented which item. You make the change using the arrow tool and the rectangle tool.

STEPS

1. **Click the Left Arrow button to the left of the Page button** [Page 1 of 1]
   Page 15, Production Costs, is displayed in Current Page view.
2. **Click the Rectangle tool**
   When you move the arrow pointer to the work area, it changes to a cross-hair pointer, indicating that you chose a drawing tool.
3. **Move the cross-hair pointer to a position to the right of the first bullet entry; press and hold the mouse button while dragging the mouse down and slightly to the right**
   This draws a small thin rectangle at the end of the first three entries.
4. **Release the mouse button and click outside the rectangle**
   When you release the mouse button, the rectangle fills with a color. Clicking outside the box deselects it. (Note: Clicking outside the box may select another area such as the text or chart box. Just click outside all areas to deselect everything.)
5. **Click the Arrow tool button**
   Again, the arrow pointer changes to a cross-hair pointer, indicating that you selected a drawing tool. Now you're ready to draw the arrow from the shaded box you just added to the corresponding data line in the chart.
6. **Position the pointer midway along the right edge of the rectangle; then press and hold the mouse button and drag the cross-hair to the top data line in the chart**
   The line stretches in the direction you drag the mouse.
7. **Release the mouse button, then click outside the line**
   The line is added and deselected. Figure 6-7 shows the rectangle and arrow created using the drawing tools.
8. **Click the File Save SmartIcon**
   If Freelance Graphics asks whether you want to replace the file GRAPHICS.PRE already saved, click Replace.

FIGURE 6-7: Results of using the drawing tools

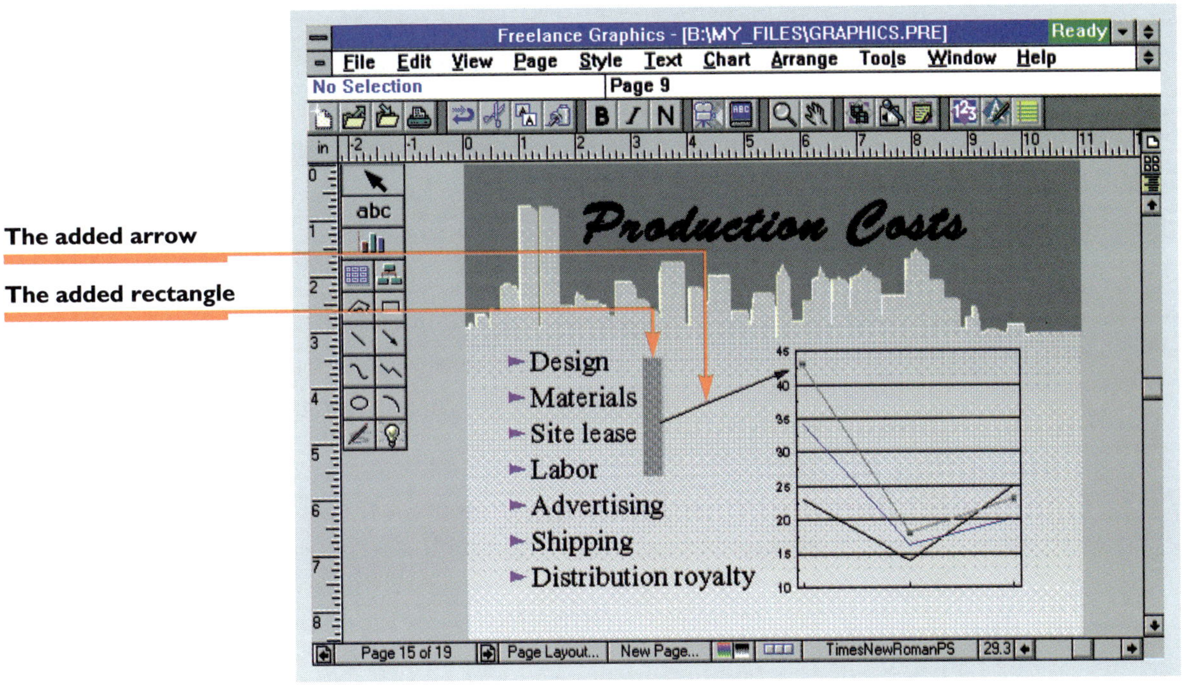

Changing shape and line color

You can change the settings for a tool you're going to use before you use it. Position the pointer on the tool you want to change settings for and double-click the mouse button. An attributes dialog box appears, as shown in Figure 6-8, in which you can set line width and color and area color and pattern. Make your choices and click OK. The shapes or lines you create with that tool appear in the settings you specified.

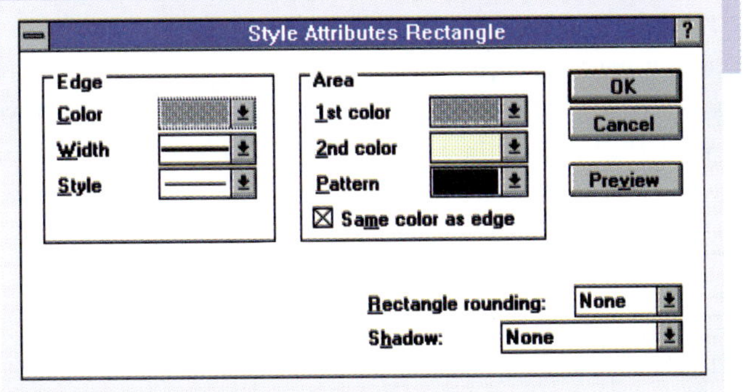

FIGURE 6-8: Displaying shape attributes

QUICK TIP

By default, after you complete an action using a drawing tool, Freelance Graphics deselects the tool and selects the pointer. If you prefer that Freelance Graphics leaves the drawing tool you used selected until you choose a different tool, click Tools in the menu bar, click User Setup, and in the Drawing tools area, click Keep tool active.

Editing graphics

After you create an object you may want to edit it. Many of the basic editing commands you can use with text and charts—cutting, copying, and pasting objects—apply also to the graphics you work with on your presentation pages. Table 6-3 lists different ways you can edit graphics. Freelance Graphics also provides a sophisticated editing feature—called **points mode**—that enables you to change the shape of virtually any line of any graphics object. ▶ Tom wants you to finish the section pages so he can present the complete first draft of the presentation to his boss.

Steps

1. **Click the Page button** Page 1 of 1 **and click 9. Part Two:**
   Page 9 appears in Current Page view.
2. **Click the symbol in the lower-right corner of the page**
   The symbol is selected, with handles on the edges and in the corners of the image. To create the effect you want, you need more of an "audience" than this symbol provides. By making another copy of the symbol and pasting it beside the original, you can create the effect of more people.
3. **Click the Copy SmartIcon**
   The symbol is copied and placed on the Windows clipboard.
4. **Click the Paste SmartIcon**
   The copied symbol is placed on top of the first symbol. However, it doesn't do you much good placed there—you need to move it beside the original.
5. **Drag the new symbol to the left, then click outside the symbol**
   This step positions the new symbol to the left of the original symbol and then deselects it.
6. **In the Toolbox, click the Freehand tool, then move the cross-hair pointer to the work area, press the mouse button, and drag to underline the text, as shown in Figure 6-9**
   As you drag the mouse, the line appears. Next you can change the curve in the line slightly by using points mode.
7. **Click Arrange in the menu bar, then click Points Mode**
   A small **Edit Pts** indicator appears in the upper-left corner of the title bar, indicating that points mode is in effect. Compare your screen to Figure 6-10.
8. **Position the pointer on the leftmost point in the line; then drag the line to the right**
   The line extends as you move the point. You can also change any or all of the internal points on the line by dragging the point to the new location. In this way, you can change the curve and length of shapes and lines as necessary.
9. **Release the mouse button and click outside the line**
   Freelance Graphics accepts the changes and deselects the line.
10. **Press [Shift][F6]**
    This turns off points mode and returns the page to normal presentation display. (If you prefer, you can click Arrange in the menu bar and click Points Mode again to deselect it.)

FIGURE 6-9: The added underline

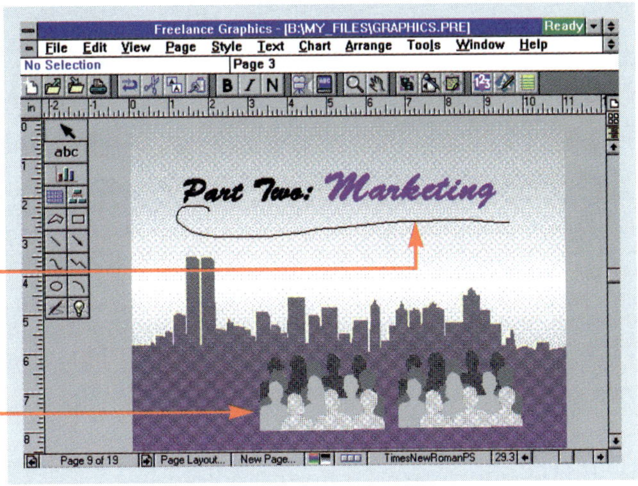

Line created with the Freehand tool

Copied and pasted symbol

FIGURE 6-10: The screen in points mode

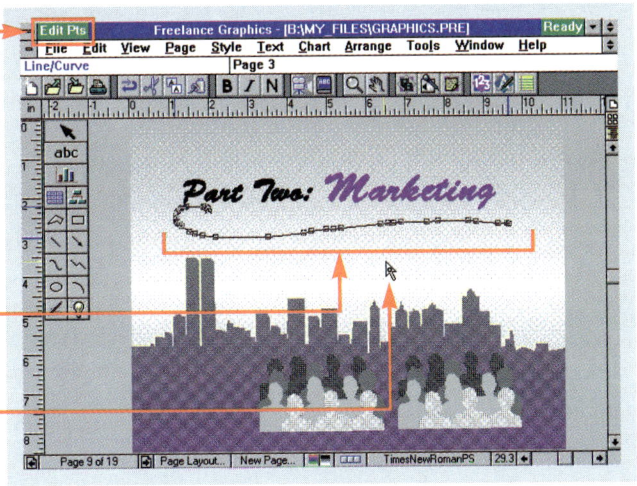

The points mode indicator

The points on the selected object

The points mode pointer

TABLE 6-3: Ways to edit graphics

IF YOU WANT TO DO THIS	FOLLOW THESE STEPS:
Delete an object	Click the object; press [Del]
Copy an object	Click the object; press [Ctrl] [C]
Paste an object	Press [Ctrl] [V] and position pasted object
Change the length of a line	Click the line; resize by dragging an end
Remove arrows from a line	Position pointer on the arrow; click right mouse button; choose Attributes in Arrowheads, click None; click OK
Change the shape of a curve	Click Arrange; click Points Mode; drag the point you want to change
Add a bend in a line or shape	Click Arrange; click Points Mode; click Add Points; click at the place on the shape or line you want to add the point; drag to create bend

Layering and grouping graphics

When creating graphics using Freelance, you are combining shapes to create a certain look. In order to get the right effect, you might want to change the layering of some objects, that is, the way they overlap. ▶ When you group selected shapes and lines, you may want to lock them together into one graphical object, so that an individual line or shape doesn't get moved accidentally. In Freelance this is called **grouping**. Table 6-4 explains the different ways you can layer and group objects. ▶ Before you let Tom look through the finished first draft, you want to layer the graphics on the section pages and then add a few small objects and group them to create a simple but striking effect.

Steps

1. **Select the leftmost symbol on the bottom of Page 9 and drag it to the left side of the page**
   The gap between the two symbols widens. Now make another copy of the symbol.
2. **Click Copy, then click Paste**
   A copy of the symbol is pasted on top of the left symbol.
3. **Drag the new symbol to overlap the left edge of the symbol on the right**
   Notice that the right side of the new symbol blends in with the first symbol. On the left side, however, the edge of the symbol is still apparent. You can solve this problem by changing the layering of the second symbol.
4. **If it's not already selected, click the second symbol; then click Arrange in the menu bar, then click Priority, and click Top**
   This tells Freelance Graphics to move the selected graphic to the top layer of the presentation page. Now you're ready to add the last touch.
5. **Click the Zoom Page SmartIcon, then move the pointer to the end of the line you added with the Freehand tool and click**
   This part of the display is magnified.
6. **Click the Line tool and draw six short lines stretching outward from a single point, pressing [Shift] as you draw to constrain the lines to straight lines**
   The addition of the lines creates a bursting-bubble effect. Compare your screen with Figure 6-11.
7. **Click the Selection tool and drag a rectangle around all the lines you just added**
   This selects all the lines at once. Each line displays its own handles. Now you can group the items into one graphic so you can easily copy and paste the graphic to other section pages later.
8. **Click Arrange, then click Group**
   The objects are all grouped into one graphic. Instead of handles appearing on each individual line, one set of handles encloses the entire object, as shown in Figure 6-12.
9. **Save and close your presentation file**
   If Freelance Graphics asks whether you want to replace the current file, click Replace.

FIGURE 6-11: Creating a graphic effect

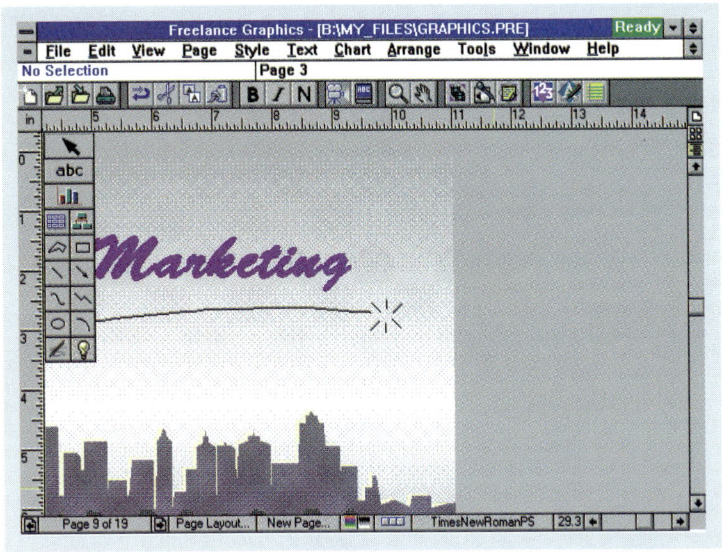

FIGURE 6-12: The grouped object

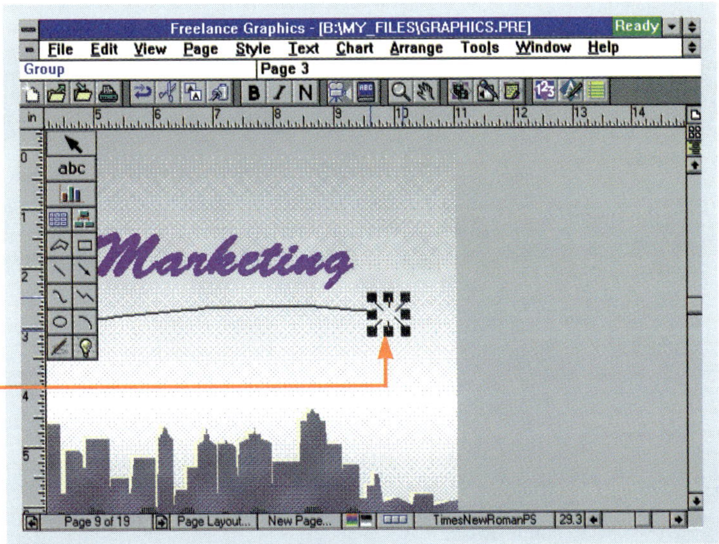

One set of handles for all items

TABLE 6-4:
Layering and grouping options

SMARTICON	NAME	DESCRIPTION
	Forward One	Moves the selected object forward one layer
	Back One	Moves the selected object backward one layer
	Bring to Front	Brings selected object to the front of all other objects
	Send to Back	Moves selected object behind all other objects
	Group	Combines selected objects into one group
	Ungroup	Separates a grouped object into individual shapes and lines

CONCEPTS REVIEW

Label the Freelance Graphics screen items shown in Figure 6-13.

FIGURE 6-13

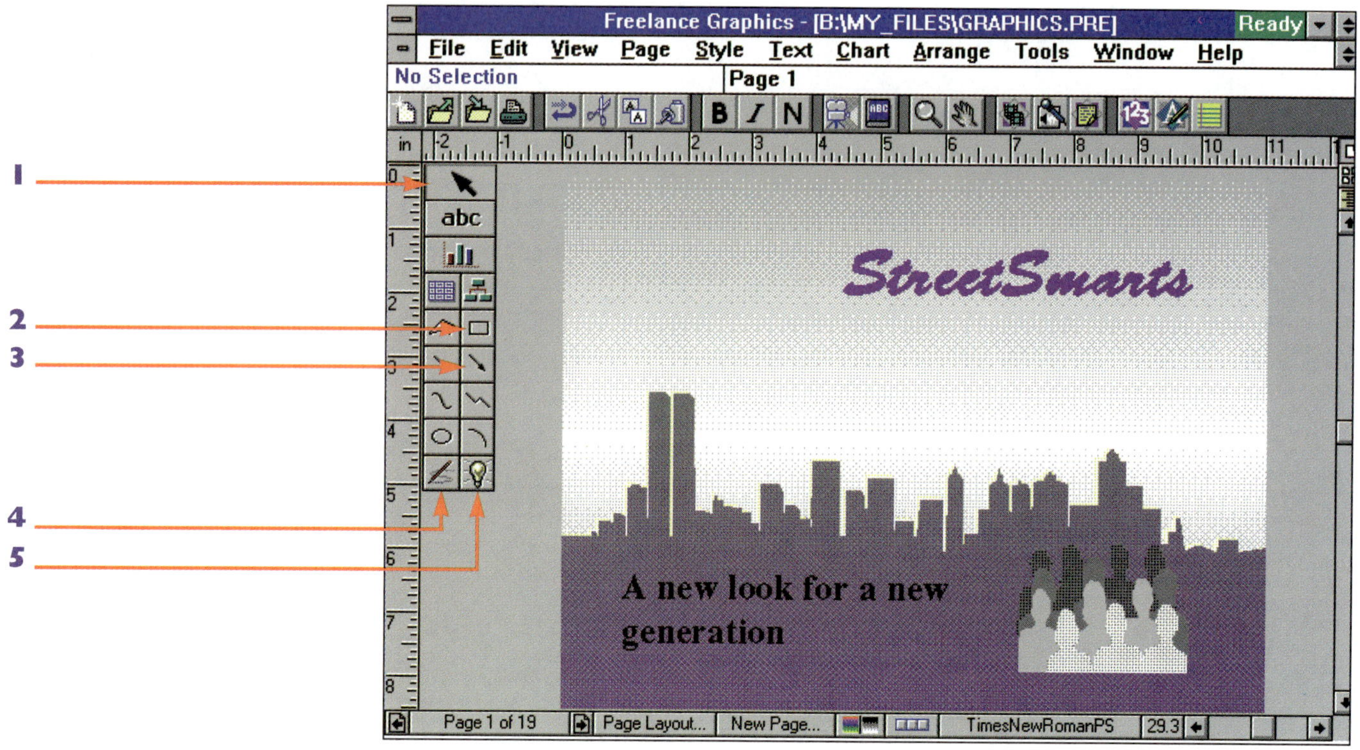

Match each definition with its element.

6 An editing feature that enables you to change the shape of lines, curves, and shapes

7 Combining an object comprised of several individual elements into one object

8 Predrawn art included with programs or purchased separately

9 Using a graphic created in another program in your Freelance Graphics presentation

10 Predrawn graphics included with Freelance Graphics

a. symbols
b. points mode
c. grouping
d. clip art
e. importing

Select the best answer from the list of choices.

11 How do you add a symbol to your presentation?
   a. Click the Symbol tool
   b. Click the Click here to add chart text
   c. Draw the graphic using the drawing tools
   d. All of the above

12 Which one of the following statements is NOT a characteristic of the graphics you create in Freelance Graphics?
   a. You can layer objects on a page
   b. You can group multiple objects into a single graphic
   c. You can display and edit the dots that comprise an object
   d. You can easily resize graphics

13 Which one of the following statements describes the function of the Freehand tool?

a. It works as a paintbrush, filling an area with color

b. It works as an eraser, erasing selected area

c. It works as a pointer, to select graphics

d. It works as a pencil, allowing you to draw on screen

14 Which one of the following statements describes the way in which the pointer changes when you select a drawing tool?

a. The arrow changes to a cross-hair pointer

b. The pointer takes on the shape of the selected tool

c. The pointer blinks like a text cursor

d. None of the above

15 Which one of the following statements best describes points mode?

a. A way of viewing small objects

b. An editing mode for modifying lines and shapes

c. A method of copying and pasting

d. A way to magnify a page

APPLICATIONSREVIEW

1 Create a new presentation.

a. Open a new presentation file.

b. Choose the motion.mas SmartMaster; click OK.

2 Create two new pages.

a. Select the Title page layout, then click OK.

b. Click the title area and type Techies, Inc.

c. Click the subtitle area and type Laughing in the face of technology.

d. Click New Page and choose Bullets & Symbol, then click OK.

e. Click the title area and type Does your PC...

f. Click the bullet area and type Purposely lock up at the worst possible times?

g. Press [Enter] and type Make you look bad in front of your coworkers?

h. Press [Enter] and type Totally control your business life? then click OK.

i. Save your presentation as TECHIE in the MY_FILES directory of Student Disk #2.

3 Add a symbol.

a. Click the arrow to the left of the Page button 

. Page 1 appears.

b. Click the Click here to add symbol prompt text.The Add Symbol to Page dialog box appears.

c. Type [C] and press [Down Arrow] until you reach cartoons.sym.

d. Click the second symbol (2 of 8).

e. Click OK. The symbol is added to the title page.

f. Click the arrow to the right of 

to display Page 2.

g. Add symbol 6 of 8 from cartoons.sym to the symbol prompt area.

h. Click outside the symbol and compare your screen with Figure 6-14.

FIGURE 6-14

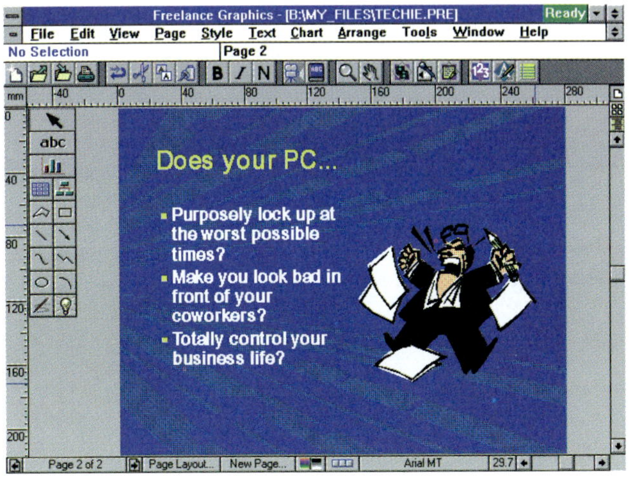

4 Resize the symbol.

a. Click the symbol to select it.

b. Position the pointer on the top center handle.

c. Drag the handle upward until it is even with the page title. The graphic lengthens.

d. Release the mouse button.

e. Click outside the symbol.

5 Use the drawing tools.

a. Click the Polygon tool .

b. Draw a five-sided shape beneath the feet of the cartoon man.

c. Position the pointer at the beginning of the first polygon line and double-click to end the polygon. Freelance Graphics fills the area with color.

(If you are using a black and white monitor, you may need to change the color of the polygon to provide more contrast. Position the mouse pointer on the shape, click the right mouse button, and choose Attributes; then choose the colors you want for the edge and area of the shape.)

6 Move the drawing back one layer.

a. Click the right mouse button on the polygon. A menu appears.

b. Click Priority.

c. Click Bottom. This tells Freelance Graphics to move the selected shape to the bottom layer. The shape will serve as the "floor" beneath the cartoon man.

d. Compare your screen with Figure 6-15.

e. Save and close your presentation.

FIGURE 6-15

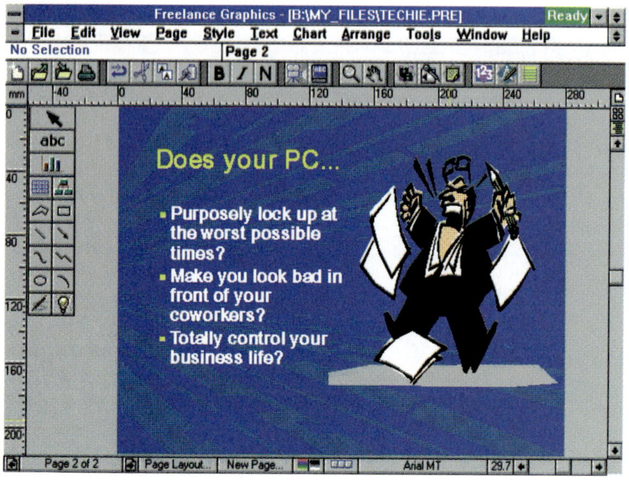

INDEPENDENT CHALLENGE

At the 4-H fair last year, the Bartholomew County Quilt Contest was a big hit. So big, in fact, that you've already received several hundred requests for information about this years' dates and times. When the president of the fair board asks you to contribute one page to a presentation she's making to the town council, you decide to design a quilt-like graphic to remind the council of the success of your contest; you really want your graphics to stand out.

To complete this independent challenge:

1 Start a new presentation, using a blank SmartMaster background.

2 Select a title page and type the title of your presentation: Bartholomew Quilters Put it All Together!

3 Create a custom graphic resembling a quilt.

Use the following tips:

- Draw a large rectangle as the basis for the quilt.
- Use squares of different colors to create a pattern.
- Rotate colored squares, if you choose, to create a different pattern. (*Note*: If you are using a black and white monitor, the squares appear in different shades of gray.)
- Remember to layer objects.
- Group each row as you finish it and copy it to another location.

4 Save the presentation as QUILT in the MY_FILES directory of Student Disk #2. Compare your screen to Figure 6-16.

5 Print a copy of the presentation page and submit it to your instructor.

FIGURE 6-16

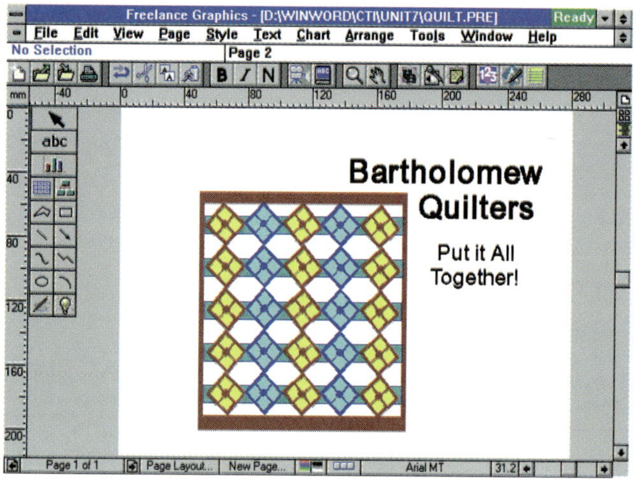

UNIT 7

OBJECTIVES

- Prepare to give the presentation
- Add special effects
- Control page advance
- Draw on screen
- Using the Freelance Graphics Control Panel
- Add buttons
- Run the screen show
- Print handouts and slides

Producing THE PRESENTATION

You have added all the necessary elements—text, charts, and graphics—on your presentation pages and have checked for accuracy, page order, and overall design. There's only one thing left to do: display the screen show. A **screen show**, in Freelance Graphics, is an on-screen presentation that enables you to display the pages full screen—unencumbered by tool bars and buttons. You can get the full effect of your work by displaying it in a screen show, and you can decide whether you want to go a step further and add special transitional effects and timing controls to give your presentation a professional touch. ▶ Tom's meeting with the managers is scheduled for tomorrow morning. You are almost finished with the presentation. You decide to explore the different display options Freelance Graphics offers and put the finishing touches on the final presentation. ▶

Preparing to give the presentation

Before producing your presentation materials, you need to consider what form the presentation will take. Do you need transparencies or slides? If so, Freelance Graphics' print options will help you print the presentation pages in the format you want. (See "Printing handouts and slides," later in this unit for more information.) Will you use your computer to give the presentation? For the Conscious Clothing presentation, you'll use Freelance Graphics' screen show feature, which includes a number of special options you can employ to create the most professional presentation possible. ▶ The following questions will help you consider these special options for your presentation:

- **What materials will you need for your presentation?**
  In most cases, it's not enough to simply stand up in front of a group of people, show a few slides or a screen show presentation, and leave. People might have questions long after the presentation is over. You can help educate your audience—and provide a more effective presentation—by preparing support materials for your audience in the form of handouts, outlines, or notes. Prepare a presentation checklist, like the one shown in Figure 7-1, to help make sure you create all the different elements you need for your presentation.

- **How will it be easiest for you to move from page to page?**
  Freelance Graphics gives you a number of options for moving from page to page. You can use the mouse buttons to move forward or backward one page at a time. You can also use the Page Up and Page Down keys on the keyboard. But you can also display the on-screen Freelance Graphics Control Panel that enables you to move forward or backward, jump to a certain page, or stop the presentation with a click of the mouse button. Additionally, you can add buttons to pages so you can move back and forth in whatever order you want.

- **Do you want to use special transitions?**
  Open the file UNIT_7-1.PRE on your Student Disk #3 and display your presentation in Page Sorter view. You can choose from a number of special transitions to vary the way pages are displayed in your presentation. You might slide one page in from the left, another in from the right, or have one appear in the center and scroll outward toward the edges. Before you begin adding transitions, think about the pages you want to use. Which of these pages would be candidates for transitions? Figure 7-2 gives you a few examples. The names of the transitional effects shown in the figure tell you what the transition resembles—Curtain looks like a theater curtain, for example, and Shade looks like a window shade. The text display effect shown in Figure 7-2, Text left, moves text in from the left onto the page.

FIGURE 7-1: A presentation checklist

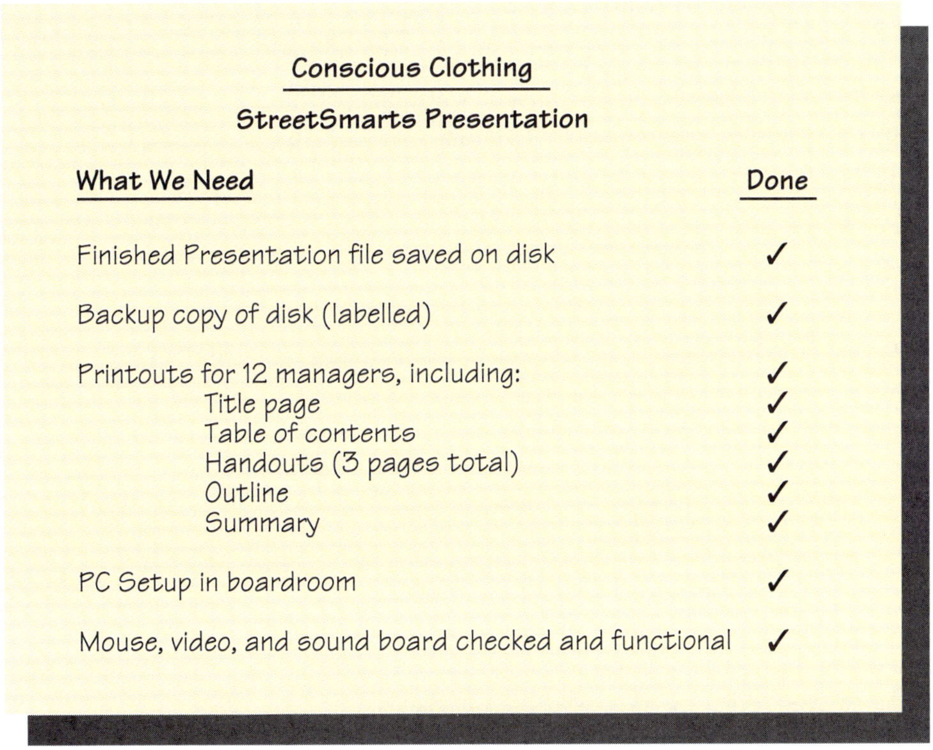

Conscious Clothing

StreetSmarts Presentation

What We Need	Done
Finished Presentation file saved on disk	✓
Backup copy of disk (labelled)	✓
Printouts for 12 managers, including:	✓
Title page	✓
Table of contents	✓
Handouts (3 pages total)	✓
Outline	✓
Summary	✓
PC Setup in boardroom	✓
Mouse, video, and sound board checked and functional	✓

FIGURE 7-2: Looking for transition opportunities

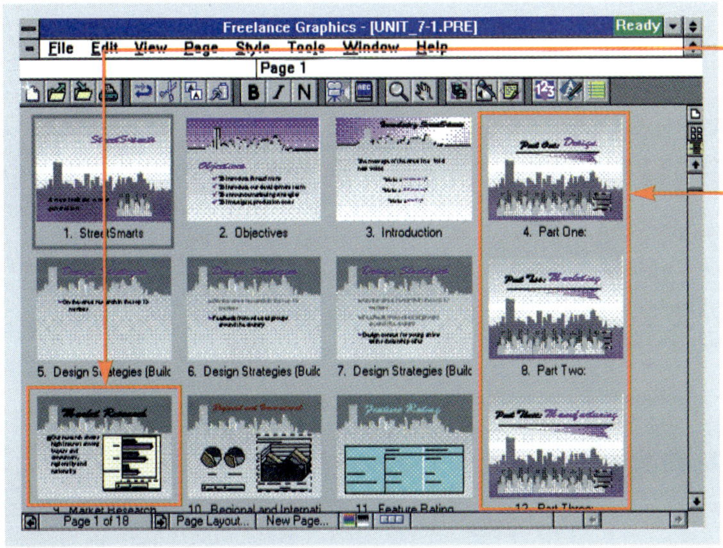

QUICK TIP

To run the spelling checker quickly before you start the presentation, click the Spell check SmartIcon in the default SmartIcon palette.

Adding special effects

Freelance Graphics provides you with a number of options—called **special effects**—you can use to customize the way pages in your presentation are displayed. You select the page you want to add the special effect to and then select a **transition**—that is, a special technique used to display the page you've selected. ▶ Add a few transitions to the Conscious Clothing presentation before you show the screen show to Tom for the first time.

STEPS

1 The file UNIT_7-1.PRE is already open on your file; save the file as SCREEN1 in the MY_FILES directory of your Student Disk #3
This creates a working copy of the unit file. If you have not yet created a MY_FILES directory on Student Disk #3, you will need to refer back to the "Working with Windows" section and the lesson entitled "Using File Manager." The presentation is displayed in Page Sorter view.

2 Click **4. Part One**
The page selection box encloses the selected page.

3 Click **View** in the menu bar, then click **Screen Show** and click **Edit Effects**
The Edit Screen Show dialog box opens, as shown in Figure 7-3.

4 In the Choose an effect window, click **Box Out**
This selects the Box Out transition. You decide to preview this effect.

5 Click **Preview Page**
The presentation page opens, beginning in the center of the screen and spreading out toward the edges.

6 Click anywhere on the page
The Edit Screen Show dialog box reopens.

7 Beneath the Choose a page window, click **Page 4 of 18**
The Choose Screen Show Page dialog box appears, as shown in Figure 7-4.

8 Click **StreetSmarts** and click **OK**
This selects the first page of your presentation and returns you to the Edit Screen Show dialog box.

9 In the Choose an effect window, scroll to **Curtains** and click it; then click **Preview Page**
A "theater curtain" closes, and opens to reveal the first page of your presentation.

10 Click anywhere on the page to return to the Edit Screen Show dialog box, then click **OK**

FIGURE 7-3: Edit Screen Show dialog box

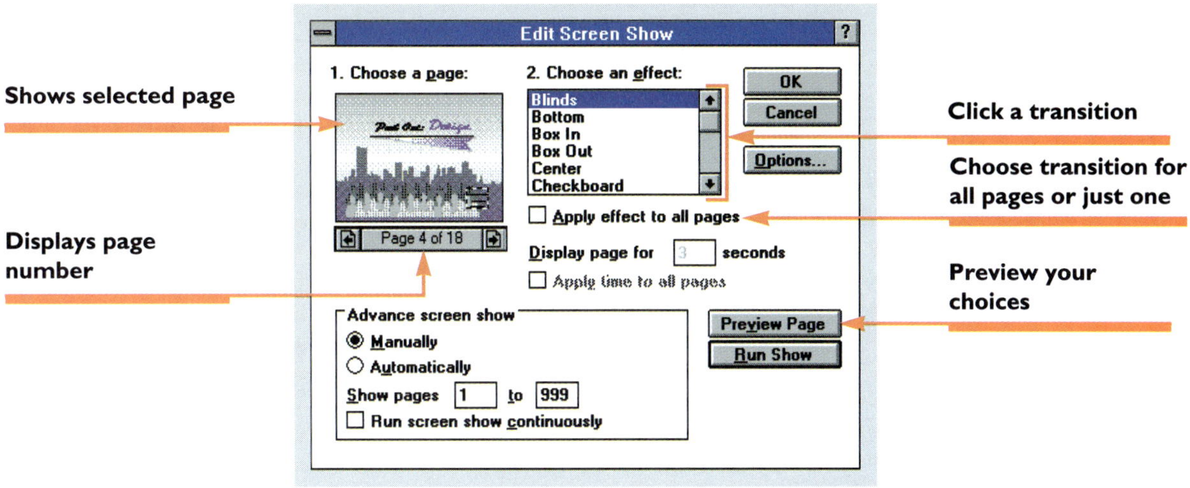

FIGURE 7-4: Screen Show effects

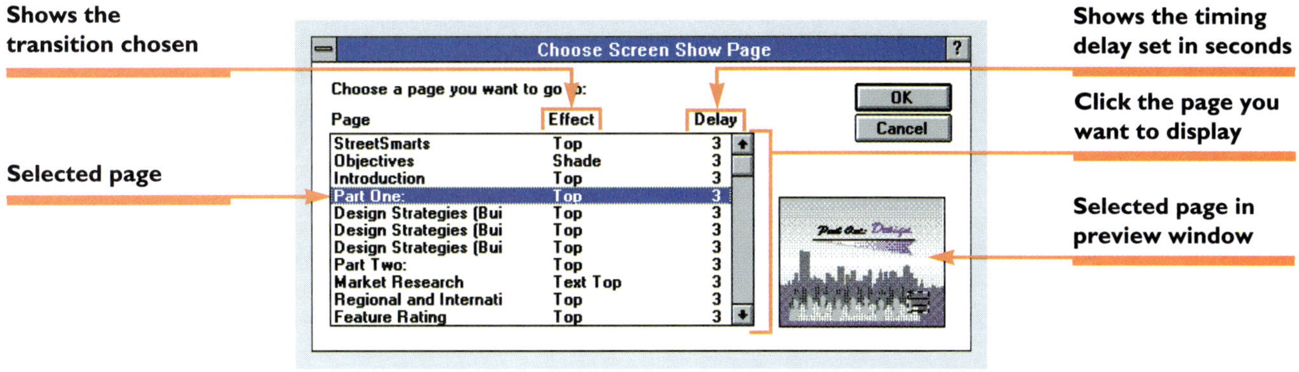

Using multimedia features in your presentation

If your computer is multimedia-ready—meaning that it has a sound board, a VGA or Super VGA monitor, and enough memory to handle large files—you have the option of adding sound or even movie files to your presentations. If you later want to enhance the Conscious Clothing presentation, for example, you could insert a recording of the new commercial tune or show a piece of a designer interview, right there on the presentation page.

Controlling page advance

The advancement and timing of the pages in a presentation can significantly affect its success. You can choose to advance the page **manually**—meaning that the presenter controls the amount of time a specific page is displayed, by clicking the mouse button or pressing Page Down to move to the next slide—or you can let Freelance Graphics **automatically** advance the pages. If you choose Automatic advance, you can set all pages to a certain time limit or you can enter a specific time value for each page. ▶ Tom wants the pages in the presentation to advance automatically. The problem is that the amount of information on the pages varies greatly. You need to select Automatic advance for this presentation, but specify longer times for slides that need more display time.

STEPS

1 Click **View** in the menu bar; then click **Screen Show** and then click **Edit Effects**

This displays the Edit Screen Show dialog box. In the lower-left corner of the dialog box, you see the Advance screen show options. Manually is selected by default. See Figure 7-5.

2 Click the **Automatically radio button**

The options above the Advance screen show options change. Now the Display page option shows the number 3, meaning that each page will be displayed automatically for three seconds before the next page appears. This is the Freelance Graphics default.

3 Double-click in the Display page for box and type **30**; then click **Apply time to all pages**

This first action records 30 seconds as the time you want to apply to the selected page (which is Page 1, StreetSmarts). The second action tells Freelance Graphics to apply the 30 second time to all slides in the presentation. But 30 seconds still isn't enough time for some of the slides in your presentation. For example, you need to allow more time for Page 2, Objectives.

4 In the Choose a page area, click the arrow to the right of Page 1 of 18

Page 2, Objectives, appears in the Choose a page window.

5 Click the **Apply time to all pages checkbox** to remove the X

Freelance Graphics changes the timimg for the selected page without modifying the time setting for the rest of the pages.

6 Double-click the **Display page for box** and type **60**

This tells Freelance Graphics to allow 60 seconds for this page, which shows a short bulleted list.

7 Click **Page 2 of 18**

The Choose Screen Show Page dialog box opens showing the changed timing. See Figure 7-6.

8 In the Choose Screen Show Page dialog box, click **OK**, then in the Edit Screen Show dialog box, click **OK**

You are returned to the presentation displayed in Page Sorter view.

9 Save your presentation and click **Replace** when prompted

This saves the changes you made in the file SCREEN1.PRE .

FIGURE 7-5: Choosing manual advance

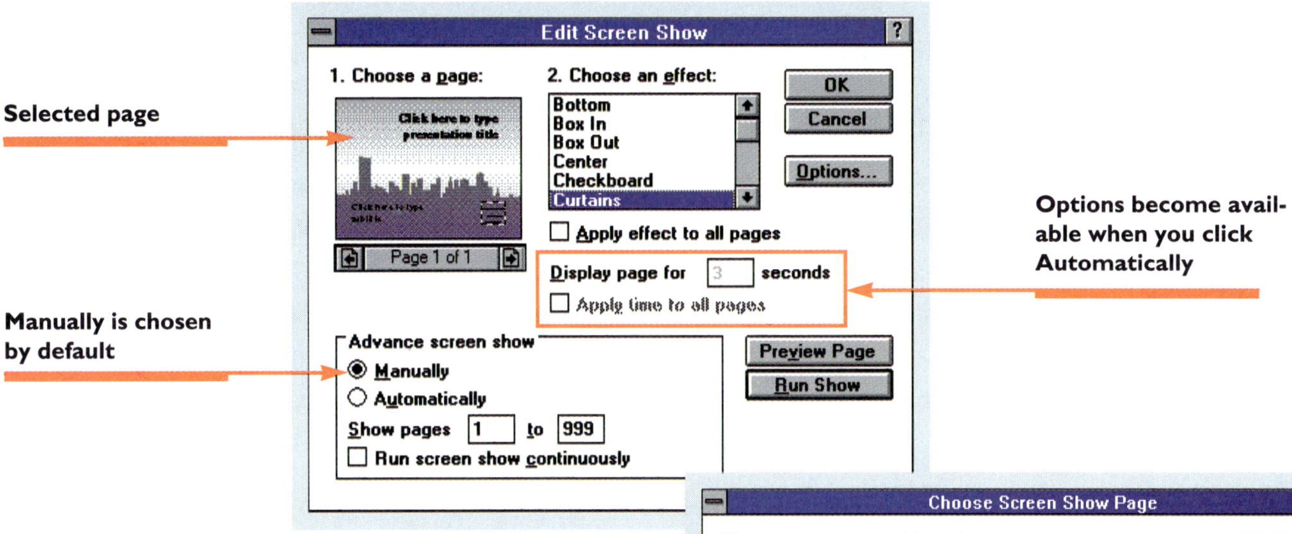

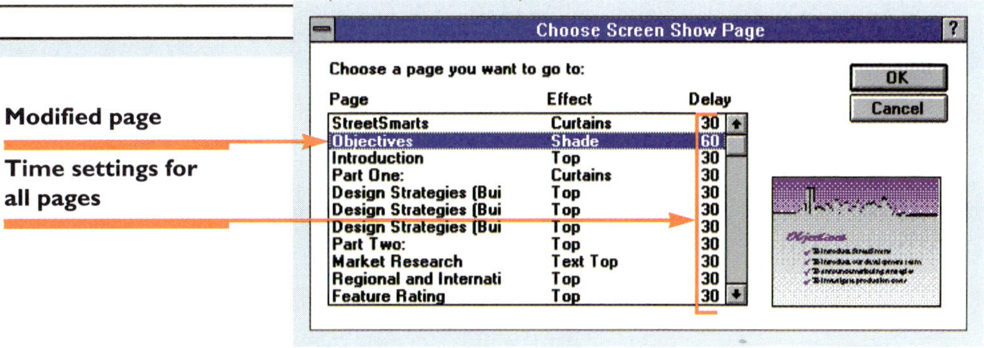

FIGURE 7-6: Checking timing settings

Running continuous screen shows

In the Advance screen show options are two enhanced features: Show pages and Run screen show continuously. If you wanted to display only selected pages—for example, if Tom wants to see only how the charts pages look—you would enter a beginning and ending value in the Show pages boxes. If you want the presentation to run over and over again—such as when you're running a self-directing demo in a booth at an industry trade show—you would click Run screen show continuously.

QUICK TIP

To suppress the display of a page without deleting it, type 0 in the Display page for option box.

Drawing on screen

Freelance Graphics knows that having the choice of adding last-minute or on-the-fly notes gives you great flexibility and can help boost your confidence when you're presenting. On screen, during your show, you can underline important phrases, circle items you don't want your audience to miss, or cross out options you hope they won't consider. ▶ Tom is a nonstop doodler so you know he's going to want on-screen drawing during the presentation. Choose a color and line thickness that will contrast against the SmartMaster you've chosen.

Steps

1. In Page Sorter view, click **3. Introduction**
   The selection box moves to Page 3.

2. Click **View** in the menu bar, then click **Screen Show**, then click **Edit Effects**
   Once again, the Edit Screen Show dialog box opens. This time you'll display the Screen Show Options.

3. Click the **Options button** in the upper-right side of the dialog box
   The Screen Show Options dialog box appears, as shown in Figure 7-7. Notice that instructions for how to draw on screen are displayed at the top of the dialog box.

4. In the On screen drawing options, click the **Color down-arrow**
   A palette of available colors appears. Contrast is important—and the background of the page is medium gray. Use a fairly dark but bright color for best results.

5. Click the red that is in the second column, fifth row from the bottom
   The color palette closes and you are returned to the Screen Show Options dialog box. The color you chose appears in the Color box.

6. In the On screen drawing options, click the **Width down-arrow**
   A drop-down list of line widths appears.

7. Click the line width third from the bottom
   The line width is selected and displayed in the Width box.

8. Click **OK** to return to the Edit Screen Show dialog box; then click **Preview Page**
   The page appears full-screen on your monitor.

9. Position the mouse pointer beneath the last line of text, press and hold the left mouse button, and drag to the end of the line
   The red line appears as you drag the mouse. Compare your screen to Figure 7-8.

10. Click anywhere on the page to return to the Edit Screen Show dialog box; then click **OK** to return to Current Page view

FIGURE 7-7: Screen Show Options dialog box

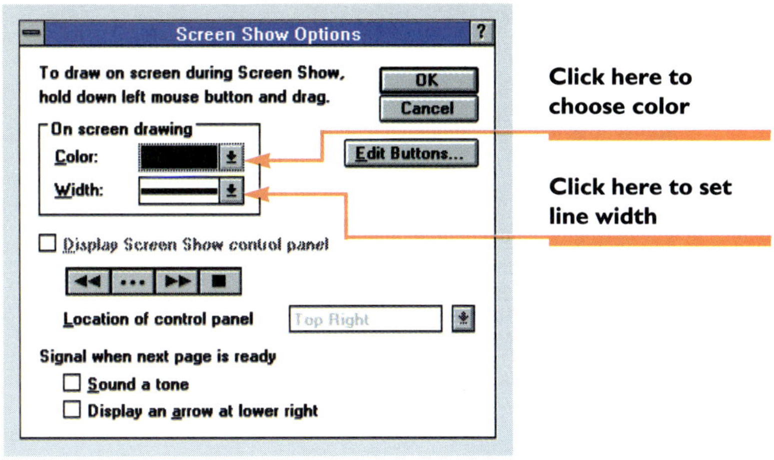

FIGURE 7-8: Drawing on screen

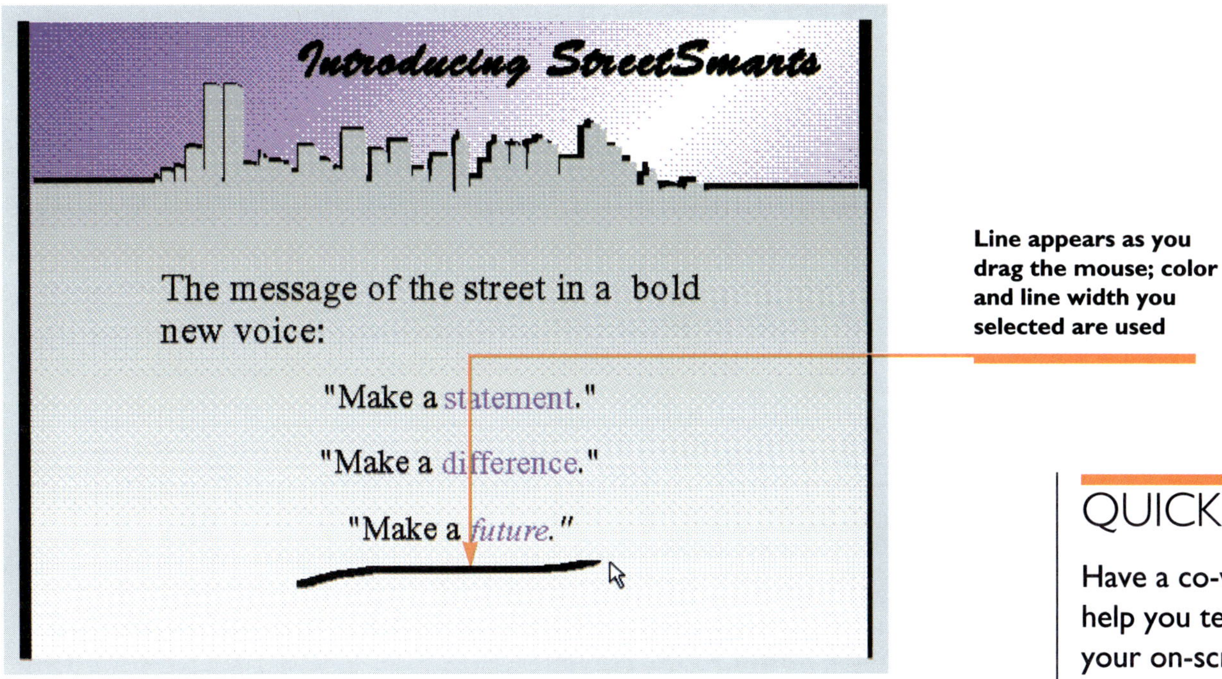

Using on-screen drawing to plan revisions

When you give a presentation, pay particular attention to the places where you find yourself drawing on screen quite a bit. As you talk, are you underlining a concept? Circling a chart? Calling attention to a particular item your audience seems to have trouble understanding? Paying attention to where you use on-screen drawing most can help you identify places where your presentation may need to be clearer. Think about adding a note to a confusing chart, for example, or underlining or boldfacing an important phrase, to cut down on the amount of on-screen drawing you do during the presentation. A little is effective, but too much makes your presentation seem incomplete.

QUICK TIP

Have a co-worker help you test the way your on-screen drawing works before you present. Start a slide show and underline text on the screen. Can your co-worker see your markings from ten feet away? Fifteen feet? Did you choose a color and line width your audience can see from a distance? If not, revise as necessary.

Using the Freelance Graphics Control Panel

Even though moving from page to page in a screen show is a simple process—just a click of the mouse will do it—Freelance Graphics provides you with other options for navigating through your presentation. One method involves displaying and using the Freelance Graphics Control Panel. Similar to buttons on a VCR, the buttons on the Control Panel enable you to move backward or forward through your presentation pages, jump to a specific page, or stop the presentation altogether. Table 7-1 explains how the buttons work. You can display the Control Panel almost anywhere on screen, which means that you can choose a spot that won't interfere with page information. ▶ As you prepare to present the screen show to Tom, you decide to add the Control Panel because he will, no doubt, interrupt you and ask you to move to various pages in the presentation.

STEPS

1. **Click View in the menu bar; then click Screen Show and click Edit Effects**
   The Edit Screen Show dialog box opens.

2. **In the Advance options, click Manually**
   This tells Freelance Graphics that you want to manually control the advancement of the pages. (Otherwise, you don't need the Control Panel. If you select Automatically, Freelance Graphics advances the pages for you.)

3. **Click the Options button**
   The Screen Show Options dialog box opens. In the center of the box, you see the Display Screen Show control panel checkbox.

4. **Click the Display Screen Show control panel checkbox**
   An X appears in the box. This turns on the Control Panel—now you need to decide where to display it.

5. **Click the Location of control panel down arrow**
   A drop-down list of possible locations for the Control Panel appears. See Figure 7-9.

6. **Click Bottom Right, then click OK**
   The Edit Screen Show dialog box reappears.

7. **Click Preview Page**
   The current page is displayed full screen. The Control Panel appears in the lower-right corner of the screen.

8. **Click anywhere on the page to redisplay the Edit Screen Show dialog box; click OK**
   Freelance Graphics returns to the presentation page.

9. **Click the Save SmartIcon**  **to save your presentation**

FIGURE 7-9:
Freelance Graphics Control Panel options

Turns display of Control Panel on and off

Select a location for the Control Panel

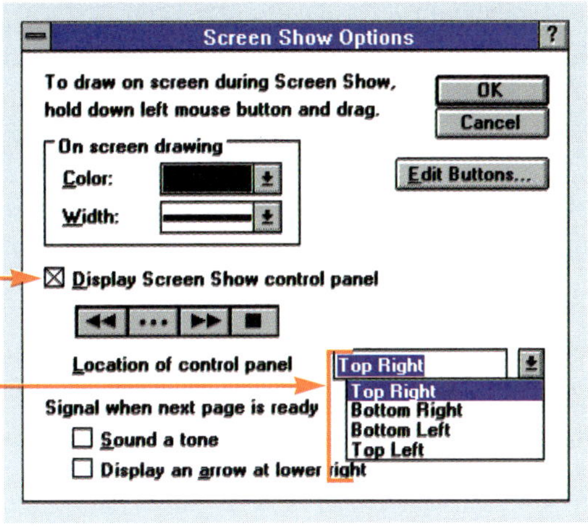

TABLE 7-1:
Freelance Graphics Control Panel buttons

BUTTON	NAME	DESCRIPTION
	Back One Page	Displays the previous page
	Jump to another Page	Displays the List Pages dialog box so that you can view another page
	Forward One Page	Displays the next page
	Quit Show	Stops the presentation and returns you to the presentation page

Alternate methods of moving through a screen show

During their presentations, some people like to wander around talking, instead of staying glued to the display screens. If you want Freelance Graphics to let you know audibly when it's time to advance to the next screen, you can elect to have the program sound a tone to alert you. Display the Screen Show Options dialog box and click the Sound a tone checkbox; then click OK. See Figure 7-10. Another way Freelance Graphics can let you know the next page is ready is by displaying an arrow in the lower-right corner of the screen, which you click to advance to the next page. The arrow appears only when it's time to turn the page, instead of continually staying visible, like the Freelance Graphics Control Panel.

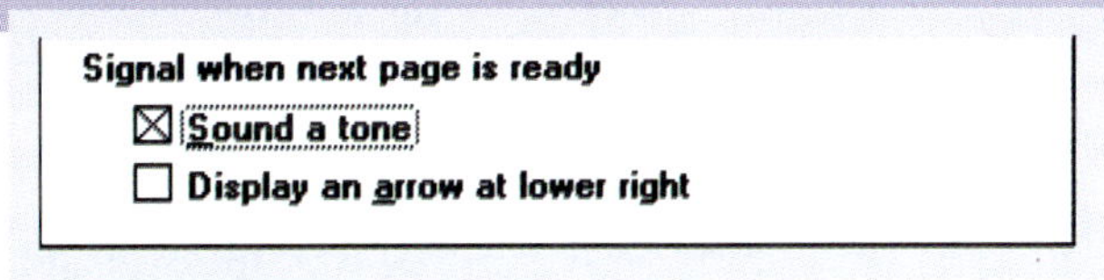

FIGURE 7-10:
Setting tone and adding arrows

Adding buttons

Another way you can navigate through document involves **buttons**. You can create buttons that enable you to move to the first or last page of the presesentation or any page in-between. You can also create buttons that actually run other programs—right from your screen show display. And another type of button allows you to run multimedia objects, if your computer is multimedia capable. ▶ After reviewing a printed copy of the charts, Tom's not completely satisfied with the two charts on Page 10. "I don't want to put them to sleep," he says. You suggest adding a button to Page 9 that is linked to Page 11—that way, if Tom feels he's losing his audience, he can skip over Page 10, move directly to the table on Page 11, and get on with the show.

STEPS

1. **Click the Page button** Page 1 of 1
   A list of presentation pages appears.
2. **Click 9. Market Research, then click Current Page**
   Page 9 appears in Current Page view. First you need to add a symbol to serve as the button.
3. **Click the Symbol tool**
   The Add Symbol to Page dialog box opens.
4. **In the Choose a symbol category area, scroll down and select buttons.sym**
   A collection of buttons appears in the Choose a symbol window.
5. **Choose the rectangular button (symbol 6 of 9), then click OK**
   The symbol is added to the presentation page, as shown in Figure 7-11. (Note: Although Freelance Graphics places the button automatically, you can move by dragging it to a new location, just as you would any Freelance Graphics object.)
6. **Click View in the menu bar, then click Screen Show and click Create/Edit Button**
   The Create/Edit Screen Show Button dialog box appears. In the Screen Show button name area, you can type a name for the button (but it's not necessary). In the Specify button behavior area, you choose whether you want the button to display a different page, start a program, or run a multimedia object.
7. **Click Jump to a page, then scroll down the list and click Feature Rating**
   This selects Page 11, Feature Rating, the page to which you want to link the button you just created. When you click the page name, the preview window shows the selected page, as shown in Figure 7-12. Later, when you display the presentation as a screen show, you can jump over Page 10 and go directly to Page 11 with a click of a button.
8. **Click OK, and then save and close the presentation**

FIGURE 7-11: Added button

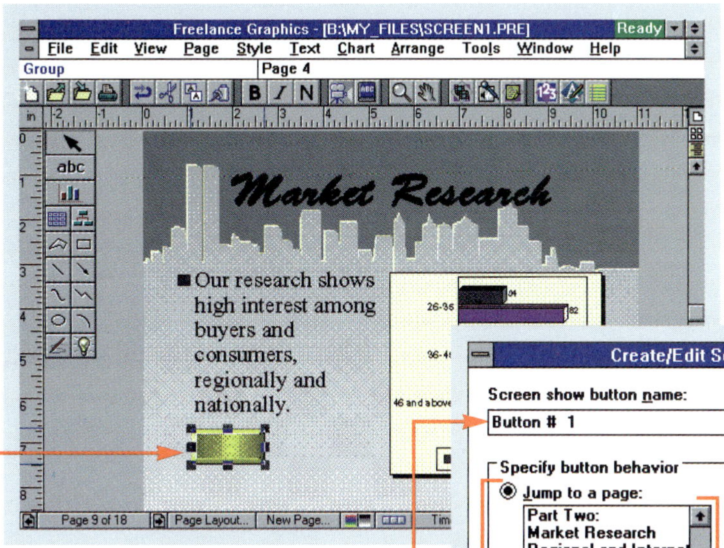

Leave the button selected

Enter a button name if you choose

Select the button function

Choose a page to move to

Selected page in preview window

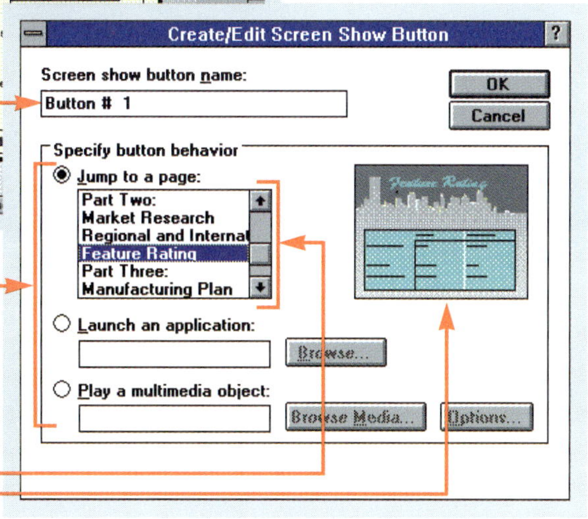

FIGURE 7-12: Create/Edit Screen Show Button dialog box

Using buttons to run other programs

You can create a button that actually runs another program during your Freelance Graphics worksession. For example, suppose that you are discussing information from a spreadsheet you originally created in Lotus 1-2-3 for Windows. You can add a button to your presentation that runs 1-2-3 if your audience members have questions related to your financial data. Select the button, click View in the menu bar, then click Screen Show, and finally click Create/Edit Button. When the Create/Edit Button dialog box appears, click the Launch an Application radio button, and then click Browse. The Launch an Application dialog box opens, in which you can locate and select the EXE file that runs the Lotus 1-2-3 program, as shown in Figure 7-13. Click OK, and then click OK again to return to the presentation page.

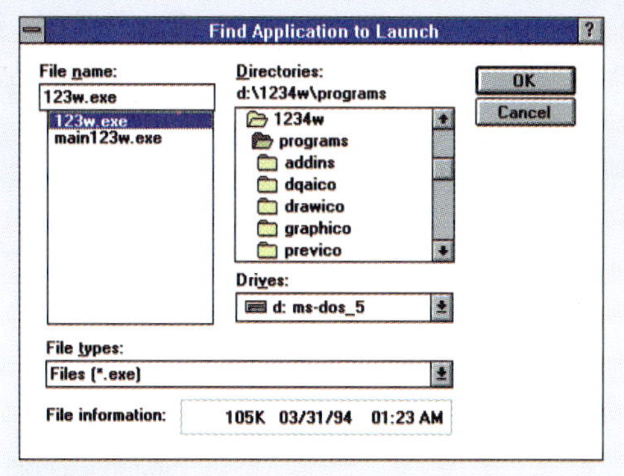

FIGURE 7-13:
Assigning another program to a button

Running the screen show

You can start a screen show two different ways: by clicking the Screen Show SmartIcon or by clicking View in the menu bar, clicking Screen Show, and then clicking Run. Table 7-2 explains the keyboard and mouse techniques you can use to move through the pages in the presentation. Remember, you can also use the Control Panel or the Automatic page advance settings to control page advancement. ▶ Tom is sitting expectantly in your office, waiting to see the presentation. For this run-through of the presentation, you have turned off the Freelance Graphics Control Panel and set the advancement option to Manually.

STEPS

1 **Open the file UNIT_7-2.PRE on Student Disk #3 and save it as SCREEN2 in the MY_FILES directory**
This creates a working copy of your presentation file.

2 Click the **Screen Show SmartIcon**
The screen goes blank, and after a few seconds, the first screen appears, as shown in Figure 7-14. Notice the curtain transitional effect, closing like a theater curtain and then opening to reveal the first page of your presentation.

3 Click the left mouse button
The second page appears. This time another transition is used. The page scrolls to the right across the screen.

4 Press **[PgDn]**
The third page appears, this time from the outer edges of the screen inward.

5 Click the right mouse button
This action displays the previous page. Again you see the transitional effect of the page scrolling from left to right.

6 Continue through the presentation, clicking the left mouse button to advance the pages; stop on Page 9, Market Research
Notice the use of special transitional effects as you move through the presentation. Which ones do you like? Which ones would you change?

7 On Page 9. Market Research, click the button in the bottom left-hand corner
Freelance Graphics carries out the action you assigned to the button earlier in the unit, that is, the screen show skips Page 10 and displays Page 11. Even though Page 10 was skipped, you can easily display it as necessary.

8 Press **[PgUp]**
Page 10, Regional and International appears.

9 Continue to the end of the presentation by clicking the left mouse button after each page
When you click the left mouse button on the last page of the presentation, you are returned to Current Page view. The last presentation page is displayed.

FIGURE 7-14: The opening page

Stopping a screen show

In some cases, you might want to stop a screen show in the middle of a presentation. Perhaps you are checking the display of a few pages and don't need to see the show in its entirety. When you want to stop the screen show, press [Esc]. The List Pages dialog box appears, as shown in Figure 7-15. In the Choose a page area, click the page you want to move to; then click Quit Show. Freelance Graphics returns you to the selected page.

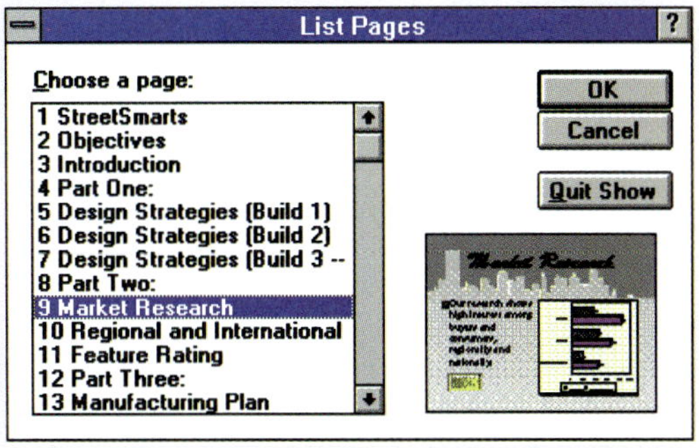

FIGURE 7-15: List Pages dialog box

TABLE 7-2:
Navigating the screen show with the mouse and keyboard

TO DISPLAY	WITH THE MOUSE	WITH THE KEYBOARD
The next page	Click the left mouse button	Press PgDn
The previous page	Click the right mouse button	Press PgUp, or Press Backspace
The List Pages dialog box		Press Esc

Printing handouts and slides

You can help viewers remember what they learned in your presentation by providing printed materials to go along with it. You might want to print the entire presentation in handout form so audience members can review it as desired. You probably want to add a line at the top of the printout, called a **header**, that gives readers information such as your company and/or department name, the date, or page number. A **footer** is the same type of information line, printed at the bottom of the page. ▶ Tom loves your presentation, but wants you to create handouts for his audience, who will be arriving shortly. He goes to the conference room to make sure the PC is set up properly while you get to work printing the presentation materials.

STEPS

1. **Click the Page button** Page 1 of 1 **and click 1. StreetSmarts**
   Page 1 appears in Current Page view.
2. **Click the Print SmartIcon**
   The Print File dialog box opens.
3. **Click the Page Setup button**
   The File Page Setup dialog box opens, as shown in Figure 7-16. For this presentation, you'll enter only a footer for the printouts.
4. **Click in the Footer text box and type Conscious Clothing |StreetSmarts line |#**
   This adds a footer with the first text section (Conscious Clothing) left-aligned; the second section (StreetSmarts line) centered; and the page number right-aligned.
5. **Click OK**
   The Print File dialog box redisplays, as shown in Figure 7-17. In the Print area, you enter the number of copies you want to print and specify a range of pages, if you want to print only selected pages in your presentation. You decide to print the current page to check the change you just made.
6. **Click Current Page only, then click Print**
   This tells Freelance Graphics to print only the current page. Now you need to print the handouts.
7. **After the page prints, click the File Print SmartIcon**
   This redisplays the Print File dialog box. Leave the settings in the Print options as they are. In the Format area, you select the type of printout you want to produce. See Figure 7-17.
8. **Click Handouts, click 6, then click Print**
   Freelance Graphics begins printing the presentation pages according to the options you specified. The presentation pages appear six on a page. The footer you added prints at the bottom of the page.
9. **Save and close your presentation file**

FIGURE 7-16: Final Page Setup dialog box

Add text for header or footer

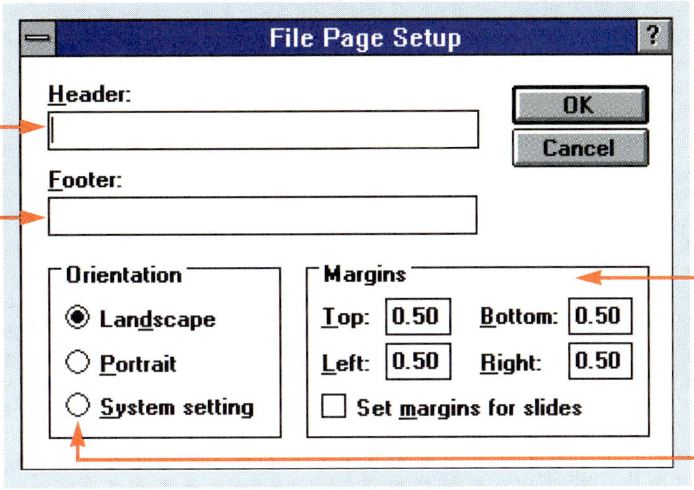

Sets margins

Choose vertical or horizontal printing

FIGURE 7-17: Print Option

Prints each presentation page on one page

Prints reduced version of presentation page and leaves space for audience write-in notes

Prints 2, 4, or 6 presentation pages per page

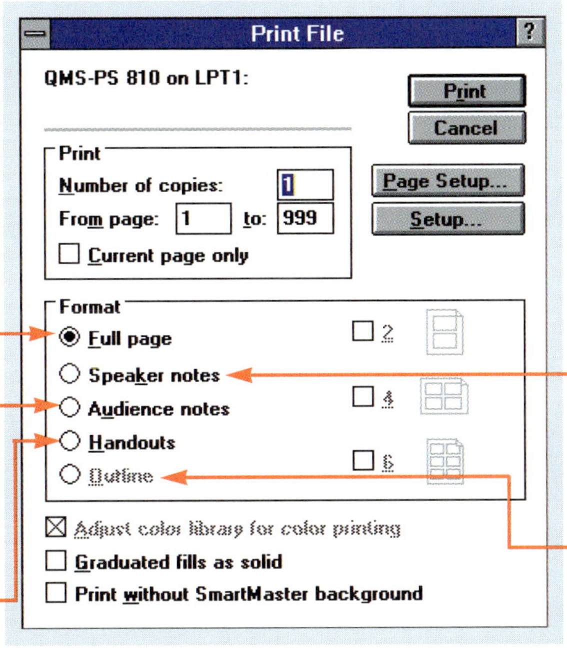

Prints the presention page reduced at top of page, and notes at the bottom of page

Available only if viewing presentation in outliner and prints only text in outline form

TROUBLE?

If your printer is not printing, check to make sure you've got the right printer selected. Click the Print SmartIcon and check the printer displayed in the top of the Print File dialog box.■

CONCEPTS REVIEW

Label the Freelance Graphics screen items shown in Figure 7-18.

1

2

3

4

5

FIGURE 7-18

Match each definition with its element.

6 Sets Freelance Graphics to advance the pages according to timing settings you enter

7 On-screen symbols that you link to other pages, applications, or multimedia objects

8 An on-screen panel that enables you to navigate through presentation pages

9 Sets Freelance Graphics to wait for you to advance the pages in a screen show by clicking the mouse button or pressing Page Down

10 Special effects that appear when a page is displayed

a. Manual timing
b. Transitional effects
c. Buttons
d. Automatic timing
e. Control panel

Select the best answer from the list of choices.

11 Where do you set transitional effects?
a. The Create/Edit Button dialog box
b. The Multimedia Options dialog box
c. The Edit Screen Show dialog box
d. The Screen Show Options dialog box

12 Which one of the following statements is NOT a characteristic of on-screen drawing?
a. The markings are stored with the page
b. You can change the line color
c. You can select from several line widths
d. You press and hold the left mouse button and drag the mouse to draw

13 Which one of the following items will you use if your presentation is set to Manual display?
a. The Control Panel

b. The Apply timing to all pages option
c. The Display pages for __ seconds option
d. None of the above

14 Which one of the following items will you use if your presentation is set to Automatic display?
a. The Control Panel
b. The Display pages for __ seconds option
c. The Sound a tone option
d. None of the above

15 Which one of the following features is NOT one of the functions of a button?
a. A way to move to a specific page
b. A way to display a text box for quick editing
c. A method of playing multimedia objects
d. A way to run an application program from a screen show

APPLICATIONS REVIEW

1 Open a new presentation file.
a. Click File in the menu bar, then click Open.
b. Select SUMMER.PRE in the MY_FILES directory of your Student Disk #3. The first page of SUMMER.PRE appears in Current Page view.
c. Save SUMMER.PRE as CAMP1 in MY_FILES directory.

2 Set transitional effects.
a. Click View in the menu bar, then click Screen Show, then click Edit Effects. The Edit Screen Show dialog box opens.
b. In the Choose an effect box, scroll through the list and highlight Fade.
c. Click Preview Page. The first page of the presentation fades in.
d. Click anywhere on the page to return to the Edge Screen Show dialog box.
e. Set transitions for the remaining pages using Table 7-3.

TABLE 7-3: Transitional effects for CAMP1.PRE

For this page:	Select this effect:
Page 2. Slept	Shade
Page 3. Ate	Text Left
Page 4. Learned	Text Right
Page 5. Camping	Box Out

3 Choose Manual timing and navigation options.
a. In the Advance page options, click Manually.
b. Click the Options button. The Screen Show Options dialog box opens.
c. Click the Display Screen Show control panel checkbox.
d. Click the Location of control panel down-arrow; then click Bottom Right.
e. Click OK. The Screen Show Options dialog box closes.
f. Click OK. The Edit Screen Show dialog box closes.

4 Run the screen show.
a. Click the Screen Show SmartIcon. The first page of the screen show appears.
b. Click the Next Page button. Page 2 is displayed.
c. Continue through the presentation until Page 5 is displayed.
d. Click the Jump to page button. The List Pages dialog box opens.
e. Click Page 3. Click OK. Page 3 appears.
f. Click Stop. You are returned to the presentation window.

5 Add a footer.
a. Click the File Print SmartIcon. The Print File dialog box opens.
b. Click Page Setup. The Page Setup dialog box opens.
c. In the Footer line, type 1994 Get-Real Campaign |#. Compare your screen to Figure 7-19.
d. Click OK.

FIGURE 7-19

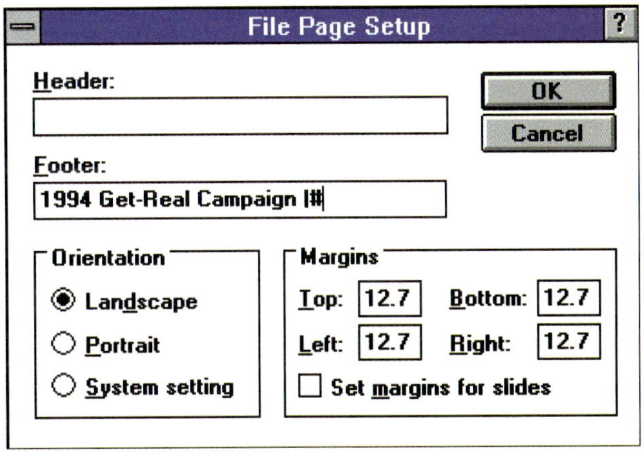

6 Print presentation pages.
a. In the Print File dialog box, click Handouts.
b. Click 2. This causes two handouts per page to be printed.
c. Click Print. The presentation is sent to the printer.

7 Save and close the presentation.

a. Click the File Close SmartIcon.

b. Click Replace. Freelance Graphics replaces the earlier version of CAMP1.PRE with the revised file.

INDEPENDENT CHALLENGE 1

It's a great idea, and unfortunately, one that hundreds of other manufacturers have thought of: fat-free foods. Your homemade cookie company, The Real McCoy, is reserving a booth at the national industry food show in Chicago this year. You envision a continuously-playing presentation in the booth, displayed on three different large-screen monitors, while your marketing assistants pass out free cookie samples. You can also see a great opportunity in adding a button that takes viewers right into another program in which they can enter their name and business affiliation, and request more information or sample packets. No more trying to decipher illegible hand-written response cards after the show—you'll have the information right there in the computer.

To complete this independent challenge:

1 Open the presentation file COOKIE.PRE on your Student Disk #3.

2 Choose effective transition effects for each of the pages; Box In, Box Out, and Scroll Left and Right are popular choices.

3 Select Automatic advance and specify an appropriate timing value. (Hint: Remember that Apply to all pages allows you to use the same timing for every page, although you can then set individual timing settings. Click the Page button to see current time values.)

4 Select the option that runs the screen show continuously.

5 Specify a new color and line thickness for on-line drawing.

6 Link the button on Page 10 to the Windows Cardfile. (Hint: This action involves clicking the Launch an Application option, clicking Browse Media, and locating the file CARDFILE.EXE, usually found in the C:\WINDOWS directory.)

7 Save the presentation as COOK1; Run the screen show.

8 Add a footer that prints The Real McCoy Cookie Company on the left and the page number on the right.

9 Print a cover page, an outline, and handouts, four to a page.

10 Submit your printed materials to your instructor.

Glossary

Area chart A type of chart that displays data as layered areas. Good for contrasting data.

Attributes Settings that apply to the selected object. Attributes for text include font, size, and color. Attributes for graphics include edge and area colors and shadow settings.

Automatic advance In a screen show, choose Automatically when you want Freelance Graphics to advance the pages automatically, without you clicking the mouse button or pressing PgDn. You specify a timing setting to tell the program how long to wait before displaying the next page.

Axis titles Titles on a chart you affix to the X or Y axes.

Backup A second copy of an important file you can put away for safekeeping.

Bar chart A type of chart that displays data series as bars set next to each other for easy comparison.

Build A bullet list that displays bullets one at a time during the screen show.

Buttons A screen show feature you can add to link one page to another or run another program from within your presentation.

Cell pointer The square highlight in the Chart Data & Titles screen that shows where data will be entered when you type.

Chart heading The text used as a title on the chart.

Chart styles Preset chart settings that help you create customized charts quickly.

Child pages The pages Freelance Graphics adds while building up to the complete build. See also *parent pages*.

Clipboard The unseen area of memory that stores text and graphics you cut, copy, and paste.

Color scheme A pre-assembled palette of colors you can use to quickly create a well-coordinated presentation.

Column labels The names displayed on the chart to identify the data series A, B, and so on.

Control Panel In a screen show, an on screen panel that enables you to move backward or forward through your presentation pages, jump to a specific page, or stop the presentation altogether.

Crosshair cursor The shape the pointer takes on when you select one of the drawing tools.

Current Page view The view in Freelance Graphics that shows the entire presentation page, similar to the way you'll see it displayed in a screen show. You enter text, create charts, and add graphics and symbols in Current Page view.

Display preferences Items such as a drawing ruler, a text block ruler, a function key panel, or a grid that you may want to use as you work on your presentation.

Drawing tools The set of drawing tools displayed in the Toolbox to the left of the work area, including polygon, rectangle, line, arrows, open arc, polyline, circle, arc, and freehand tools.

Data series An individual item (or group) of data being charted.

Edit line The line below the menu bar that displays the name of the current page and identifies the selected object.

Edit Pts An indicator that appears in the upper left corner of the title bar, which shows points mode is in effect.

File extension The last three letters of a file name, occurring after the period that indicate filetype. For example, in PRESENT.PRE, the final three letters—PRE—are the extension and indicate a presentation file.

Font One size and style of a particular typeface, such as Times Roman 10-point bold.

Footer A line that prints at the bottom of your printouts, usually including information about your department or project.

Graphics Art used in Freelance Graphics. The art may include one of Freelance Graphic's symbols from the Symbol Gallery, objects drawn with the drawing tools, or graphics imported from another program.

Gridlines Horizontal lines on a chart that help viewers determine data values.

Grouping The process of selecting several objects and locking them together as a single object.

Handles Small black squares on the corners and along the sides of a selected object.

Header A line that prints at the top of your printouts, usually providing information like your company and/or department name, the date, or the current page number.

High-Low-Close-Open chart A chart type that displays a range of items for each data set displayed, including high value, low value, opening value, and closing value. Use to show stock price changes, temperature changes, or other items that show a fluctuation in value during a specific period of time.

Highlighting The process of marking text as a text block.

Importing The process of opening a file created in another program for use with Freelance Graphics. You can import text, spreadsheet, and graphics files from selected programs.

Indicator bar A vertical bar in Page Sorter view that shows the cursor position as you move pages.

Justification The horizontal alignment of text in the selected box. See also *Vertical Justification.*

Keyboard shortcuts A method of opening menus or selecting commands by using using the keyboard. Keyboard shortcuts may be key combinations, such as the Alt+F shortcut used to open the File menu, or a single letter underlined in a dialog box command (such as Create a new presentation, in the Welcome to Freelance Graphics dialog box).

Legend The key in a chart that helps viewers identify the data series.

Line chart A type of chart that shows data series as points on a line. Good for showing the results over time.

Manual advance In a screen show, choose Manually when you want to control when the next page is displayed by clicking the mouse button or pressing PgDn. See also *automatic advance.*

Menu bar The bar below the title bar that contains the 11 different menus available in Freelance Graphics. Each menu contains commands related to a different aspect of the presentation.

Organizational chart A chart type that shows relationships, such as the hierarchy of corporate employees.

Outdents The process of assigning text to a higher level (for example, when you outdent a third-level bullet, it becomes a second-level bullet).

Outline A plan of topics and subtopics organized in the way you intend to present them.

Outliner view The view that shows the text content and organization of your presentation.

Page background The color and graphics of the page behind the prompt text boxes.

Page buttons The buttons in the far left side of the horizontal scroll bar that enable you to move among pages (the Page button), choose a different layout (Page Layout), and add a new page easily (New Page).

Page layout A preset page format contains areas for text, charts, or graphics (depending on the layout you select). Freelance Graphics provides you with 11 different page layouts from which you can choose, plus one that lets you add a totally blank page.

Page Sorter view The view that displays your presentation pages in a reduced size so you can check page order, change the arrangement of pages if necessary, copy, cut, and move pages, and add special screen show effects and timing settings.

Paragraph style A group of text settings—such as indent level, font, bullet, and alignment—that affect the text in the selected box.

Parent page The original bullet page containing all the bullet items used in a build. See also *build.*

Pie chart A type of chart that displays data series as slices of a pie. Good for displaying how segments relate to the whole.

Points A typographical measurement roughly equivalent to 1/72 of an inch. A 72-point character is 1-inch high.

Points mode A method of editing graphics objects and lines by changing individual points on a line or edge.

Presentation graphics program A program you run on a personal computer that enables you to create slides, transparencies, and handouts for all kinds of presentations.

Presentation window The Freelance Graphics screen, including the title bar, SmartIcon palette, toolbox, work area, and scroll bars.

Prompt text Text on the Freelance Graphics page that prompts you to click at that point to add your own text, chart, or symbol.

Radar chart A chart that shows each data series as a line connecting in a hexagon shape. Use to plot several related data sets, like the products sold over a specific period of time.

RAM An acronym for Random-Access Memory, RAM can store information only temporarily—when power goes off, all the data in RAM is erased.

Root The first part of a file name (up to eight characters before the period). In the file name PRESENT.PRE, PRESENT is the root.

Saving The process of writing the information stored in RAM to a more permanent storage medium, usually a 5.25- or 3.5-inch disk you insert in a disk drive, or a hard disk.

Screen show An on-screen presentation in which you can display special transition effects, control timing, and add other features like on-screen drawing or the Control Panel.

Selection box A box in Page Sorter view that encloses the selected page.

SmartIcons Special buttons that help you carry out often-used procedures quickly. With just a click of a SmartIcon, you can open the Print dialog box, copy a text block, boldface selected text and perform many other common operations.

SmartMaster A predesigned presentation template that contains page layouts, color selections, font choices, and may contain sample graphics. When you choose one of Freelance Graphics' 60 SmartMasters, the design is already done—all you need to do is enter the text.

Symbol Gallery A collection of over 100 different ready-to-use symbol files you can add to your presentation pages. The Gallery divides the symbols into a number of different categories—animals, shapes, people, business, finance, etc.—so you can easily locate the symbols you need.

Symbols Professionally created graphics included with Freelance Graphics you can use in your own presentations.

Table Text aligned in columns and rows.

Text block Any highlighted text. A text block can be of any length from a single character to an entire presentation. (*Note*: You can select text across pages only if you are working in the Outliner.)

Text display effect A type of transition that controls how the text appears on the page. In Text Left, for example, the page background, graphics, and chart appears as usual, but the text moves in from the left.

Text level The level of indention assigned to bullet text.

Timing settings Settings that enable you to control the length of time pages are displayed.

Title bar The bar at the top of the presentation window that shows the program name (in this case, Freelance Graphics) and the name of the current file.

Toolbox A set of tools on the left side of the work area that contains the selection tool, text tool, chart tool, table tool, organizational chart tool, and variety of drawing and symbol tools. See also *drawing tools*.

Transitional effects Effects in a screen show you can add to control how subsequent pages appear. For example, you might assign the Curtain effect to a page to display a theatrical curtain that closes and then opens to show the page.

Typeface The overall type family of a particular font.

Vertical justification The vertical alignment of text in the selected box.

View buttons Buttons in the upper portion of the vertical scroll bar that enable you to display your presentation in different ways. The top button displays Current Page view; the middle button displays Page Sorter view; and the bottom button displays Outliner view.

X axis The horizontal axis on a chart from which data items are displayed.

XY (Scatter) chart A type of chart that displays data series as independent points. Good for contrasting two or more data sets to see whether there is a correlation between the sets.

Y axis The vertical axis in a chart along which data items are measured.

Index